Colorado

Jon Klusmire
Photography by Paul Chesley

COMPASS AMERICAN GUIDES
An Imprint of Fodor's Travel Publications, Inc.

Colorado

Fourth Edition

Copyright 1998 Fodor's Travel Publications, Inc.
Maps Copyright 1998 Fodor's Travel Publications, Inc.

Library of Congress Cataloging-In-Publication-Data
Klusmire, Jon, 1956
   Colorado/Jon Klusmire; photography by Paul Chesley. —4th ed.
     p. cm. — (Compass American guides)
   Includes bibliographical references and index
   ISBN 0-679-00027-5
   1. Colorado—Guidebooks. I. Chesley, Paul, 1946- II. Title.
   III. Series: Compass American guides (Series)
   F774.3.K57 1998   97-47187
   917.8804'33—dc 21   CIP

Editors: Kit Duane, Julia Dillon, Nancy Falk   Designers: David Hurst, Christopher Burt
Managing Editor: Kit Duane   Map Design: Eureka Cartography; Mark Stroud,
Photo Editor: Christopher Burt   Moon Street Cartography

First published in 1992 by **Compass American Guides, Inc.**
5332 College Ave, Suite 201, Oakland, CA 94618, USA
Production house: Twin Age Ltd., Hong Kong   Printed in China

10 9 8 7 6 5 4 3 2 1

Cover: The Maroon Bells and Pyramid Mountain dominate an aspen-filled valley in the central Rockies.

COMPASS AMERICAN GUIDES ACKNOWLEDGES the following institutions and individuals for the use of their photographs and/or illustrations: Colorado Historical Society, pp. 21, 24, 39, 58, 92, 96, 101, 103, 104, 108-109, 110, 175, 196, 200, 227, 228, 306; the Museum of Western Art in Denver, pp. 25, 29, 132-133, 172; Denver Public Library, Western History Department, pp. 143, 170, 171, 249; Pueblo Library District, p. 81; Center of Southwest Studies, Fort Lewis College, Durango, p. 192; Museum of New Mexico p. 186. Mural on pp. 156-157 used with permission from the Peabody Museum at Yale University. U.C. Berkeley paleontologist Mark Goodwin contributed the essay on p. 155.

THE AUTHOR ACKNOWLEDGES all those chambers of commerce across Colorado whose information helped immeasurably in the preparation of this book. I also want to thank Abbott Fay, one of my former history professors, for the time he spent listening to my initial brainstorming and for reading the finished manuscript.
 The staffs at the Colorado Historical Society; Denver Public Library, Western History Collection; the Museum of Western Art; and Colorado Ski Museum were all accommodating. Likewise for the crew at my local library, the Glenwood Springs Branch of the Garfield County Library.

This book is dedicated to my grandparents, Eldo and Gladys Klusmire,
who brought the Klusmire clan to Aspen in the 1940s, and to my Uncle Bob,
a man who never met a shot of whiskey he couldn't drink, a horse he couldn't ride,
or a bull elk he couldn't shoot and haul down a mountainside.

■ PHOTOGRAPHER'S DEDICATION

A special thank you to my parents, Frank and Jean who first brought me to Colorado with my Brownie camera when I was a young boy. It was an inspiration to later return and live in Colorado and capture the beauty of my new home state. I also want to thank Carole Lee for her extensive research and organization of the photos.

C O N T E N T S

Topical Essays

Maps

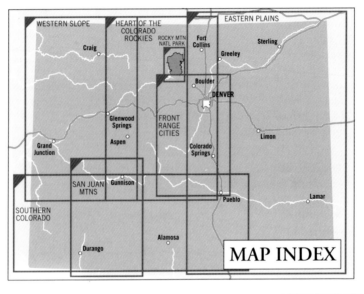

MAP INDEX

Literary Excerpts

AUTHOR'S PREFACE

AT FIRST BLUSH, I THOUGHT WRITING THIS BOOK WOULD BE a mere finger exercise at the old word processor. Hey, I was born here, lived here all my life, have a degree in history, am a working journalist, have forgotten more about Colorado than most people know, and was more than ready to write the guide of guides: no hagiography here, no siree, the real stuff, the good stuff, nothing but the truth, babble babble, dribble dribble, mutter mutter.

Fired with enthusiasm and hubris, I started. But something happened to my bluster and bombast as I dug into the state I thought I knew so well.

Thankfully, this isn't another "been everywhere twice, talked to everyone once," Colorado guide. My goal is not to inform the reader if lox and bagels are available in Ordway or to rehash the history of the Centennial State and its people. Instead, what I have tried to do is provide an interesting glimpse of a fascinating state, to give the reader a feel for what made the state what it is and what it wants to be.

But this is also intended to be a guidebook, albeit a more selective guide than some of the encyclopedic items already available. Thus, it includes a solid selection of information to help you discover and enjoy a good cross-section of Colorado's famed attractions.

What I set out to do after I uncovered favored and unique restaurants, motels, and fishing holes was to discover the links between how the past helped shape the present and how the past and present—whether embodied by the Mining Law of 1872 or the high-speed Information Superhighway—might combine to signal the future.

It didn't take me long to realize that I had indeed forgotten a lot about Colorado, that some of my assumptions were a bit outdated, that my home state proved to be a whole lot more interesting and intriguing than I had remembered.

Fortunately, Paul Chesley's photos meant I wouldn't have to keep finding new combinations of words (how many times can you say breathtaking?) to describe Colorado's indescribable scenery. Instead, I'll just let his work speak for itself.

Tracking down comfy beds, T-bone steaks, good elk hunting, and the fastest ski lift while trying to explain the essence of what makes Colorado Colorado proved to be a tremendous challenge. Don't feel too sorry for me though. It was also a delightful challenge that gave me a grand excuse to tour the state and spruce up, dust off, or throw away my pet theories about how Colorado evolved into the intriguing and internationally renowned place it has become.

I certainly had a wonderful time doing that, and I hope the fruits of my efforts will provide the reader an entertaining look at a state that certainly holds plenty of entertaining and educational surprises for any visitor, or even for a certain, once cocksure, lifelong resident.

OVERVIEW

■ EASTERN PLAINS

Acre upon acre of corn, wheat, soybeans, and silence are your companions as you drive through Colorado's flat eastern plains. Small towns and farms dot a vast landscape with wide horizons, where long ago the Comanche hunted buffalo.

■ FRONT RANGE CITIES

Boulder, Denver, Colorado Springs, and **Pueblo** are strung along the base of the Rockies. These vital, youthful cities boast burgeoning populations, excellent restaurants and accommodations, and proximity to the mountains.

■ ROCKY MOUNTAINS

High mountains and pristine lakes make the Rockies a place to enjoy hiking, mountain biking, fishing, and skiing. Added to this are the pleasures of famous ski resorts at **Vail, Aspen,** and **Breckenridge,** unique old mining towns, and some excellent cuisine and lodging.

■ SAN JUAN MOUNTAINS

The **San Juans**, an isolated southern spur of the Rocky Mountains, are still lonely and wild—in fact the grizzly bear is being reintroduced there. High in the rugged hills are old mining towns, ghost towns, and thriving **Telluride**, famous for its skiing and film festival.

■ WESTERN SLOPE

In the long tilting plateau stretching west from the flanks of the Rockies, lie badlands, wide empty reaches of arid land, rich irrigated farmland, and forests. This is an area of mineral mining, small towns, and rural living.

■ SOUTHERN COLORADO

In the dry southern reaches of Colorado are the lands of the Ute Indians and one of the grandest and most mysterious of the deserted cities abandoned by the mysterious Anasazi people, the Mesa Verde.

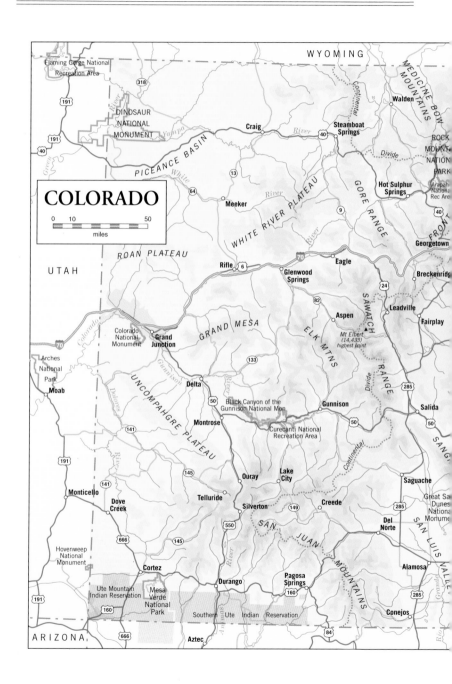

COLORADO

0   10   50
miles

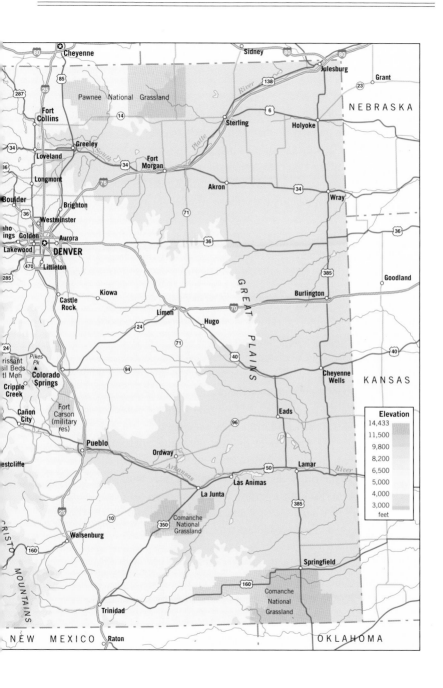

INTRODUCTION

COLORADO IS A SPRAWLING WESTERN STATE whose Rocky Mountain spine of towering snowcapped peaks is bracketed by a vast prairie on the east and a dry, windswept desert on the west. To the south, mystery reigns.

All of Colorado provides postcard images. If a picture is worth a thousand words, pictures of many Colorado scenes are worth a thesaurus. And even that can't describe the beauty, tranquility, and almost spiritual feel that can overtake mere mortals when escaping into the millions of acres of Colorado plains, mountains, and deserts.

Whether it's the stability of small town life on the plains, brightly clad skiers busting through piles of "champagne powder," or a sunrise splashing color across a desert moonscape, nature can provide visitors to Colorado more than enough goosebumps.

Goosebumps aside, there's more than postcard images in Colorado. There is also the Oil Shale Capital of the World, the world's highest town (railroad, paved road, and suspension bridge), enough natural hot springs to soak away half the world's fatigue, the world's biggest underground hole filled with military brass (and we're not talking ammo dump), and the sweetest peaches this side of paradise.

Although this book can't reproduce the taste of those peaches, it can give you a taste of and feel for the parts that make Colorado a unique whole, while pointing out each area's sights, scenes, and history. As with any story, there are characters, and Colorado is full of them, from the first optimistic gold miners and silver barons to the current crop of peach growers on the Western Slope.

Before most people get to the Rocky Mountains, they cross or fly over Colorado's eastern plains. Running right up to the mountains, the plains are flat as a pancake, and full of wheat, tractors, and tornados. (If Dorothy and Toto had flown back from Oz and wakened in eastern Colorado, they'd have thought they'd landed in Kansas.)

The string of cities along the Front Range of the Rockies popped to life to supply the booming gold and silver towns deeper into the mountains. Once the gold and silver boom busted, the Front Range cities worked to become bastions of civilization in an untamed land, and then found themselves in the right spot at the right time to become the federal government's western hub.

A forest dressed in its finest foliage.

The Colorado mountains remain the state's biggest draw and biggest bragging point. The mountains first beckoned the mountain men and fur trappers who truly explored the rugged backcountry. Next came the gold and silver miners who scattered throughout the state, from Boulder to Durango, in search of the minerals of which Victorian dreams were made.

Today, millions of acres of national forest, national parks and recreation areas, and public land draw visitors from around the globe. Whether it's to fish, backpack, bike, camp, hunt, or just try to get back in touch with land that has not been scarred or trampled by civilization, Colorado is more than accommodating.

The same is true for the state's famed mountain resorts. Entire communities have been created from scratch to itch the urge to ski. Mining towns down on their ore learned how to mine powder or historic charm instead of minerals. The transformation has been dazzling. Formerly dilapidated Victorian downtowns now boast everything from living history to the latest fashions.

Traveling toward the western side of the Rocky Mountains, it's possible, within a couple of hours, to drive from a 10,000-foot mountain pass down to sprawling farm and ranch land where the myth of the West with its fiercely independent farmers and ranchers is still alive and well. From there it's on into a hot western desert full of rattlesnakes and wind-carved rock formations.

Turning south, the traveler finds more subtle transformations, in mysteries of the past and mixtures of cultures. It was here that ancient Native American artisans created stunning cliff dwellings, and it was through this area that Spanish explorers traveled in the fifteenth century searching for the legendary Seven Cities of Gold. Later, a colonial Spanish/Hispanic culture, emanating from Santa Fe to the south, flourished and was eventually challenged by American settlers arriving from the east. Among other things, the Americans decided that southwestern Colorado was just the spot for the state's indigenous Ute Indians. As a result, the area is a true melting pot of people and heritage.

A common bond is shared by all Coloradoans: a reliance on natural resources and the surrounding environment for a livelihood. That, in turn, has created and is still creating another enduring Colorado feature: cycles of boom and bust. First it was gold, then silver, then coal, oil, oil shale, and uranium. Colorado still contains valuable minerals waiting to be mined, but today those hoping to recover them often find themselves in conflict with those whose livelihood depends on preservation of Colorado's environmental treasures. That the representatives of these two treasure troves collide on a regular basis keeps things interesting, if not downright exciting.

Thanks to its history and its people, Colorado is a state that is used to remaking itself whenever it has to. It is an amazing testament to the state's bountiful natural resources and resourceful citizens that it has been able to adjust and survive in an ever-changing world, while retaining its famous, almost magical reality.

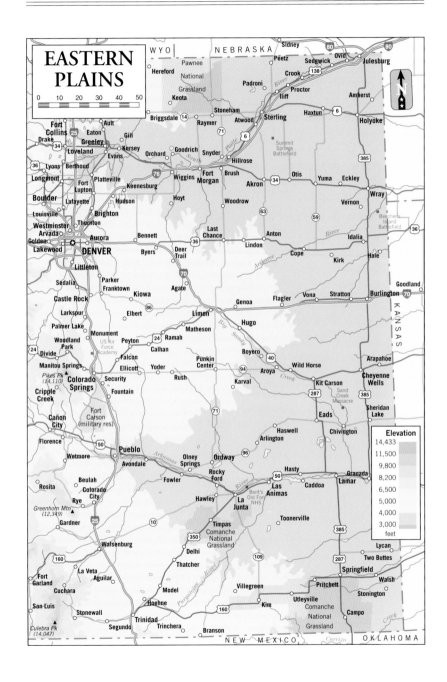

EASTERN PLAINS

THE SILENCE IS PALPABLE AS YOU TRAVEL across Colorado's eastern plains, either on two-lane, straight-as-a-string state highways; on Interstate 70, which cuts through the middle of the state; or on Interstate 76, which angles across the northern plains from Nebraska to Denver. Acre upon acre of corn, wheat, soybeans, and silence are your only companions.

The first trappers, explorers, and gold seekers traveling across America's Great Plains probably broke that silence with swear words and vile oaths about this Great American Desert which was just an obstacle to overcome and appeared to be a totally worthless pain in the butt. (Ride a mule a for a month; you'll understand.) Your seating arrangements are probably much more comfortable, but one look at a map might lead you to agree that the plains are to be sped through with a minimum of stopping and a maximum of miles per hour.

Don't be so hasty. Not only will you be missing a large part of the state's history and more than a few significant attractions, you might also bypass some of the last bastions of real American small-town life, a life that has survived the frantic freeways, crammed shopping malls, crime, stress, and anxiety that you are speeding away from.

■ BENT'S FORT AND THE SANTA FE TRAIL

The men who set out into the Colorado Rockies between 1820 and 1840 came in all shapes, sizes, colors, and nationalities. They were the mountain men and fur trappers who, with a horse to ride and another to carry their traps and scant provisions, truly explored Colorado's mountains. Frenchmen, Americans, Mexicans, and Indians all plunged into the state's frozen streams to supply the beaver pelts that fashioned fashionable men's hats from New York to Paris.

The trappers would head out into the mountains in the fall, trap all winter, and return, if lucky enough to keep their own pelts on their own heads, with enough beaver "plews" to sustain them for the rest of the year.

The fickle finger of fashion finished off the beaver trade about the same time the trappers finished off the beavers. By the 1840s, with silk hats riding high on sophisticated heads, the beaver business was dead. Another animal's shaggy, fashionable head, however, reared up just in time to coat the southern plains with commerce. Buffalo robes replaced beaver pelts in the world of fashion and the traveling trappers' carnival called the "rendezvous" was replaced by permanent trading posts and forts to take advantage of the buffalo robe trade.

Bent's Fort was one of the most successful trading posts in the West during the buffalo robe stampede. Built in 1833 on the American side of the Arkansas River between present-day La Junta and Las Animas, its thick adobe walls, secure lodging, and store of trading goods made it a welcome sight to anyone coming out of Colorado's southern mountains or across the plains on the **Mountain Branch of the Santa Fe Trail.**

Brothers Charles and William Bent and Ceran St. Vrain operated the original fort and several others for 17 years. They were successful in part due to innate business sense, and in part due to their ability to respect the cultures and peoples upon which their trade depended.

This was a heady time. Until the Mexicans won their independence from Spain in 1821 and freed themselves from colonial domination, Santa Fe was prevented by the King of Spain from trading with the United States. Once Spanish rule ended, land and trade opened up, and the effect was electrifying.

Authenticity is the stock and trade at Bent's Old Fort.

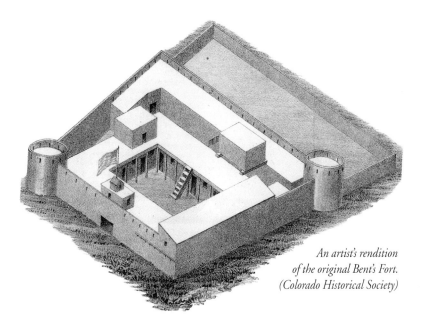

*An artist's rendition
of the original Bent's Fort.
(Colorado Historical Society)*

It was a time when skin color didn't matter, Spanish or American political shenanigans were old news with no practical effect, paperwork was unheard of, governments' approving or disapproving hand was invisible, and you didn't need lawyers and accountants to seal a deal or assure that promises once made were kept. All you needed were mutual respect for those you encountered, an appreciation of their labors and wares, a little haggling, a firm handshake, and a shot of trading post whiskey, which in its earliest incarnation was grain alcohol flavored with red pepper. (Does that give you a clue to the derivation of the word "firewater?")

The male Plains Indians, not white hunters, killed the buffalo, and the women prepared the robes, thus good relations with the Indians were a necessity. Fair trading and the marriage of William Bent to Owl Woman, a Cheyenne, cemented the Bents' tie to the Natives. Neither could the Bents indulge in disrespect or disregard for the American, Mexican, and Spanish traders and travelers who plied the Santa Fe Trail.

Once inside the *placita* (the open courtyard inside the fort's walls), nationalities and cultural differences were forgotten, for a time at least, to be replaced by security, commerce, and companionship.

Maybe that's why, over 100 years and millions of politicians, lawyers, and bickering bureaucrats later, **Bent's Old Fort National Historic Site** has become one of Colorado's première tourist attractions. It's also a nice rest after fishing, floating, or hunting along the Arkansas River. *(See* "GREAT OUTDOORS," *beginning on page 203, for more on the area's recreational possibilities.)*

Within sight of plains and mountains, visitors can amble through the fort's gates into the *placita* and back into a simpler time. Volunteer interpreters dressed in buckskins and sombreros staff the trading post, which is filled with all the goods needed to refresh an average mountain man or weary traveler on the way to Santa Fe. You can rest in the shade under the adobe awning that rings the inside of the fort, cuss the end of the beaver empire with the bearded trapper next to you, get a tip about a rapid route across the Rockies from a nearby mountain man, or just sit and wonder what life was like when a man's word was his bond, his handshake his seal, his life untroubled by contracts, lawyers, accountants, and politicians. *Six miles east of La Junta on Colorado 194 (Trail Road); (719) 384-2596.*

■ COMANCHE NATIONAL GRASSLAND

If that reflective mood remains after a trip to Bent's Fort, you can travel back to La Junta on Colorado 194, then take Colorado 109 or US 350 through the **Comanche National Grassland**. Here you can see how the Great American Desert looked before the plow turned under the buffalo grass and native plants that were once a part of the plains' barren beauty. Let your mind wander back to the time when all a man needed was a horse to hunt and fight from, buffalo meat and robes, his family and his tribe, and respect for the Creator who provided all of life's necessities. Unfortunately, fierce competition, a little war with Mexico, a gold rush in the Rockies, and the arrival of thousands of settlers made sure the peaceful days of collaboration on the plains between the whites and the Indians ended.

The trials and tribulations of the gold-seekers rushing to California, Nevada, and Colorado from the late 1840s to the 1860s are both humorous and tragic. Even those with scant sense realized winter was the wrong time to trek across the prairie, so summer was the only traveling season. Few tried it alone. Many were never heard of again. Horses and mules were the preferred beasts of burden, but humans tried to fill those horseshoes by pushing wheelbarrows or carts themselves,

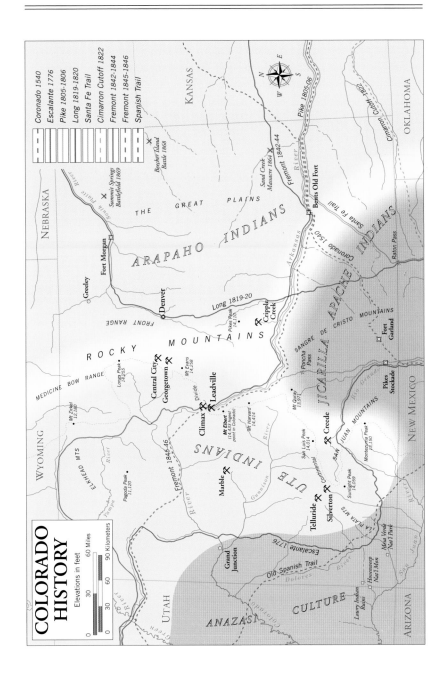

COLORADO HISTORY

Elevations in feet

Coronado 1540
Escalante 1776
Pike 1805-1806
Long 1819-1820
Santa Fe Trail
Cimarron Cutoff 1822
Fremont 1842-1844
Fremont 1845-1846
Spanish Trail

and some even tried crude backpacks, a much ridiculed choice. One enterprising soul decided to make the wind do the work by attaching a sail to a regular wagon. It worked for a while before unceremoniously sinking miles before making port.

Information on Comanche National Grassland is available at the Visitor Center, 1420 E. Third Street, La Junta, CO 81050; (719) 384-2181.

■ SETTLERS VERSUS INDIANS

Generally, until after the Civil War, Colorado's plains were just an obstacle to overcome. But the sodbusters—those not seeking quick riches, but merely farmland—saw something else under the buffalo grass sod: fertile soil. And on Colorado's eastern plains, they saw something even more important: water for irrigation.

As the sodbusters got closer to the Rockies they noticed a difference from the pancake-flat plains they had crossed. Before hitting the mountains, they started encountering everything from little streams to sizable rivers coming off the eastern side of the Continental Divide. For instance, over 50 smaller streams or rivers feed the Arkansas River before it crosses into Kansas. Between the Arkansas and the

Sod houses and solid citizens settled the plains for farming. (Colorado Historical Society)

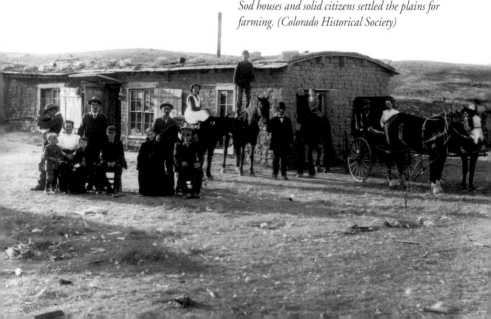

"The Chinook Wind" by Harvey Dun. (Museum of Western Art)

South Platte, another score of streams flow through the plains, and the South Platte is also fed by dozens of streams great and small.

In 1860 the federal government squeezed the Cheyennes and Arapahos into a triangular reservation between the Arkansas River and Sand Creek, about 40 miles west of the present-day Kansas border and 30 miles north of the Arkansas River. The once free-roaming hunters got a measly 40 acres per family, along with machinery, money, and instruction on how to pull the plow. Some younger braves roamed from the unfenced, unguarded reservation, attacked an occasional supply wagon, and didn't quite seem to respect the whites' generosity or boundaries.

Those forays, and the fear of more of them, helped convince many settlers that the plains would never be "safe" until even the vaguest threat of Indian attack was removed. That meant removing all the Indians.

This determination led to breaking the silence of the plains with booming cannon fire, crackling rifle shots, chilling war hoops, and the screams of wounded and dying men, women, and children.

Those sounds of conflict have long since been swept away by the wind, but are recalled by the names now proudly taken by many counties and towns on the eastern plains. Names like Pawnee, Cheyenne Wells, Kiowa, Arapaho, Comanche,

EATING DOG WITH THE INDIANS

*T*he lodge of my host, Kongra Tonga, or the Big Crow, presented a picturesque spectacle that evening. A score or more of Indians were seated around it in a circle, their dark naked forms just visible by the dull light of the smouldering fire in the centre. The pipe glowing brightly in the gloom as it passed from hand to hand around the lodge. Then a squaw would drop a piece of buffalo-fat on the dull embers. Instantly a bright glancing flame would leap up, darting its clear light to the very apex of the tall conical structure, where the tops of the slender poles that supported its covering of leather were gathered together. It gilded the features of the Indians, as with animated gestures they sat around it, telling their endless stories of war and hunting. It displayed rude garments of skins that hung around the lodge; the bow, quiver, and lance, suspended over the resting-place of the chief, and the rifles and powder-horns of the two white guests. For a moment all would be bright as day; then the flames would die away, and fitful flashes from the embers would illumine the lodge, and then leave it in darkness. Then all the light would wholly fade, and the lodge and all within it be involved again in obscurity.

As I left the lodge next morning I was saluted by howling and yelping from all around the village, and half its canine population rushed forth to the attack. Being as cowardly as they were clamorous, they kept jumping around me at the distance of a few yards, only one little cur, about ten inches long, having spirit enough to make a direct assault. He dashed valiantly at the leather tassel which in the Dahcotah fashion was trailing behind the heel of my moccason, and kept his hold, growling and snarling all the while, though every step I made almost jerked him over on his back. As I knew that the eyes of the whole village were on the watch to see if I showed any sign of apprehension, I walked forward without looking to the right or left, surrounded wherever I went by this magic circle of dogs. When I came to Reynal's lodge I sat down by it, on which the dogs dispersed growling to their respective quarters. Only one large white one remained, who kept running about before me and showing his teeth. I called him but he only growled the more. I looked at him well. He was fat and sleek; just such a dog as I wanted. "My friend," thought I, "you shall pay for this! I will have you eaten this very morning!"

I intended that day to give the Indians a feast, by way of conveying a favorable impression of my character and dignity; and a white dog is the dish which the customs of the Dahcotah prescribe for all occasions of formality and importance. I consulted Reynal; he soon discovered that an old woman in the next lodge was owner of the white dog. I took a gaudy cotton handkerchief, and laying it on the ground, arranged some vermilion, beads, and other trinkets upon it. Then the old squaw was summoned. I pointed to the dog and to the handkerchief. She gave a scream of delight, snatched up the prize, and vanished with it into her lodge. For a few more trifles I engaged the services of two other squaws, each of whom took the white dog by one of his paws, and led him away behind the lodges, while he kept looking up at them with a face of innocent surprise. Having killed him they threw him into a fire to singe; then chopped him up and put him into two large kettles to boil. Meanwhile I told Raymond to fry in buffalo-fat what little flour we had left, and also to make a kettle of tea as an additional item of the repast.

The Big Crow's squaw was briskly at work sweeping out the lodge for the approaching festivity. I confided to my host himself the task of inviting the guests, thinking that I might thereby shift from my own shoulders the odium of fancied neglect and oversight.

When feasting is in question, one hour of the day serves an Indian as well as another. My entertainment came off about eleven o'clock. At that hour, Reynal and Raymond walked across the area of the village, to the admiration of the inhabitants, carrying the two kettles of dog-meat slung on a pole between them. These they placed in the centre of the lodge, and then went back for the bread and the tea. Meanwhile I had put on a pair of brilliant moccasons, and substituted for my old buck-skin frock a coat which I had brought with me in view of such public occasions. I also made careful use of the razor, an operation which no man will neglect who desires to gain the good opinion of Indians. Thus attired, I seated myself between Reynal and Raymond at the head of the lodge. Only a few minutes elapsed before all the guests had come in and were seated on the ground, wedged together in a close circle around the lodge. Each brought with him a wooden bowl to hold his share of the repast. When all were assembled, two of the officials, called "soldiers" by the white men, came forward with ladles made of the horn of the Rocky Mountain sheep, and began to distribute the feast, always assigning a double share to the old men and chiefs. The dog vanished with astonishing celerity, and each guest turned his dish bottom upward to show that all was gone. Then the bread was distributed in its turn, and finally the tea. As the soldiers poured it out into the same wooden bowls that had served for the substantial part of the meal, I thought it had a particularly curious and uninviting color.

"Oh!" said Reynal, "there was not tea enough, so I stirred some soot in the kettle, to make it look strong."

Fortunately an Indian's palate is not very discriminating. The tea was well sweetened, and that was all they cared for.

—Francis Parkman, Jr., *The California and Oregon Trail, Being Sketches of Prairie and Rocky Mountain Life*, 1849

Neeso Pah, or Chivington. Or names like Sand Creek and Beecher's Island, the two major "battles" on the eastern plains which eventually led to the Indians' final removal.

But Sand Creek and Beecher's Island were as different as night and day; the first being the era's equivalent of throwing the Christians to the lions (with a Methodist minister doing the throwing), the second being one of the most astounding displays of stamina and courage during the Indian Wars and an example of superior technology (firepower) being the key to military victory.

The Cheyennes and Arapahos settled into the Sand Creek reservation and from 1860 to 1863 things went pretty smoothly except for a little horse stealing and minor conflicts. The Civil War had slowed the flow of settlers and in 1864 Indian raiding and rowdiness grew as roving bands struck along the Arkansas River Valley. In June, some Indians killed the Hungate family a mere 25 miles south of Denver. When the five white, scalped, and mutilated bodies were brought to town for display, terror and outrage struck. The city was certain that complete annihilation by hordes of Indians was imminent.

Arapaho and Cheyenne leaders met with Territorial Gov. John Evans (Colorado became a U.S. Territory in 1861), state officials, and military leaders. The Indians left the meeting seemingly satisfied and went back to their camps to prepare for a peaceful winter. They hadn't counted on political maneuvering or the power of public opinion. The white officials made conflicting reports of the meeting and the public and press wouldn't drop demands for outright warfare.

■ SAND CREEK MASSACRE

In August, Governor Evans, being a sensitive politician, said anyone who wanted to fight Indians could volunteer for 100 days in the Third Colorado Militia. Commanding the militia was Col. John Chivington, a Methodist minister who had served with distinction during the Civil War. With no Indians on the warpath, it appeared no action would take place before the 100-day enlistment ended, and Chivington's troops began to be ridiculed as the "Bloodless Third."

When Evans—who was pushing for statehood because a mere territory couldn't handle murderous Indians—left for Washington, Chivington decided it was time for action to satisfy the public demand for a "Bloody Third." He moved his troops

BLACK ELK SPEAKS

*W*e made these little gray houses of logs that you see, and they are square. It is a bad way to live, for there can be no power in a square.

You have noticed that everything an Indian does is in a circle, and that is because the Power of the World always works in circles, and everything tries to be round. In the old days when we were a strong and happy people, all our power came to us from the sacred hoop of the nation, and so long as the hoop was unbroken, the people flourished. The flowering tree was the living center of the hoop, and the circle of the four quarters nourished it. The east gave peace and light, the south gave warmth, the west gave rain, and the north with its cold and mighty wind gave strength and endurance. This knowledge came to us from the outer world with our religion. Everything the Power of the World does is done in a circle. The sky is round . . . and so are all the stars. The wind, in its greatest power, whirls. Birds make their nests in circles, for theirs is the same religion as ours. The sun comes forth and goes down again in circle. The moon does the same and both are round. Even the seasons form a great circle in their changing, and always come back again to where they were. The life of a man is a circle from childhood to childhood, and so it is in everything where power moves. Our teepees were round like the nests of birds, and these were always set in a circle, the nation's hoop, a nest of many nests, where the Great Spirit meant for us to hatch our children.

But the Wasichus (whites) have put us in these square boxes. Our power is gone and we are dying, for the power is not in us anymore.

—John G. Neihardt, *Black Elk Speaks,* 1932

"What an Indian Thinks," by Maynard Dixon. (Museum of Western Art)

into position around the Sand Creek Reservation on November 29, 1864, and, without warning, gave the order to attack. That's all the citizen soldiers needed to hear. They ran amok. It wasn't an attack. It was a slaughter. During an all-day battle (which shamed Chivington because the Indians were outnumbered and outgunned) no Indian prisoners were taken. Whether armed or unarmed, any Indian, including the women and children running from the scene, was summarily tracked down and killed.

Some Coloradoans thought the move long overdue and applauded the "battle," including the killing of the children. "Nits make lice," was one oft-used quote that justified such cold-blooded action. The nation didn't see things in such glowing terms. Congress reprimanded Chivington and called the action "a foul and dastardly massacre which would have disgraced the veriest savages." Famed scout Kit Carson said of Sand Creek:

> The pore Injuns had our flag flyin' over 'em, that same old stars and strips that we all love and honor . . . then here come along that durned Chivington and his cusses. They'd bin out huntin' hostile Injuns, and couldn't find none no whar . . . . So they just pitched into these friendlies, and massa-creed them—yes sir, literally massa-creed them in col' blood, in spite of our flag thar—women and little children even . . . And ye call these civilized men Christians; and the Injuns savages, du ye?

The Indian response to Sand Creek was immediate. Violence broke out all along the frontier from New Mexico to Montana. More than 20 stage stations were destroyed; the town of Julesburg, Colorado, was burned to the ground; and hundreds of people died on both sides over the next two years.

Today, on Colorado 96, north of the town of Chivington and Chivington Reservoir, a Kiowa County road leads to a small monument marking the Sand Creek Massacre.

■ Beecher's Island

The final major Indian battle in Colorado was a far different story since it was a battle in every sense of the word. The Arapaho and Cheyenne had been officially moved to Indian Territory in 1867 but still had hunting privileges and the spunk to raid isolated farms or supply wagons, which kept the public wary of "the Red Menace."

In September of 1868, about 1,000 Indians met a patrol of 50 Army scouts under Capt. John Forsyth, who quickly took refuge on an island near the Arikaree Fork of the Republican River, about 11 miles west of the current Kansas border and about 15 miles south of Wray. (This island was later named Beecher's Island in honor of a soldier killed in the attack.) The scouts delivered withering firepower thanks to a new weapon: the Spencer rifle. Instead of the old single-shot muzzle-loader of Civil War fame, the Spencer used a single cartridge, and thus could be reloaded and re-fired much more quickly. After holding off the Indians for nine days and killing famed Chief Roman Nose, the scouts were rescued by the Tenth Cavalry Regiment, an all-black force based at Fort Wallace, and took a place of honor amongst the era's Indian fighters.

By 1870, the Indians were permanently banished to reservations, the bison herds were rapidly dwindling, and settlers had begun plowing under the virgin prairie.

■ GREELEY

In 1872, Colorado set up a Board of Immigration—a forerunner of the modern chamber of commerce, to attract settlers by publicizing the state's virtues. The word "publicizing" doesn't quite express the vigor of the board's approach. How about screaming to high heaven about what a Garden of Eden this place called Colorado was? That's better.

Anyway, the publicity, willingness of emigrants to set out to newly opened land, and Americans' general feeling that things are better just over the horizon attracted settlers. It also attracted an unusual number of "colonies" or "cooperatives" in which members would share work, profits, and decisions to create a successful town.

These idealists decided this new land, especially in the northern plains near the Front Range, was the perfect place to start new communities and generally show the world just exactly how to run a perfect little farming town. **Greeley** was the most famous, and successful, of the utopian endeavors.

In 1869, a tour of the West by Nathan C. Meeker, the Agricultural Editor of the New York *Tribune*, convinced him that Colorado was perfect for a cooperative

(following pages) Irrigation greened "The Great American Desert."

farm colony. The *Tribune* was owned by Horace Greeley, and Meeker took Greeley's advice to "Go West Young Man, Go West." A public meeting in New York lined up followers willing to pay $155 a head to take part in the effort, of which Meeker was elected president. *(For more about Meeker, see page 161.)*

The promised land was purchased near the confluence of the Cache la Poudre and South Platte rivers. The settlers started arriving in the spring of 1870, imposed a total booze ban, and established the settlement of Greeley.

The big guy, Horace Greeley, came out to visit and encourage the operation. Whether it was his encouragement, a virtual absence of hangovers, or just outstanding land and plenty of irrigation water, the town of Greeley started to prosper. Extensive irrigation led to outstanding crops and an almost unheard of experiment in those days of the open range: fencing cattle off the land. Of course, a cynic or two thought the $20,000 fence was merely an effort to keep the sinners from non-utopian communities away from the saints at Greeley. Intermingling, however, took place, especially in the colony of Evans, begun in 1871 just to the south. In its saloons one could usually find a Greeleyite temporarily testing or tasting where the grass was truly greener.

Soon Greeley had a buffalo hide processing plant, museum, library, and lyceum, and by 1880, when the colony's charter had expired, the original utopianists had created the beginnings of present-day Greeley (which, by the way, retained its anti-booze law until after World War II). Not every colonist thought Greeley was a utopia. Many arrived, looked around, and left; or arrived, tried to live within the rules, then left for other plains towns or to homestead their own farms.

■ MORE UTOPIAS SPROUT

The **Longmont** colony, started in 1871 about 30 miles north of Denver, was another success story, thanks to support from rich New Yorker, Elizabeth Thompson. But good management, ample irrigation water, and hard-working colonists didn't hurt either.

Fort Collins, 30 miles north of Longmont, another colony started at this time, is still spreading the good word. In 1879 it secured Colorado State Agricultural and Mechanical College. Farmers soon reaped the benefits by getting the most from their land by using information from the school's farmer/scientists about

continues on page 39

ROUND 'EM UP, HEAD 'EM OUT
ACROSS THE PLAINS

You'd think anyone with about 30 percent of their brain cells in working order could figure out that the stupidest and most expensive way to get Texas cattle to Eastern markets would be to drive them northwest across the prairie to railheads in Colorado and Kansas where they would then be shipped back east. Why not angle those herds toward Chicago and be done with it? But there were good reasons Texas cattlemen decided to undertake epic northwest cattle drives from the 1860s to the 1880s.

One reason was that during the Civil War, the Union Army held the northern Mississippi River. In 1863, the fall of Vicksburg, Mississippi, effectively closed off the southern market for Texas cattle. Besides, no self-respecting Texas Rebel would sell anything to those damn Yankees. Thus arrived the great Texas cattle glut. Prices were a joke, even if buyers could be found. Meanwhile, without Texas cattle, beef prices back East soared. That's why Rebel cows started making their way to Colorado in earnest in 1864.

But even after the war, the direct route from Texas east wasn't the most profitable. It was impossible to drive thousands of cows through established, usually fenced, farmland, and pay every farmer for every chomp of corn consumed.

The great, open plains, on the other hand, featured miles of fenceless range and all the prairie grass a cow could eat. So it was cheaper to start from Texas in March with skinny cows and head north across the plains, letting the cattle arrive at the railhead with plenty of meat on their bones (some claim this easy eating started the federal grazing subsidies that have kept the cattle industry fat to this day, at taxpayers' expense).

Great herds—often numbering in the thousands—kept coming, especially when the train reached Denver in 1870. But getting there wasn't always that easy. The drovers had to avoid those pesky homesteaders and their fences, find water every few days, and face truly life-threatening, not to mention profit-reducing, troubles. As usual, as soon as it was apparent money could be made in cattle, large operators and corporations arrived to dominate the scene. Colorado cattle barons accumulated huge acreage and herds along the Arkansas and South Platte rivers. Some real barons from England and Ireland also invested heavily in the Western cattle industry, and the international connection helped provide the cash to create corporate farming.

continues on page 38

(following pages) Cattle ranching is still the backbone of the high plains economy.

continued from page 35

By the 1880s the open range era started to wane. Overgrazing occurred as the cattle vied for less and less grass. More homesteaders were irrigating the plains and fencing their property (in 1874, an effective barbed wire machine allowed farmers to fence on the cheap). To this day, the rule is you have to fence cattle and sheep OFF your property. If 300 cows come through a hole in your fence and eat all your hay, what a bummer, fix your fence.

By the mid-1890s the open range was pretty much closed, but it lingers in two significant ways. Stories recalling the open range and cattle drives immediately put all Americans' brain cells on hold, especially John Wayne fans. Those days are indelibly etched on America's collective vision of the West.

Everyone knows the story: a rancher facing financial ruin turns into a tough but fair trail boss, assembles an unlikely crew of misfits, drunks, and amateurs to herd his thousands of cattle across the plains. They fight the weather, Indians, each other, and finally meld together as a team, make it to the railhead, get drunk, say their emotional (for men) good-byes, and head off into the sunset and the next drive.

More importantly for Colorado, the cattle industry gave the state one more economic leg to stand on and boosted Denver's importance as a regional transportation hub. And the open range is really alive and well, now it's just described as national forests and Bureau of Land Management land.

The proliferation of cattle spreads large and small led to the creation of stockmen's associations in the 1880s. Originally started to coordinate roundups and institute a rational branding system, the associations quickly became powerful political forces. And they were instrumental in promoting the idea that cattle had a "right" to graze public land. On the Western Slope, the cattlemen fought not only the railroads and legislature, but the sheepmen. The name "Night Riders" gives you a pretty good clue about the cowboys' methods when sheepmen were the target.

The sheepmen's and cattlemen's associations, which today display only minor undercurrents of antagonism against each other, are still kicking and still have the ear of more than one local, state, and national legislator. You can hear them behind the podium, in Meeker, Denver, or Washington, D.C., recalling the heritage of the open range before launching into a biting chant about the vital importance of protecting cattle and sheep grazing rights on that huge public trough called federal land.

better irrigation and dryland farming techniques, crop rotations, profitable cash crops like sugar beets, and effective mechanization. Today, the school's extension agents still dispense the latest agricultural information and advice to farmers and ranchers throughout the state.

Longmont and Greeley were the exceptions to the rule when it came to colonies. Most colonization efforts were launched by companies in New York and Chicago that pulled cash out of innocents' pockets and sent them to barren stretches of Colorado. Several ethnic varieties of colonies were tried, and failed. The Mormons (in the San Luis Valley), the German Colonization Society (Colfax), and a Jewish settlement (Cotopaxi) all met the same fate—they failed as utopias but lived on as towns.

Sterling, which straddles Interstate 76 in the middle of the northeastern plains, was founded in 1873–74, but quickly dumped idealism and embraced pragmatism. The townsfolk offered to move lock, stock, and barrel, and toss in 80 acres of free land, if the Union Pacific Railroad would locate a division point for its line three miles (five km) northeast of the original town. The railroad accepted and the whole town picked up and moved to the new location.

Intensive tillage contributed to dust storms, such as this one outside of Lamar in 1937 during the Great Depression. (Colorado Historical Society)

Some aspects of farm life never change.

Ironically, while the utopionists were busy trying to use "civilization" to create a utopia, they overlooked the type of utopia Mother Nature laid at their feet: the prairie itself. Today, a bit of that natural utopia is preserved in the **Pawnee National Grassland,** located north of Colorado 14, which links Fort Collins and Sterling. No plows slashed through the buffalo grass and other native prairie plants. Creeks still run free, and during the four seasons the wind, rain, snow, and sunshine still play on the natural prairie much as they did when the wagonloads of wide-eyed optimists rolled through on their way to their version of utopia. *Information on Pawnee National Grassland is available from the Forest Service office in Greeley at 660 O Street; (970) 346-5000.*

By the turn of the century the colony craze had cooled. Towns had been established, the good land claimed, the bad abandoned, and favorable court rulings had secured a steady supply of irrigation water. By 1907, six million acres of Colorado farmland had been irrigated, most of it on the eastern plains.

In the decades that followed, all that was left for those who found themselves in the small towns dotting the eastern plains was the choice between staying and putting down roots and making this land theirs and their children's, or bolting from the serenity and set ways of the eastern plains for bigger, more exciting environs.

IT'S THE REAL AMERICA:
SMALL TOWNS OF THE EASTERN PLAINS

In between the plain's main arteries—the interstate highways and the Arkansas River—are small farm towns sheltering anywhere from a couple dozen to 10,000 residents and accessible only by those straight-as-a-string blue-line highways. They are intriguing, sometimes mysterious, usually misunderstood. Often they operate under a different set of rules than their urban counterparts, and they can, among those who know them well, quickly generate deep, almost mystical affection or a cold sneer of contempt.

Along the interstate highways are some plains towns urging motorists to pull off for some gas, a meal, and maybe a night of rest. But most of the plains towns are untainted by tourism. Conversely, plains towns also remain free of tourism's benefits—cultural events, upscale eateries (cuisine, not food), art galleries, and international fame.

The eastern plains towns have experienced a natural, slow evolution and are peopled by those who have found something special, something intriguing in the way of life sustained in an intimate community. The people who choose to live in small towns infuse them with civic parallels of their own personalities.

The common characteristics of most small towns are cited by fans and foes alike as either the basis for a passion for such a way of life, or dread of the same.

WHERE NEIGHBORS STILL CARE

Fans celebrate the small town as a final remnant of "real America," an America where neighbors still care about neighbors and the good of the community, a community where "values" are more than stock market quotes. They are places where:

+ If you need to go to the bank you can park in the middle of the street, run inside, do your business, trot back to your car, and wave at the cop driving by, who just waves back and shakes his head a little.

+ You usually lock your doors at night, but if you wake up at midnight and realize you forgot, you don't sit upright in bed and break out in a cold sweat.

+ The blaring of the fire siren to call out the volunteer fire department sends people racing out of the Elks Club meeting. Or the Rotary Club. Or the chamber of commerce.

+ You don't have to go to town council meetings because you already stopped the mayor on the street and gave him an earful.

+ Without the help of the local newspaper, you know what's happened, what should have happened, and what probably will happen, because that's what always happens.

+ On most summer weekdays the cheering of the spectators at the slow-pitch softball game drowns out the traffic noise on the main drag.

+ Half the population makes the trek, convoy style, to root for the high school team at state championships.

+ You shop downtown, even if it costs a little more than the big mall, because, well, just because it's your downtown.

+ It takes 15 minutes to work your way through the coffee shop because you have to say "hi" to everyone and generally get caught up.

+ It's easy to appreciate and benefit from a family's roots because they are generations deep.

WHERE LIFE'S TOO SLOW

On the other hand, to the foes of small towns, life seems stifled—a stodgy anachronism. They see them as mere backwaters, as holding tanks for those who didn't have the talent or gumption to swim in a bigger pond. For these people small towns are places where:

+ The police decide on the spot who should spend the night in jail, who should go home and sleep it off, and when a bus ticket to Denver solves a transient problem.

+ Playing golf with the town judge or poker with the police chief can keep little "indiscretions" under wraps and keep the scales of justice tipping the right way, toward the "right" people.

+ The same group, usually of men, seems to always get elected to the town council. And they include the president of the Elks. And the president of the Rotary. And the president of the chamber of commerce.

+ There is nothing else to do on a weekday summer night but play slow-pitch softball or cruise the main drag.

+ Everyone that counts plays high school sports, and scoring 30 points in a basketball game just might improve a student's comprehension of the Civil War.

◆ Shopping means filling out catalog order forms and waiting for the UPS truck.

◆ The coffee shop crew knows all about that intimate nightcap you enjoyed with your new flame. And the sight of a local's car in the parking lot at the Dew Drop Inn informs everyone in town whose spouse is out of town.

◆ If you don't have grandparents buried in the town cemetery, you're going to be a newcomer for quite a while.

So which is it? Shangri-la or Living Hell? Here's one hint: small town life must be pretty appealing or there would be more ghost towns on Colorado's eastern plains than in its mineral-rich mountains, which are full of them.

Speaking of life in the slow lane, try a stagecoach ride.

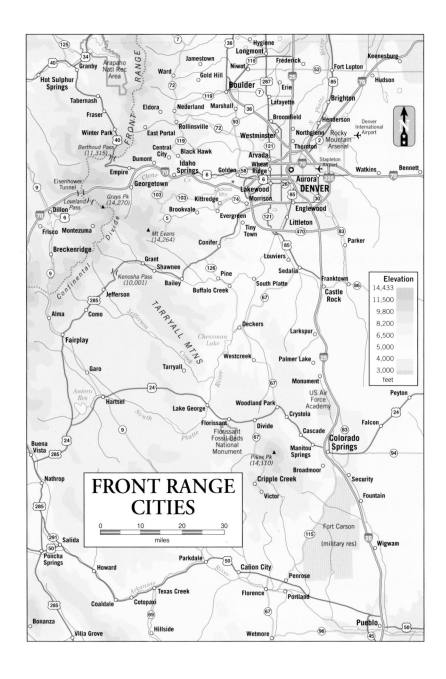

FRONT RANGE CITIES

0   10   20   30
miles

Elevation
14,433
11,500
9,800
8,200
6,500
5,000
4,000
3,000
feet

FRONT RANGE CITIES
DENVER, BOULDER, COLORADO SPRINGS, PUEBLO

WHEN PRESIDENT DWIGHT D. EISENHOWER FLEW INTO DENVER in the mid-1950s on his way to do a little fishing, the media followed. Their stories and photos revealed a surprise to the nation: the cities along Colorado's Front Range had evolved from a string of rough frontier towns into unique, modern cities primed to lead the West into the future. That attention also alerted the nation to the special combination of attitude and natural allure of Front Range cities that would eventually be dubbed "quality of life."

■ URBAN HISTORY

Until World War II, Colorado's Front Range cities—Denver, Boulder, Colorado Springs, and Pueblo—weren't much to brag about. Towns at the base of the Rockies had existed in part to supply mines, miners, and prospectors. Later they supported smelting, minting, or other forms of finagling gold and silver into "useful financial instruments" or hornswaggling investors into thinking a piece of paper with a mine's name on it would make them rich. Which was not bad work, if you could find it.

Despite the best efforts of civic boosters and the newly minted mining tycoons, the urban scene resembled little more than the squalid, ramshackle slums of older, more established eastern cities. The gold and silver barons tried to dress up the drab little cities with stately brick mansions and plush hotels, but those bits of Victorian refinement swam against the tide in a sea of mud streets and slap-dash building. During most of the nineteenth century, Colorado's "cities" seemed to be frontier outposts at best and muck holes at worst, full of hayseeds, bums, fools called prospectors, and much of the nation's undesirable or immoral population. By the early twentieth century, urban Colorado, if more respectable, was still a backwater.

The booming metropolis of Denver with its historic clocktower in the foreground.

■ MOVING INTO THE MODERN ERA

Mining made **Denver** the state's transportation and financial center, so it remained a city to be reckoned with. "Quality of life" was probably an alien term to Robert W. Speer, but as mayor of Denver in 1904, he knew it was lacking. First he tackled small things, like cleaning up Cherry Creek, building sewers and storm drains, and actually laying out streets and lining them with trees. Bigger items were next, like dotting the town with parks and starting a Greek-style Civic Center Auditorium. Thus a little quality was added to life in Denver.

Then came "Cow Town" days, a tag Denver sought during the 1880s, was glad to have during the Depression, and in fact deserved after the Monfort family, in 1930, came up with a new way to raise and fatten cattle. Instead of letting cows roam around eating whatever range grass was handy, the Monfort clan penned them up and stuffed them with hay, corn, and grain. Thus was born the modern cattle feedlot wherein a skinny calf could become a fattened calf in no time. And in no time all those cattle were being shipped through the cow town of Denver.

Denver's railroad yards expanded into a spaghetti-like swirling of tracks and spurs to accommodate huge stockyards. Although Denver never matched Chicago's "brawny shoulders" when it came to stockyards, it wasn't exactly a 98-pound weakling either. The city welcomed the jobs, although the accompanying, er, well, aroma, wasn't listed in chamber of commerce brochures.

By the 1970s, Denver had decided to go upscale, and it's been trying to live down its cow town image ever since.

The college town of **Boulder** (University of Colorado) just kind of chugged along, thanks to an ability to lure Eastern "adventurers" wanting a taste of the West along with a taste of Plato and beer.

Colorado Springs, thanks to General William Palmer and Pikes Peak, was one huge chamber of commerce brochure. A true tourist city, it relied on a flow of visitors, rather than natural resources, for its livelihood.

Down south a bit farther, **Pueblo** took almost everything in stride because it was a steel town whose furnaces stayed hot, thanks to Colorado Fuel and Iron (CF&I) and the coal and coke fields near Trinidad. As the first fully integrated steel mill in the West, the Pueblo works had a jump on the competition, a jump that kept it ahead of the crowd for almost 70 years and kept Pueblo a stable, blue-collar city.

Stockyards fueled the growth of the city after the mining boom faded.

The front door of NORAD/U.S. Space Command, Cheyenne Mountain Operations, weighs 30 tons and is three feet thick. Supposedly,, it can withstand a direct nuclear attack.

■ THE MILITARY MOVES IN AND OUT

Starting with adobe forts and tent garrisons during the pioneer days, the military has maintained a constant presence in Colorado. World War II prompted a full-scale military assault on the state's land and economy. Existing military installations were expanded, and the Front Range welcomed new army bases, hospitals, and air fields.

Another type of "installation" also called Colorado home, but it is not mentioned today with much pride. A relocation camp on the eastern plains near Granada held thousands of Japanese Americans for the duration of the war.

After the war the boom kept going. Colorado Springs became the site of the U.S. Air Force Academy in 1958, and the North American Air Defense Command Center (NORAD) burrowed into nearby Cheyenne Mountain a few years later. The Rocky Mountain Arsenal, located just outside Denver, became one of the nation's biggest producers of chemical and nuclear weapons.

The peak of the military boom came in the early 1980s when the Air Force Space Operations Center at Colorado Springs was chosen to coordinate and oversee the "Star Wars" defense program. Colorado's lucrative link to the military pork barrel had many convinced this was one economic boom that would not end with a bust, as had many before.

They were wrong. When the Iron Curtain came crashing down, Colorado's high-flying defense industry took a nose dive. Military facilities were closed. The teams at norad and Star Wars scrambled to redefine their missions amidst drastic budget cuts. The technicians and bomb makers at the Rocky Mountain Arsenal were sent packing, replaced by cleanup experts who attacked the radioactive and toxic residues left behind after decades of haphazard hazardous waste disposal.

An improbable benefit came to light with the closure of the arsenal. The facility had made use of only a small fraction of the acreage assigned to it. Hundreds of acres of grasslands remained untouched as the surrounding area succumbed to urbanization.

The bulk of the arsenal's land was preserved in its natural state and dedicated as a wildlife refuge, harboring hundreds of species of native plants and animals, including deer and bald eagles. This startling transformation allows Colorado to boast of one of the nation's largest wildlife preserves located ridiculously close to the sprawling urban centers of Denver and Boulder.

■ ABOUT DENVER

When the nation was suffering through the assorted energy crises of the 1970s and early 1980s, Denver was delighted. Situated in the heart of a region overflowing with coal, natural gas, oil, uranium, and oil shale, Denver saw itself in the hub of a monster boom. It was almost as good as the gold and silver days.

Skyscrapers popped up so quickly in downtown Denver it was suggested the state bird should be the elevated building crane instead of the lark bunting. Most major energy companies set up regional offices, uncounted independent and smaller companies also flocked in, and Denver became a high-flying energy boom town. As oil prices kept rising, bulldozers kept digging away at oil shale, drilling rigs kept popping up and drilling down, and Denver kept soaring.

The energy bust, of course, eventually came, but when Denver performed a slow swan dive into it, Denverites didn't gnash their teeth or whine. Instead, they

DENVER IN 1865

*I*n that period Denver was appropriately called the "City of the Plains." Situated sixteen miles from the base of the nearest Rocky Mountain peak, and six hundred and fifty miles from Atchison, Kansas, the nearest town to the east, . . . its population numbered about five thousand souls. Here was to be found the illiterate man—but a grade above coyote—lawbreakers of every kind and from every land, to men of culture and refinement.

Here it stood, a typical mining town, a monument to the indomitable energy of man in his efforts to settle that barren and almost endless plain and open to the world the Rocky's unlimited hidden gold. Here were brick structures modern for that day, the brick being made from the soil of the territory; a United States mint, a church, a school house, large warehouses, stores, and the home of the *Rocky Mountain Daily News,* which kept one partially in touch with happenings in the faraway states. Isolated from the outside world, it was an ideal place of refuge for those anxious to escape the outraged law. Knights of the green cloth held full sway. Men in every walk of life gambled. A dead man for breakfast was not an uncommon heading for the menu card, the old tree on the west bank of Cherry Creek furnishing the man. Society was just a little exclusive and to gain admission the pass was, "Where are you from?" and in some cases, "Your name in the east?"

Desperadoes made one attempt to lay the city in ashes and certainly would have accomplished their purpose had it not been for the timely action of the Vigilance Committee in hanging the ring-leaders. When the guilt of a suspect for any crime was in doubt, he was presented with a horse or mule and ordered to leave between sun and sun and never return.

—Charles E. Young
Dangers of the Trail in 1865

took stock of what they had and set about going after what they wanted.

Denver was still the biggest city in the inter-mountain West, still a regional transportation, financial, and supply hub, with more federal workers than any city but Washington, D.C. The half-empty skyscrapers presented an opportunity to lure new companies into town with plenty of cheap office space.

Sizing up its assets, Denver decided to pour its efforts into rejuvenating its downtown core. A new convention center was built. The performing arts center was expanded and polished to a high sheen. The city turned urban renewal into a contact sport, offering help and tax cuts and partnerships to businesses willing to set up shop in the city.

To keep congestion to a minimum, the city installed a light-rail line through downtown and beefed up bus service, meaning visitors and locals alike could park their cars and leave the driving to someone else.

Then lower downtown (known as LoDo) landed two prizes: Elitch Gardens and Coors Field. Fun-lovers flocked to Elitch's, baseball fans flocked to Coors Field, and developers flocked into LoDo.

In almost no time at all, a rundown warehouse district was transformed into a place to go and a place to live. Shops, galleries, and night spots opened at street level, and people began to move into large, renovated lofts above, providing something previously unheard in Denver: a growing population of affluent downtown dwellers.

Looking to keep and expand its role as the region's premiere airline hub, Denver, with help from the rest of the state, built Denver International Airport on 34,000 acres of prairie east of town. After a bumpy construction period, the terminal's distinctive tent-like outline stands as an impressive piece of imaginative engineering. Capable of handling over 1,200 flights a day, DIA provides a modern, reliable air link to the rest of the world, even during the worst winter weather.

And to secure its reputation as a "big league city," Denver landed a major league baseball franchise, christened the Colorado Rockies, and a hockey team, dubbed the Colorado Avalanche. With the Broncos (football) and the Nuggets (baseball) already in town, Denver became one of a handful of cities in the nation with four major professional sports teams.

■ EXPLORING DENVER

Denver is a city of brick homes, tree-lined streets, and a settled, comfortable feel, a city where roots have taken hold. Two decades of urban renewal have spared most of the historic center, spruced it up, and provided new reasons to visit Denver. To assist you in learning what they are, pick up a free copy of Westword, Denver's award-winning weekly arts and entertainment newspaper. For help in getting around call the RTD or drop in on one of its information centers. *Colfax and Broadway, or Market and 16th; (303) 299-6000.*

A glance at the map should convince most visitors to explore downtown Denver by foot. Most of the sights are conveniently contained in an area of about 20 blocks. And driving through the maze of one-way streets, three-way intersections, triangular buildings, and general confusion requires—or becomes—an extensive education. The city was laid out at the confluence of the South Platte River and Cherry Creek, making the concept "grid system" a joke.

If driving into downtown on the I-25, a good option is to park in the garage at Broadway and Kentucky and catch the RTD light rail into downtown. Or you can take your chances and just drive toward the center until you can't go any farther—you will no doubt be facing a one-way street—and a garage or parking lot will probably appear as an answered prayer. Once within the downtown area, you can walk just about anywhere, and when your feet fail you, hop aboard the free shuttle on the mile-long Sixteenth Street Mall and ride from the Civic Center to Market Street, two blocks from LoDo.

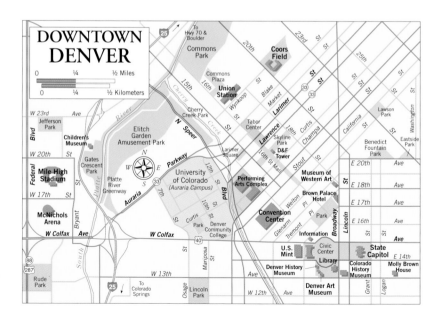

Downtown Denver Highlights

State Capitol Building. Built in 1894, the capitol features a gold dome and opulent appointments that would make a silver baron blush. The interior makes use of the world's entire supply of rose onyx. Free tours are offered on weekdays, and if you can make it up a 93-step staircase you'll be treated to a stunning view of the Rocky Mountains and the rest of Denver. *Broadway and Colfax Avenue; (303) 866-2604.*

Molly Brown House. Two blocks behind the state capitol, Pennsylvania Street runs atop just the slightest of hills, where those who grew rich in Colorado's gold and silver rush built their mansions. Of the score of elegant nineteenth-century homes that remain, one stands apart, not only because of the two sculpted lions guarding its opulence, but because of who happened to call it home: the Unsinkable Molly Brown. *(See page 58).* The home has been restored and filled with period furniture and Molly memorabilia. *1340 Pennsylvania Street; (303) 832-4092.*

The Colorado History Museum. A wide variety of displays and attractions tell the story of the state. Some of the finest examples of Anasazi pottery available are on display, along with detailed dioramas depicting frontier forts, buffalo hunts, and mining techniques. On a larger scale are pieces of mining equipment, a covered wagon, a sod house, and a huge model of Denver as it was in 1860 before it was razed by fire. A 150-year time-line and research library let you trace the state's history and dig as deeply as you want into the people, places, and events that shaped Colorado. *13th and Broadway; (303) 866-3682.*

Byers-Evans House and Denver History Museum. Built in 1883 for William Byers, founder of the *Rocky Mountain News,* and then occupied by John Evans, the state's second governor. A guided tour of the home gives a glimpse of the good life in post–World War I Colorado. The carriage house contains exhibits and interactive videos on Denver history. *13th and Bannock; (303) 620-4933.*

Denver Public Library. Its renowned, irreplaceable Western History collection has long sent historians of the West into Pavlovian pantings. Since the dramatic new building, designed by Michael Graves, opened in 1995, the library has become a must-see spot for the tourist as well. Architectural tours and tours of the collection are offered daily. *10 W. 14th Avenue Parkway; (303) 640-6206.*

Denver Art Museum. This modern 10-story structure was designed by Gio Ponti and completed in 1971. Windows

continues on page 54

seem to have been set at random into the building's 28 sides. (The windows were placed as they are to reveal "living art;" that is, looking from the inside out.) It's eye catching, but is it art? Inside are what many consider to be the world's finest examples of Native American art. *100 W. 14th Avenue Parkway; (303) 844-3582.*

United States Mint. This Italian Renaissance-style monolith with its four-and-a-half foot thick walls was built in 1904 and has become an extremely popular tourist attraction. Weekday tours are free, but not samples of its wares, which include the nation's second largest stash of gold bullion. *320 W. Colfax Avenue at Cherokee Avenue; (303) 844-3582.*

Brown Palace Hotel. Comfortably nestled in amongst the imposing glass and steel skyscrapers of downtown Denver, this now stubby sandstone rectangle of a building is a living reminder of gold and silver's glory days, complete with Victorian art deco delights and a nine-story atrium topped with Tiffany stained glass that was the talk of its day when it was built in 1892. Now into its second century, the hotel hasn't lost its sheen. *321 17th Street.*

The Museum of Western Art. This building with a past houses a fine collection of Western art, including more than 125 paintings and bronze sculptures which trace the development of the Western frontier from the Fur Trapper Era through World War II. The building was once a bordello and gambling hall to which silver barons and cattle kings traveled surreptitiously through a sub-floor tunnel from the Brown Palace Hotel across the street. *1727 Tremont Place; (303) 296-1880.*

Sixteenth Street Mall. This mile-long, pedestrian zone is a commercial center rather than a tourist attraction, but it's a better-than-average way to get from here to there, by foot or free shuttle bus. Along the way, you'll see fountains, trees, shops, restaurants, and espresso stands. *16th Street between Colfax and Market.*

D&F Tower on the Sixteenth Street Mall is a bit of history poking its head into the skyline. At a whopping 325 feet, it was the tallest building west of the Mississippi upon completion in 1910 and intended to resemble the campanile at San Marco in Venice. *16th Street and Arapahoe.*

Tabor Center, also on the mall, uses three levels of glass, chrome, towering skylights, a 550-foot long greenhouse and every other modern architectural trick to set the scene for the center's 70 shops and restaurants. *16th Street between Larimer and Arapahoe.*

continues on page 56

The State Capitol Building presides over gardens of Civic Center Park (top). The 67-acre Elitch Gardens Amusement Park is the first such to relocate into a downtown.

Larimer Square The historic Victorian buildings on Denver's oldest commercial street have been restored to their former splendor, and lodge an eclectic sprinkling of establishments, from art galleries and outdoor cafes to unique shops and bistros. *1400 block of Larimer.*

Lower Downtown (LoDo)

The neighborhood bounded by Union Station, Larimer Square, Coors Field, and Cherry Creek has become one of the hottest spots in town, with dozens of art galleries and scores of shops, restaurants, jazz joints, night spots, and sports bars. It is liveliest on summer nights.

Elitch Garden Amusement Park. This century-old institution reopened in 1995 in its LoDo location as a spanking new, cleanly scrubbed, high-speed, modern version of an amusement park. *I-25 and Speer Boulevard. (Exit 212A); (303) 595-4386.*

The LoDo, or "Lower Downtown" historic district has become a popular locale for restaurants, galleries, and micro-breweries (above).

The recently restored clocktower of the D&F Tower overlooks the Sixteenth Street Mall. (right)

UNSINKABLE MOLLY BROWN

A Missouri native, Molly Tobin hit Leadville in the early 1880s. It took a few years, but in 1886 she finally snagged her man: James J. Brown, superintendent of the Little Johnny Mine. Brown's mere one-eighth share of the mine's wealth made him a millionaire and allowed the couple to move to lavish digs, complete with sculpted lions at the entrance, in Denver's most stylish neighborhood. Molly decided to conquer Denver's close-knit upper crust, the so-called "sacred 36," only to be constantly rebuked. Denver's prominent families thought she was not merely a social climber, but a social leaper, if not a broad jumper, and took great delight in snubbing her.

That's why midnight, April 14, 1912, was lucky for Molly. That's when the *Titanic* sunk and she boarded lifeboat number six. Rallying the scared survivors, she scared the hell out of the helmsman, took a turn at the oars, shared her clothing with those colder than herself, and became the heroine of the *Titanic* tragedy, or so said the newspapers of the day.

At any rate, she was generally credited with extraordinary effort and general gutsiness throughout the whole affair. After that, the doors of Denver society grudgingly swung open for the now "Unsinkable" Molly Brown, and she reached the high point of her life.

Things got messy after that. Jim Brown died in 1922, leaving no will, just legal entanglements. Her

"The Unsinkable Molly Brown" afloat in Victorian finery. (Colorado Historical Society)

riches might have been slowly shrinking, but her bravado never did. She kept swaggering through exclusive hotels in Palm Beach, New York, and Europe in lavish, if not exactly stylish, clothes.

She still remembered Leadville, though, by offering to supply the town's children with mittens and presents during the Depression. She didn't have enough money for the gifts, but her family members quietly fulfilled the promise.

The Unsinkable Molly Brown died in 1932, her wardrobe in tatters, bills for back-rent and other legal problems still dogging her, but not depressing her unsinkable determination to never give up the grand life she had, for the most part, created for herself.

GREATER DENVER DIVERSIONS

Denver is not just a downtown; its many diversions can keep you busy for days. **City Park,** on Colorado Boulevard just north of Speer Boulevard, contains a day's worth of activities for kids and adults, including the zoo and natural history museum, described below.

Denver Zoo. One of the nation's top ten, the Denver zoo has innovative natural habitats and fine new exhibits. *In City Park at East 23rd Avenue and Steele Street; (303) 331-4100.*

Denver Museum of Natural History. This popular museum features good old Colorado dinosaurs and over 90 other dioramas displaying North America's plants and animals. The museum also hosts national traveling historic exhibitions, as well as a fine mineral display, including "Tom's Baby," Colorado's largest gold nugget. **The** IMAX **Theater,** with a screen four-and-a-half stories high by six-and-a-half-stories wide, brings everything into sharp focus, as does the **Charles C. Gates Planetarium,** which features the solar system in multimedia splendor and laser shows that are, shall we say, hot.

Lakeside Amusement Park. Here is the relaxed, old-fashioned counterpoint to Elitch Gardens. Lakeside has all the requisite rides, including a wonderful wooden roller coaster that lets you feel the rattles and shakes, making it king of the hill for aficionados in the "vomit comet" world. The park wears its age with pride. Oh, and it's cheaper than Elitch's, too. *4601 Sheridan Boulevard at I-70; (303) 477-1621.*

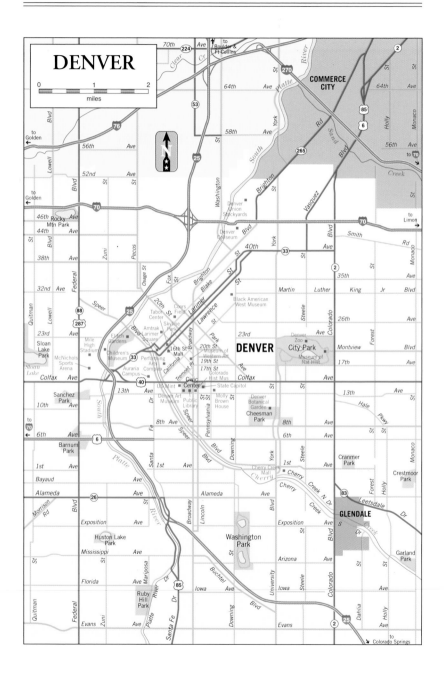

DAY TRIPS FROM DENVER

Coors Brewery. Perhaps the most popular day trip from Denver is the 12-mile drive on US 6 to Golden. Once there, people foam at the mouth to tour the **Adolf Coors Brewing Company**, the world's largest single brewing facility. If you're of age, you can sample the company's products, to a point, of course. *13th Avenue and Ford Street, Golden; (303) ₁277-BEER.*

Buffalo Bill's Grave and Museum. Buffalo Bill, the West's best known frontiersman and showman, didn't really want to be buried on Lookout Mountain 20 miles outside Denver, as the folks remind anyone who asks in Cody, Wyoming, and North Platte, Nebraska, where Bill had ranches and lived. But he died at a relative's house in Denver, and well, civic pride and a little quick talking landed Bill atop the hill. The museum contains posters, guns, outfits, and other remnants from Cody's Wild West Show, along with exhibits on frontier life and the Pony Express, which had a station in Julesburg on the eastern plains. *On Lookout Mountain Road, Golden. Exit 256 off I-70; (303) 526-0747.*

Mount Evans and Echo Lake. This is what the Rocky Mountains are all about. Mount Evans is located just 40 miles west of Denver, on Colorado 103 off Interstate 70. Once the road is cleared of snow around the end of May, you can drive right to the top of this 14,260-foot peak and breathe the rarified air usually reserved for those with large lungs and climbing gear. At the base of the mountain, Echo Lake Park features picnic spots, fishing, and views of the surrounding, usually snowcapped, peaks.

Gold Mining Towns

Some of the West's most famous gold mining towns are within an hour's drive of Denver. Central City, Breckenridge, Georgetown, and Silver Plume, to name just a few, were once boomtowns and have recently been reborn with their golden history intact. *(See following chapter,* "ROCKY MOUNTAINS," *page 84.)*

Rocky Mountain National Park *(see page 124)* and several ski areas, such as Arapahoe Basin, Eldora, and Loveland *(see page 240)* are all within an hour's drive of Denver.

■ BOULDER

When prospectors hit a legitimate mother lode on Gold Hill, just west of town, Boulder found itself leading the state into the 1860s' gold boom. A steadier source of employment, however, quickly became the center of Boulder—the University of Colorado—which has since kept the city on an even keel. When the computer age dawned, Boulder became home to a fast growing, high-tech explosion that has made it one of the nation's top computer and high-tech startup zones.

Then there's the sports boom. Boulder has long been the home training ground for many of the nation's top-notch runners, cyclists, and triathletes. It has produced runners such as Frank Shorter and Arturo Barrios; cyclists Davis Phinney and Connie Carpenter, and triathletes Mark Allen and Scot Molina—just to get the list started. The town continues to attract young athletes who hope to fill, then pass, their heroes' fast-moving shoes.

Why is Boulder such hot training ground?

Well, the pleasant winters allow for year-round training (with a little spunk and the right gear, that is); the altitude (5,363 feet) makes the air seem thicker almost anywhere else; and a large athletic community provides support, world-class training partners, and, because stars are so commonplace, some anonymity.

Thanks to Eldorado Canyon, Boulder Canyon, and Flagstaff Mountain, all just minutes from town, rock climbers of all abilities consider Boulder a mecca. The climbing community in Boulder is large, supportive, and growing almost daily. More than one mountaineer got his or her start by crawling and clawing to the top of a chute or wall in one of these climbing hot spots, then deciding that Boulder was the perfect base camp from which to launch wholeheartedly into the demanding sport.

Combine a beautiful setting, university eggheads, computer nerds, a horde of outdoor-loving athletes, and an environmentalist on every corner and you have quality-of-life becoming almost a religion in Boulder. A little touchy-feely for some, a bit far-out for others, seemingly extreme by some standards, but jealously guarded and paying off for Boulder, regardless.

To some, it's paying off too well. Boulder's expansive public parks, aggressive open space program, and slow-growth political climate have given it a well-deserved reputation as a city on the cutting edge of urban planning. But those policies cut both ways. Boulder's amenities attract an ever-increasing number of

The Flat Irons rise above Chautauqua Park on the edge of Boulder—a town justly famous for its myriad of recreational areas in and around town.

people concerned about quality of life. The city is constantly grappling with growing pains and working to ensure that growth will not destroy those qualities which attracted newcomers in the first place.

Boulder has embarked on a long-range plan to limit the type and amount of both commercial and residential growth within its boundaries. Boulder, in other words, is in the enviable position of being able to say it doesn't want to grow much more, and it is more than willing to turn people and businesses away so it can give its full attention to making the city a better, not necessarily bigger, place to live.

Those who enter Boulder via US 36 are greeted by a big mall, but entrances to cities can be deceiving. Keep going. Hit Baseline, turn off at Broadway, and you're heading for the heart of Boulder.

An aerial view (looking to the southwest) of the University of Colorado campus.

to
Rocky Mtn
Natl Park

Sixmile
Reservoir

to
Longmont

Lee   Hill
Dr

36

119

Violet   Ave

Wonderland
Lake

Wonderland
Lake Park

Poplar   Ave

7

Broadway

Jay   Rd

Twin
Lakes

Norwood   Ave

19th St

26th St

Diagonal

47th St

57th St

Independence   Rd

Rustic
Knolls

Linden   Dr

Linden   Ave

Hawthorne Ave

Iris   Ave

119

Hayden
Lake

Boulder
Municipal
Airport

North
Boulder
Park

Balsam   Ave

119

Valmont   Rd

63rd St

4th St

Alpine   Ave

36

BOULDER

Leggett
Owens
Res

Mapleton   Ave

9th

Broadway

Pearl   Pkwy

BOULDER
MOUNTAIN
PARK

Pearl   St
Pearl
Street
Mall

7

28th St

30th St

Foothills

Creek

55th St

Arapahoe   Rd   7

Canyon

Blvd

119

City Hall

Arapahoe   Ave

119

to
Boulder
Canyon &
Nederland

Central Park

Boulder

Bike

Carpenter
Park

University of
Colorado
(East Campus)

Arapahoe   Rd

Panorama
Point

Historical
Museum

Macky
Auditorium

Path

Folsom
Stadium

Colorado   Ave

Eisenhower

St

Flagstaff

College   Ave

University of
Colorado

93

Events
Center

Pennsylvania   Ave

Baseline
Heights

Rd

Aurora   Ave

6th St

14th St

Fiske
Planetarium

Aurora   Ave

Mohawk   Dr

Baseline   Rd

Baseline   Rd

Chautauqua
Park

Broadway

Moorhead

Pawnee

157

Baseline
Reservoir

BOULDER

MOUNTAIN

PARK

Dartmouth   Ave

Ash   Ave

Martin   Dr

36

Boulder

Martin
Park   Dr

S

Boulder   Rd

Cherryvale Rd

National
Center for
Atmospheric
Research

Table St

Mesa

Denver-Boulder Turnpike

to
Denver

Lehigh St

Emerson   Ave

Gillaspie Dr

Broadway

South

Viele
Lake

Harlow
Platts
Park   Blvd

93

Greenbriar

BOULDER

0   1
mile

(following pages) The Flat Iron Mountains rise abruptly above the city of Boulder. Howling
chinook winds of hurricane force occasionally blast out of the canyons and over the city.

EXPLORING BOULDER

University of Colorado. The campus, with its tree-lined walkways and solidly academic-looking brick buildings topped by red tile, is the first attraction. A second is the frenzy of college students trying to look cool while rushing to their next class. By comparison the lunch bunch at Colorado Springs' Air Force Academy looks a bit rigid. *Broadway between Arapahoe Avenue and Baseline Road; (303) 492-6301.*

The Hill. The area where College and Broadway come together is filled with shops and cafes for the college crowd when they're feeling less frenetic. This is the place to relive your college days or bemoan the fate of the nation at the thought that what you're seeing is our "best and brightest."

Pearl Street Mall. This pedestrian mall is always alive and usually bizarre enough to bring a grin or an incredulous look from some. Entertainment runs from sidewalk jugglers and singers to painters to organized concerts and educational seminars. Food ranges from basic burgers to such foreign-sounding stuff that you don't dare ask about ingredients. This combination of Berkeley and Haight Street, plus a few Bermuda-short types

from Des Moines thrown in to add some color, makes the mall a "don't miss." *Pearl Street between 11th and 15th Streets.*

Boulder Creek Path. A unique feature of Boulder is that it has brought the outside inside town. The **Boulder Creek Bike/ Pedestrian Trail** winds through town from east to west and delivers a refreshing dose of the outside to all the urbanity. *55th Street and Pearl Parkway to Arapahoe Avenue and Canyon Boulevard; (303) 441-3407.*

Boulder Canyon, Flagstaff Mountain, and Eldorado Canyon. Get a real taste of Boulder's outdoor life in the easily accessible mountain parks that offer serious climbing routes for serious rock climbers and trails for mere hikers. If you've ever wondered why people tie themselves to ropes and scale a sheer rock wall or shimmy up cracks in said wall, you can watch climbers displaying the combination of strength, grace, quick thinking, and determination that make this a unique and rapidly expanding pursuit. *Boulder Canyon is west of town on Colorado 119; Flagstaff Mountain is off Baseline Road; Eldorado Canyon is off Colorado 93.*

Farther Afield. Those not wanting to sweat their way into the wilds can take a number of scenic drives through the foothills and hit high-mountain scenery on one end, history on the other. West of Boulder on Colorado 119 is **Nederland,** an old gold mining town starting to modernize while retaining small-town charms. Take Colorado 72 north and you will eventually end up at the resort town of **Estes Park** and **Rocky Mountain National Park,** or stay on 119 south and you'll find yourself in the revived gold rush towns of **Black Hawk** and **Central City.** *(See* "ROCKY MOUNTAINS," *page 93, for more on these historic settlements.)*

■ COLORADO SPRINGS

Colorado Springs has always been an exception to its Front Range brethren, because it was designed from the very beginning to attract tourists. Broad boulevards—neatly laid out to accommodate the carriages of the rich and stylish of the late 1800s—and the fine Broadmoor Hotel were all part of a plan to turn the town of Colorado Springs into a European-style vacation spa and resort.

Those efforts, proximity to Pikes Peak and the Garden of the Gods, as well as such visitor amenities as the first golf links west of the Mississippi, made Colorado Springs the Front Range's original tourist city.

Spirited promotion kept the tourists coming. Pikes Peak became the nation's most famous mountain, even though it isn't Colorado's highest or even its most dynamic-looking peak. Assuring the peak's fame was the second oldest car race in America: the **Pikes Peak Hillclimb,** organized in 1915. Only the Indianapolis 500 is older, but Indy lacks 156 hairpin turns up a gravel mountain road.

Colorado Springs took its quality of life to the bank for over a century, but it also realized it couldn't rest atop Pikes Peak twiddling its thumbs while waiting for more bankable deliveries. So it began courting the military, and in the post-World War II era, the military delivered. The military brass liked the view of Pikes Peak so much it virtually encircled the town with bases, airfields, and command posts. Colorado Springs scored the North American Air Defense Command Center (NORAD) in 1957. This little enterprise entailed digging a huge cave deep into Cheyenne Mountain from which to operate the nation's nuclear wars come hell or commie nukes. The Air Force Academy came to town in 1958 and those crafty Colorado Springers quickly repeated their Pikes Peak performance and turned the Academy and its unique chapel into one of the state's largest tourist attractions. A real double-dipper, in other words.

Double back-flips occupied the city as it worked to become the nation's Olympic city. The U.S. Olympic Committee, headquarters for the Olympic training centers, and 20 sports national governing bodies now call Colorado Springs home. With Colorado Springs' track record, it seems a safe bet that the city, thanks to its diverse economic base, will keep huffing and puffing along into the future.

Fanatic Air Force Falcon football fans jam Falcon Field. Colorado Springs is also home to the U.S. Olympic Committee and its training centers.

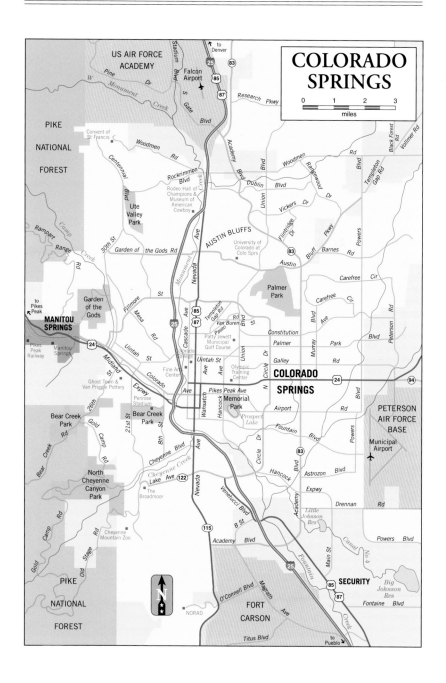

COLORADO SPRINGS

0   1   2   3
miles

(top) Cyberspace cowboy David Hughes sends e-mail to President Clinton at Rogers Bar in Colorado Springs. (above) Air Force cadets drilling their honor code.

EXPLORING COLORADO SPRINGS

U.S. Air Force Academy. Visitors aren't necessarily drawn here by a yearning to see young men and women with snappy uniforms and sabers, although at lunchtime that's the scene. The **Cadet Chapel,** with its 17 spires pointing 150 feet skyward, is the place's truly inspiring sight. *North of Colorado Springs on I-25; (719) 333-8723 (visitor center); (719) 333-2636 (chapel).*

Garden of the Gods. This 1350-acre park lives up to its name, with spectacular naturally carved red-rock formations. You can either drive through for a quick look or take one of the many trails to get a feel for its mix of strange and fascinating rocks, earth, and plants. Colorado's version of Eden contains windswept rock formations and sandstone towers with names like "Kissing Camels" and "Weeping Indian" jutting from the flat ground. *US 24 northwest to 30th Street or I-25 to Garden of the Gods Road to 30th Street; (719) 634-6666.*

U.S. Olympic Complex. About 350 inspired athletes sweat out gold medal dreams here. The 37-acre complex hosts over 500 programs, including training camps, seminars, clinics, and anything else loosely tied to our nation's Olympic effort. *1750 E. Boulder Street; (719) 578-4618.*

Cheyenne Mountain Zoo. Along with the NORAD command center, Cheyenne Mountain is also home to this unique zoo. What makes it unique is not the animals but the setting. The various animal enclosures are tucked into the side of the mountain. A trail meanders up the mountainside, flanked by ponderosa pines and native grasses, shrubs, and undergrowth, and delivers visitors to each animal exhibit. To round a corner, peer through the branches of pine trees and scrub oak, and discover a snarling mountain lion staring straight at you is quite a thrill, even after you make out the outline of the fence that surrounds the large-toothed feline's neck of the woods. *4250 Cheyenne Mountain Zoo Road; (719) 633-9925.*

Broadmoor Hotel. Still Colorado Springs' centerpiece, the original hotel has been augmented by every conceivable type of visitor service and attraction to become a formidable resort complex offering everything from a ski hill to three golf courses.

"AMERICA THE BEAUTIFUL"

Katherine Lee Bates probably didn't give much thought to, or receive much inspiration from, the miles of prairie she traveled through on her way to Colorado in the summer of 1893. She was not writing a guidebook and she probably had no burning interest in the latest grain-producing techniques of the day.

Instead, she was a well-respected professor of English Literature at Wellesley College, in Wellesley, Massachusetts, who was making the time-consuming, arduous, cross-country journey to spend a summer as a visiting professor at Colorado College, located in Colorado Springs.

Like most visitors to Colorado Springs, she was urged to make a trip to the top of the legendary Pikes Peak. The trip was not exactly a wilderness adventure or a physical challenge since a cog railway and carriage road had been ferrying sightseers to the summit for the past three years. Bates succumbed to the urgings and found herself atop the most famous mountain in Colorado.

From that perch she could see the miles of planted prairie stretching eastward. She looked into the distance in every direction across the top of the Rockies and saw nothing but beautiful skies. And then there were the dark, brooding Rocky Mountains themselves, towering to the north, south, and west.

Poetic inspiration did not hit, it slam-dunked this matronly English teacher from back East. Her poetic mind was sent reeling by the combination of Colorado's Rocky Mountains jutting almost straight up from the flat eastern plains to touch the sky with their ragged peaks. This unique combination, this stunning juxtaposition, seemed to sum up not only the West, but the entire nation.

She eventually found the right words to express the feelings that swept through her on top of Pikes Peak that day:

> Oh beautiful for spacious skies,
> For amber waves of grain:
> For purple mountain majesties
> Above the fruited plain—
> America, America, God shed his grace on thee,
> And crown thy good with brotherhood
> From sea to shining sea . . .

Surprisingly, the poem "America the Beautiful" did not appear in print until 1911, when it was the featured poem in one of Bates' many books of poetry. By then she had published ten other books of poetry, and would eventually pen a total of 15 volumes before dying in 1929 at the age of 70.

However, as soon as "America the Beautiful" was released, it was set to music. It became Bates' most enduring and inspirational work, and many consider it this nation's real national anthem.

Garden of the Gods is Colorado Springs' most popular attraction.

■ PIKES PEAK HIGHWAY AND MANITOU SPRINGS

Manitou Springs is the gateway that opens to the Pikes Peak Highway, which allows unfettered access to the states most publicized peak. (Remember "Pike's Peak or Bust"?)

Manitou Springs takes its name from the famous water, which flows from ten springs throughout the town. Brave souls can step up to a pagoda-like public fountain in the middle of town and take a few gulps of the highly touted, "soda spring water" from the Cheyenne Spring. The water's virtues were first discovered and extolled by the Ute Indians, who declared the springs a sacred healing site and named them "Manitou," which translates into "the God of all."

A wall fresco in Manitou Springs depicts an Indian weaver.

In 1872, Dr. William A. Bell built the first water bottling plant in town. By the turn of the century, a horde of patent medicine men had created one of the first bottled water crazes by bottling the spring water and ascribing to the liquid all manner of miraculous curative powers.

Manitou Springs is also the hub of all the action up Pikes Peak, from the road races, marathons, a cog railroad *(see page 304),* and the plain old drive to the peak in the family car. Manitou also boasts of some cliff dwellings built by the locals, but at best the effort just whets your appetite for the real items in Mesa Verde National Park. *(See page 180.)*

Before Perrier, there was Manitou soda.

Florissant Fossil Beds National Park, on the other hand, is the real thing. About an hour's drive from Colorado Springs on US 94, the 6,000-acre park provides a glimpse of the tiny, prehistoric world. Insects and plants from the Eocene period are preserved in all their fragile beauty. You can marvel at the delicate wings of long extinct insects and trace the intricate patterns of fossilized leaves and plants. *Take US 24 east to Florissant, about 35 miles, and go two miles south on Teller County Road 1; (719) 748-3253.*

PIKE DIDN'T HAVE A PEAK EXPERIENCE

All the fame, notoriety, and mountain-naming generated by a little hike through Colorado by a man named **Lt. Zebulon Pike** is a little hard to understand if you just look at the bare outlines of his famous expedition of 1806.

After successfully crossing the Great Plains and meeting with various Plains Indian tribes, Pike and his crew couldn't seem to get much right once they got inside the borders of present-day Colorado.

When they first sighted the Rocky Mountains they raised a huzza for the *Mexican Mountains.* They camped near present-day **Pueblo** and peered up at the huge peak that had caught their eye from the prairie. They tried to climb it. Sorry, wrong mountain. They realized the peak they were seeking was even farther away, and probably couldn't be climbed by anyone. Wrong again.

The party moved west and discovered the **Royal Gorge,** which made Pike think he was near the headwaters of the Arkansas River, which he thought would lead him to the Red River, his ultimate goal. Then he blew it. He headed north, explored South Park, didn't find the Red River, but did find quite a red blush on his face when he came back through the gorge to where he had started.

Now we're talking dead of winter. The party kept going south, somehow crossed the Sangre de Cristo mountains, and landed in the **San Luis Valley** on the west side of the Rio Grande, placing them in Spanish territory.

But they thought they were on American soil, so, near the present-day town of **Sanford,** they built the first fort in Colorado, actually a fairly impressive stockade, and flew the stars and stripes. **Pike's Stockade** (which has been restored) and his flag, however, didn't impress the Spanish who, in February 1807, not so politely invited him to finish wintering in Santa Fe. Pike might have missed his mountain count, but he could count muskets and politely accepted. Convinced that Pike and his men were spies, the province's governor sent the travelers 550 miles south to Chihuahua for more fun in the sun. The governor of that province, however, merely took Pike's notes and sent the crew off toward Texas, which they reached in July.

Pike pulled his fat out of the fire and forever etched his name in Colorado history and stone by an amazing bit of memory. Without notes, he penned the story of his trip. The public ate it up, and he reached the peak of his fame. Not only was his book a pretty good adventure story, it also gave the nation its first feel for the southwestern stretches of land west of the Mississippi that it had scored in the Louisiana Purchase of 1803.

The mountain that Pike and his men couldn't climb but could see became Pikes Peak and "Pikes Peak or Bust" became the rallying cry for the thousands who would cross the prairie in search of Colorado. Of course, they didn't end up near Pike's Peak, they were all heading for the gold and silver fields hundreds of miles away, but then again, Mr. Pike wasn't exactly a good example when it came to knowing where you are heading or where you would eventually end up.

Pike avoided putting his well-traveled foot in his mouth, a fate Colorado's other famous explorer experienced, toe, heel, and legging. But the party of **Maj. Stephen Long** did manage to climb Pike's Peak, so maybe it's a historical draw. Like Pike, Long really didn't discover much. His expedition was almost a wander in the woods compared to Pike's adventures.

In June 1820, Long's party, which included a biologist, naturalist, geologist, and other men of learning, spotted the Rockies. And spotted was about all they settled for, besides naming a peak or two, like the mountain now called **Longs Peak,** but which they called by the inspired name of **Highest Peak.** They came down the South Platte River and generally took a nice little ride down the Front Range, except for the three-day trek up Pike's Peak, and by the end of September the whole thing was over.

It was after the trip that Long and his men of learning blew it.

Long proclaimed the Great Plains to be **"The Great American Desert."** He compared them to sandy African deserts, predicted that "vegetable matter" would never grow there, and generally consigned the plains to be forever the domain of the Indians, rabbits, and buffalo. The name stuck. For decades afterwards the plains were marked "The Great American Desert" on most U.S. maps.

But the truth about the Rockies and its peaks and rivers and the plains and their fertility eventually came out. It would take the fur-trapping mountain men and prospectors—not the numerous military or government explorers who came after Pike—to really traverse the state from top to bottom, and a crop of industrious farmers and a sprinkling of water to turn "The Great American Desert" into part of "The Breadbasket of the World."

■ PUEBLO: A STEEL CITY

The folks in Pueblo, Colorado's "Steel City," have had a chance to prove that they can be pretty steely-eyed in the face of adversity.

Located south of Colorado Springs along Interstate 25, and north of the prolific coal fields around Trinidad, CF&I's steel plants were stoking Pueblo's economy before the turn of the century. Over 9,000 workers toiled at the plants during the 1950s, but in the early 1980s new technology cooled the blast furnaces, costing Pueblo 3,300 jobs. Once the smoke cleared, the town decided it was time to quit waiting for corporate accountants to decide its future, dusted itself off, and went to work on itself, for itself.

Surrounding natural amenities, an entrenched blue-collar work ethic, and extra effort to spruce up the town (quality of life again) assured that it didn't take long for many companies to discover Pueblo was a pretty good place do business.

A decade after the shock at the steel mills, Pueblo had lured a diverse batch of businesses to the area and generated enough growth, and new jobs, to more than replace those lost at the steel mills and put the city back on its economic feet.

Pueblo lies along the Arkansas River, 42 miles south of Colorado Springs on I-25. Even Puebloans admit their city isn't in itself a great tourist attraction, but it does have attractive aspects.

PUEBLO HIGHLIGHTS

Colorado State Fair. For almost two weeks every August, the fair brings thousands of people to town. This is a real state fair. Grandmothers with their preserves and peach farmers with their peaches vie for blue ribbons while eager 4-H kids wash, shave, polish, and preen their animals for judging. The fair is a reminder that from the mountains to plains, the sturdy folks relying on ranching and farming still play a key role in the state. Top-name country-western singers, carnivals, parades, and a week of professional rodeos are also on the bill of fare. *(See page 295.)*

Union Avenue Historic District. Downtown Pueblo's historic center has become the focal point for the city's rejuvenation and revival. Although the area is tucked in the middle of town, visitors need only follow the ample signs, starting at I-5 and continuing through town, to find *continues on page 82*

Eunice Winkless takes a dive on a dare at the Pueblo State Fair in 1905.
(Pueblo Library District)

this corner of historic Pueblo. Extra wide and pedestrian friendly, Union Avenue is lined with dozens of renovated Victorian and turn-of-the-century brick buildings, housing various shops and restaurants.

Anchoring the area is the towering presence of the 1870-vintage **Pueblo Union Depot** train station. The four-story, Romanesque Revival building, complete with massive clock tower, has been restored to its historic elegance and renovated to accommodate a variety of shops and offices. A string of new shops and buildings have sprung up to flank the depot. *Union Avenue between the Arkansas River and First Street; (719) 542-1704.*

Rosemount Victorian House Museum. Often mentioned as one of the state's finest examples of Victorian architecture, the 24,000-square-foot mansion contains a conglomeration of period furniture and finery. The exterior is decorated with turrets, chimneys, a sun porch, and just about every other bit of delightful gingerbread ornamentation imaginable. *419 West 14th Street; (719) 545-5290.*

Pueblo Zoo. The zoo lays claim to fame as the state's largest collection of cold-blooded animals (deduct two points if the words "investment banker" came to mind). *In City Park at Goodnight and Pueblo boulevards; (719) 561-9664.*

Arkansas River Greenway and Nature Center, is 20 miles' worth of outdoor action, from hiking to wildlife viewing to biking. *On the western edge of the city limits at 5200 Nature Center Road.*

Pueblo Reservoir, which includes 60 miles of shoreline bordered by limestone cliffs with mountain views in the background, offers anglers, boaters, and layabouts the chance to indulge in their particular pastimes.

The Royal Gorge, home to the country's highest suspension bridge—a mere 1,053 feet above the Arkansas River—is an hour's drive from Pueblo on US 50 through Cañon City. The canyon itself is stunning, if not scary, as solid granite walls too steep to tinker with roar up at visitors on the rim. To see into the canyon, you can pay to drive across the bridge, take a tramway over the gorge, loop around the edge on an old-fashioned railroad, or just park your car and peek over for free.

The Royal Gorge: a great sight if you don't have a fear of heights.

ROCKY MOUNTAINS
GOLD AND SILVER TOWNS

IT'S THE MOTHER LODE WITH A BOOMING TENT CITY with mud streets and miners turned millionaires building opera houses and stores and bars and hotels better start cutting down every tree in sight to build this town into a city for thousands by God let's just keep digging and firing smelters and shipping out the riches yippee the train is here the road is open life can only get better this is the mother lode and it ain't ever gonna end.

What?

The mines are giving out?

Those damn Eastern politicians won't buy silver?

The millionaires are going broke?

Let's get the hell out of here, this place is dead, but there's another mother lode, just over the next ridge, or maybe two mountains ranges west, come on, let's go, the mother lode is still out there, somewhere.

■ GOLDEN BEGINNINGS

From 1859 to 1893, the search for the next mother lode sent miners out from Denver into the Rocky Mountains. First they scurried through the foothills, scratching here, digging there, and panning any stream to be found. Towering mountains that don't lose their snowcaps until midsummer didn't stop the miners' westward surge, nor did the dense stands of pine and fir trees they fought through as they kept plunging deeper into the Rockies in an arc from Steamboat Springs to Aspen to Cripple Creek. The gold seekers raced across the huge open meadows tucked in between mountain ranges because gold was in the hills and along the streambeds.

In those moments when their eyes weren't focused on gold, a few must have marveled at the pure beauty of their surroundings—steep canyons, rolling mountains, herds of deer and elk, and a deep blue sky slowly turning an orange-red at sunset or sunrise.

But what really got their attention was news of a good strike in a good location. It took transportation, smelters, and capital to make a mining town boom, so once

The old mining town of Summitville now sits uninhabited in the San Juan Mountains.

The 1872 Mining Act allows gold miners to still "dig" Aspen Mountain.

a town like Leadville or Breckenridge boomed, the miners would stream out of isolated cabins high in the Rockies and descend on the boom towns like locusts. Although prospectors' footprints covered most of the Rockies, today millions of acres of forested slopes beneath snowcapped peaks, along with wide-open meadows and their free-flowing creeks, remain relatively unscarred by the gold boom.

Mining's booms and busts are alive today in those Colorado towns that have retained their Victorian roots and enthralling mining history. The state still disgorges significant amounts of minerals from its mountainous bowels and continues to bounce in and out of the ranks of the nation's top gold- and mineral-producing states. So who knows, you might want to keep an eye on the streambed the next time you're fishing or hiking, because you might find a vein of gold as thick as your leg and stumble on the next mother lode. Mining has long been considered a reputable occupation in Colorado, even if Mark Twain did claim that a mine is "a hole in the ground owned by a liar."

■ FIBBING IN 1858

Colorado's gold rush had a rather dubious beginning when a Georgian named William Green Russell led a small party to the confluence of Cherry Creek and the

WYOMING

230 230

HEART OF THE COLORADO ROCKIES

⚒ Mining Towns

0 10 20 30
miles

125 127 Kings Canyon

Columbine
Mt Zirkel *(12,180)*
Cowdrey
Hahns Peak
Bears Ear Peak *(10,661)*
Glendevey
Walden
Mt Ethel *(11,924)*
Coalmont
ARAPAHO NATIONAL WILDLIFE REFUGE 14
Fort Collins
Milner
Steamboat Springs
Rand
Masonville
Eaton
Hayden
Glen Haven
Windsor Greeley
Drake 34 Loveland
Estes Park
Berthoud
Johnstown
40
Oak Creek
Continental
125
Lyons
Mead
Gilcrest
Phippsburg
ROCKY MOUNTAIN NATIONAL PARK
Longs Peak *(14,255)*
Grand Lake
66
Yampa
Hot Sulphur Springs
Lake Granby
Niwot
Longmont
Toponas 131
Arapaho National Rec Area
Jamestown
Gold Hill 119 Erie 25
Brighton
Kremmling
Granby
72
7
36
Louisville
Sheep Mountain *(12,246)*
McCoy
Parshall
Tabernash
Eldora
Boulder
93
Burns
Radium
Fraser
East Portal
119 72
Thornton
Bond
Winter Park
Central City
Black Hawk
Arvada
State Bridge
Berthoud Pass
9
Golden
Aurora
Wolcott
⚒ Silver Plume
Idaho Springs
70
Gypsum 6
Edwards
Vail
Dillon Loveland Pass
Georgetown ⚒
DENVER
Dostero
Eagle
Vail Pass
Frisco
Grays Pk *(14,270)*
Evergreen
470
Englewood
GLENWOOD CANYON 70
Keystone
Conifer
Littleton 83
Glenwood Springs
Minturn
Gilman
Breckenridge ⚒
Mount of the Holy Cross *(14,005)*
Copper Mountain
70
Carbondale ⚒
Meredith
24
Shawnee
Bailey
Pine
Sedalia
Basalt
Climax ⚒
Buffalo Creek
Castle Rock
Snowmass 82
Alma
Como
126
Larkspur
133
Aspen
Leadville ⚒
Fairplay
Palmer Lake
Redstone
Independence Pass *(12,095)*
Mt Elbert *(14,433)*
Garo
Westcreek 67
Monument
Marble ⚒
Castle Peak *(14,265)*
Granite
24
Woodland Park
25
Twin Lakes
Hartsel
Lake George
US Air Force Academy
Florissant
Cascade

Elevation

feet
14,433
11,500
9,800
8,200
6,500
5,000
4,000
3,000

Crested Butte ⚒
Buena Vista
Florissant Fossil Beds National Mon
Pikes Peak *(14,110)*
Colorado Springs
Taylor Park
Nathrop
Guffey
Cripple Creek ⚒
Victor ⚒
Security
135
St Elmo
Almont
Pitkin
Mt Antero *(14,269)*
Maysville
Salida
Cañon City
Fort Carson *(military res)*
Gunnison
Ohio
Poncha Springs
Howard
Parkdale
Penrose
Doyleville
50
Florence
Portland 50
Sargents
Texas Creek
Cotopaxi
149
Powderhorn
114
Coaldale
Hillside
Wetmore
Bonanza
Villa Grove
69
Mineral Hot Springs

South Platte River in 1858. The party had partaken of the Georgia gold rush, and these Colorado streams looked just as peachy and golden as Georgia's. The men panned a little gold, nosed around, assumed there should be more somewhere, and decided to stay the winter and start serious prospecting in the spring.

Even in the 1850s, it was hard to keep any nugget of good gold news a secret. Word of their meager find got back to towns like Kansas City and Omaha, which had prospered supplying the forty-niners on their way to the California gold rush. Stuck in the Depression of 1857, they hated to let facts get in their way, so they declared a full-blown Colorado gold rush. Sales in the mercantiles picked up dramatically as 100,000 people headed west in the spring of 1859. Half of them never made it to Colorado. They either suffered prairie paranoia, died, got lost, or came to their senses when they arrived and saw impassable mountains, icy streams, and riverbanks lined with rocks instead of gold nuggets.

■ HEADY YEARS IN GOLD COUNTRY

The first real gold strikes were by George A. Jackson and John H. Gregory, miners who independently discovered veins on Clear Creek in 1858. Two years later, substantial discoveries were also made at Gold Hill west of Boulder. That was all it took. A boom was on. Of course, having Horace Greeley pan a little Colorado gold, a fact he loudly touted in his New York *Tribune*, didn't hurt. (Could someone the night before have dropped a little gold in the spot Horace was supposed to pan? Well . . . you never can tell about such things.)

It also became obvious that Cherry Creek, where all the hullabaloo started, contained about as much gold as the below-average bottles of whiskey being shipped by the wagon load to the gold diggers from the infant towns of Denver and Auraria, which straddled Cherry Creek and battled each other for urban supremacy. Look at a current state map and you will know who won.

Those first heady years created the myth of a lone prospector and his burro striking gold deep in the hills and coming back to town with a sack of gold nuggets that would make him a rich man. For some, that fantasy became reality. But not for many. Tugging gold out of freezing mountain streams was hard work and gold veins also put up quite a fight. As the easy gold along the river banks gave out, the gold pan was replaced by the sluice box or rockers—two-man contraptions filled with dirt that was washed away, hopefully to reveal gold.

GOLD STRIKE AT CHERRY CREEK

*T*he month of May had appeared and yet no signs of a change to the better had become manifest. The gold regions were, on the contrary, passing through the darkest days they were destined to see. The cheerless prospect exercised a depressing influence upon everything. Utter stagnation characterized material life, and hopefulness weighed heavily on the minds of all the sojourners on Cherry Creek. Everybody had the blues. Even the most sanguine became dispirited, and the idea of a general abandonment of the country was the subject of frequent discussion.

Thus affairs stood, when in the course of the afternoon of the second Sunday in May [1858], we were seated in the long-house that then represented the express office, in company with Dr. J. M. Fox, the general agent of the Express Company, and Mr. Joseph Heywood, a well known Californian, and formerly resident of Cincinnati. The trio were just discussing the unpromising aspect of things, when a short, slender, heavily bearded individual, in miner's garb, entered the room and inquired for letters. He was invited to a seat, and soon got to talking about the resources of the country. Contrary to expectation, he seemed to believe firmly in its mineral wealth. Being asked for his experience in the mountains from which he claimed to have just arrived, he stated, after a few moments of apparent hesitation, that a little more than a week ago, while following up the north fork of Clear Creek, in company with John H. Gregory and several others, he had discovered gold-bearing dirt in the vicinity of streaks of quartz rock, that ran over the mountains, in a ravine adjoining the valley of the creek. The dirt, he asserted, had yielded him as much as a dollar's worth of gold to the pan. Perceiving a manifestation of incredulity on the part of his listeners, he produced, in corroboration of his statement, a bottle containing about forty dollars' worth of flour gold, and also several fragments of a hard substance which he designated as decomposed gold-bearing quartz. Mr. Heywood stepped outdoors with one of the pieces for the purpose of examining it with a magnifying glass. He soon called out Dr. Fox, whom he told that the specimen he held in his hand was as fine quartz as he had seen in the richest quartz veins in California. Several persons having, in the meantime, entered the office and showing upon hearing the miner's tale a disposition to doubt its truthfulness, the latter grew rather excited, repeated what he had said, and asserted most emphatically that he would warrant one dollar to the pan of dirt to any number of men that would follow him to the locality in question, and added that they might bring a rope along and swing him up in case he should be found a liar.

This was the first news of the discovery of the Gregory mines that reached us. Its bearer, who had come to the Cherry Creek towns for a new supply of provisions, returned to the mountains on the following day, in company with several others, who intended to sift his story by a visit to the scene of the alleged discovery.

A few more dull days elapsed without throwing any further light on the subject, and the spark of hope kindled by the miner's apparently earnest story had nearly been lost sight of amidst the surrounding darkness, when on the fifth day a Mr. Bates, late of Dubuque, Iowa, made his appearance in Auraria with a vial full of gold, representing a value of about eighty dollars, which he claimed to have washed out of thirty-nine pans of dirt, obtained not far from the spot on which Gregory had made his discovery. Mr. Bates being known as a reliable man, his story was at once credited and he and his bottle taken from cabin to cabin. The sight of his gold forthwith produced an intense excitement, and the news of his luck spread like wild-fire and at once moved the hearts of the denizens of the two towns with gladdening sensations. Individuals could be heard every[where] on the streets shouting to each other, "We are all right now," "the stuff is here after all," "the country is safe," &c.

On the following day a universal exodus took place in the direction of North Clear Creek. Whoever could raise enough provisions for a protracted stay in the mountains sallied out without delay. Traders locked up their stores; bar-keepers disappeared with their bottles of whiskey, the few mechanics that were busy building houses, abandoned their work, the county judge and sheriff, lawyers and doctors, and even the editor of the *Rocky Mountain News,* joined in the general rush.

—Henry Villard
The Past and Present of the Pike's Peak Gold Regions, 1932

■ TECHNOLOGY AND CAPITAL

As time went on, more dirt had to be sluiced to produce less gold, leading to new and expensive technology. Coffer dams were unleashed to clean out whole stretches of streambeds. Hydraulic mining used hoses and pipes to blast away all the dirt around the stream so it could be set aside and sifted. Lode gold, or veins, quickly became the domain of mining companies that could afford to hire miners, crush tons of ore, and then ship and sell the resulting gold.

The Crystal Mill, near the ghost town of Crystal and Marble.

New technology and capital didn't stop the solitary miner and his burro. Lone prospectors still set out into unexplored territory, but if they found gold, instead of mining the claim, they would more than likely arrange a friendly corporate take-over with a well-heeled mining company, but not before securing a "golden parachute" from a percentage of earnings.

By 1865, an estimated 100 million tons of freight were being hauled to Denver by wagon. Getting as far as Denver was the easy part; hauling supplies up into the Rockies was something else again. It wasn't long before sharp-eyed and deep-pocketed men began to think about building railroads into the booming mining districts.

The lone prospector in all his "romantic" glory—Pat Lynch, 1910.
(Colorado Historical Society)

In 1867 the Union Pacific Transcontinental Railroad hit Wyoming. Three years later a Union Pacific spur reached Denver and the Kansas Pacific made a straight shot across the prairie into town. Then Gen. William Palmer created the Denver & Rio Grande Railroad and pushed its lines south to Colorado Springs, Canon City, Pueblo, and Trinidad.

Rail links still didn't make investors' eyes glow over Colorado gold. A chunk of granite and gold was a tough nut to crack, especially when the cracking was done by stamp mills that pounded the hell out of the ore to break the granite's grip on the gold. Nathaniel P. Hill, a chemist from Brown University, got the gold boom cooking in 1868 when he developed a smelter that would heat the ore, bake away the granite, and attach gold or silver to copper mattes for extraction. Forget smashing high grade ore, now you could cook low grade ore and still make money.

■ BLACK HAWK AND CENTRAL CITY

Hill's smelter and William A. H. Loveland's Colorado Central Railroad, completed in 1877, made Black Hawk and Central City "the richest square mile on earth." Thanks to legalized gambling, they're booming once more.

To get there, drive due west from Denver on US 6, get off on US 119, and you'll find yourself winding through Clear Creek Canyon, where the creek banks reveal piles of rocks left by the placers and hydraulic miners. The closer you get to Black Hawk, the more mining debris, of the metal variety, there is, and when you get to town you'll see the leftovers of Hill's inventions rusting around everywhere.

Just up the road a bit is **Central City**, and the emphasis here is on *up*. It's hard to imagine thousands of people living in the valley of this steep little canyon. A closer look at the hills—dotted, crisscrossed, and covered with tailings piles, roads, and assorted miners' marks—makes you wonder if the miners could even swing a pick without hitting some other miner's foot or head. The town's few paved streets quickly give way to dirt roads steep enough to make a mule snort.

It's the buildings, not the roads, that enthrall. After the town burned to the ground a couple of times, a "bricks, or stone, or nothing-doing" building code was imposed. Thus, Central City probably has the state's best collection of original block, brick, and stone Victorian buildings, and they're all jammed right into a couple of easy strolling blocks. The crown jewel is the rejuvenated **Central City Opera House**, home to a summer season of opera unmatched in Colorado. Next to the

The Face on the Barroom Floor

"…I was a painter…not one that daubed on bricks and wood,
But an artist, and for my age, was rated pretty good,
And then I met a woman…now comes the funny part,
With eyes that petrified my brain and sank into my heart.

"I was working on a portrait, one afternoon in May,
Of a fair-haired boy, a friend of mine, who lived across the way,
And Madeline admired it, and much to my surprise,
Said she'd like to know the man that had such dreamy eyes.

"It took not long to know him and before the month had flown,
My friend…he stole my darling, and I was left alone,
Give me that piece of chalk that marks up the baseball score
And you'll see the lovely Madeline upon the barroom floor.

"Another drink…" with chalk in hand, the vagabond began
To sketch a face that well might buy the soul of any man.
Then, as he placed another lock upon the shapely head,
With fearful shriek, he leaped, and fell across the picture…dead.

The Teller House
Hotel's famous
"barroom floor"
image.

"The Richest Square Mile on Earth."

opera house is the famed **Teller House,** home to the equally famous "Face on the Barroom Floor," belonging to the lovely Madeline and painted by her jilted lover right before he died atop his masterpiece/mistresspiece.

The introduction of limited stakes gambling was intended to add tourist appeal to Central City and Black Hawk by reproducing the long-lost taste and feel of the wild silver camps. The quaint vision presented by gambling's backers had the town's existing mom-and-pop businesses, from shirt shops to gas stations, installing a few slot machines to augment their income. Local bars and restaurants would also put in a row or two of the one-armed bandits and set up blackjack and poker tables where visitors could idle away an hour or so in a casual card game.

Well, it didn't quite turn out that way. Granted, gambling created a new gold rush mentality that more than equalled the boom town era, but the quaint idea that the towns could retain their small-town charms didn't quite pan out.

Everyone seems to have underestimated the power of gambling fever. The idea of making slot machines another curio in a curio shop soon gave way to the idea that the big money was in slot machines, not selling coffee mugs. Hardware stores, T-shirt shops, and even the town's sole gas station were replaced with gambling emporiums.

"The Smelting Capital of the World."

Central City, primitive but pulsating in the 1860s. (Colorado Historical Society)

Then, in an ironic replay of the corporate buyout of the lone prospector a hundred years earlier, the big boys came to the gaming table. Huge, full-blown casinos popped up, featuring hundreds of slot machines, day-care centers and video arcades for the kids, and in-house souvenir shops. Unable to compete, the mom-and-pop shops quickly sold out to the corporate chains.

Historic Black Hawk, which had more vacant land before the gambling boom, was engulfed and overshadowed by towering, sparkling gambling palaces. Every vaguely vacant parcel in Central City also found itself home to a big new gambling edifice. The casino building boom crawled up the narrow valley and now, instead of being two distinct towns a mile apart, Black Hawk and Central City have coalesced into a single gambling conglomerate.

Instead of the rough and tumble of a 19th-century mining town, the flashy new casinos present an almost Disney-like facade, where gambling is just good, clean, family fun. The historic brick buildings in downtown Central City have been restored and sandblasted to a rosy sheen. Every Victorian flourish has been accentuated with fresh paint or bronze. Methinks the original silver boom town wasn't quite this tidy.

Then there's the noise. In the summer, all doors are open and all manner of bells and whistles whine from slot machines that have just paid, say, eight dollars on a two-dollar bet. On each casino doorstep a costumed greeter hails passersby with coupons, spiels, and other tricks of the barker's trade.

Unintended consequences aside, gambling has accomplished two things. First, Central City and Black Hawk are once again filled year round with treasure-seekers. Second, and most important for the state as a whole, gambling taxes have put an appreciable bulge in the state's historic preservation coffers. Towns across Colorado have used the money to preserve their historic buildings and attractions.

For the purists, however, changing the historic character of Black Hawk and Central City, two of the state's best-known links to its mining heyday, is a heavy price to pay for assuring that the rest of the state's historic heritage doesn't succumb to commercialization and exploitation.

As for gamblers, hey, a slot machine is a slot machine is a slot machine, whether it's in Las Vegas or an old Colorado silver town.

■ IDAHO SPRINGS, GEORGETOWN, AND SILVER PLUME

These three towns, which rest one after another about an hour's drive west of Denver on I-70, once swarmed with miners, and the hillsides around them were dotted with gold and silver mines.

The coming of the Colorado Central Railroad in 1877 assured the boom wouldn't die. Steep mountains blocked the line from reaching the prolific mines of **Silver Plume**. When Jay Gould bought the Colorado Central, he decided to extend the line, a decision that led to the **Georgetown Loop**, an iron train trestle that rises up 638 feet and was considered one of the greatest engineering feats of the day *(also see page 304)*.

As riders peek down from 638 feet above ground while riding "the Loop," many gasp, either in awe of the engineering and the beauty of the valley, or from a fear of heights and anxiety that those tiny little iron sticks can't really hold up a passenger-filled, steam-powered train. Atop the trestle (while in the train) is the best place to view Georgetown and the surrounding mountains, which are steep, rocky, and still dotted with dozens of yellowish mine tailings amongst the pines.

Argo Gold Mine and Mill in the Idaho Springs area.

Nestled in the valley, Georgetown's downtown (not the conglomeration of banality at the interstate off-ramp) hasn't been ruined with renovation. The back streets, and the original brick and wooden Victorian buildings downtown, evoke a comfortable, lived-in feel. This is a place where selling tee-shirts isn't the only business at hand.

Silver Plume, which once contained some of the richest gold ore in the state, is interestingly Victorian once you get away from the freeway ramps, and many a mining remain is still jammed into the narrow canyon. You can relive some of the good times by taking any number of gold mine tours, the biggest being that of the huge **Argo Gold Mill** (proving there's more than one way to make money on Colorado gold). *Off I-20 at 2350 Riverside Drive, Idaho Springs; (303) 567-2421.*

■ CRIPPLE CREEK AND VICTOR

Latecomers to the gold rush, these towns were nevertheless comers. After an 1891 gold strike, Cripple Creek boomed. By 1900, 475 mining companies were in operation and the town's population reached 25,000. Labor troubles and falling prices beginning with the financial panic of 1907, combined with devastating fires, ended the boom almost as quickly as it started. The gold remains today, as do the miners, who now use cyanide-leech-field mining to extract the ore.

❖

A new gold rush, based on limited-stakes gambling, descended on Cripple Creek in 1991. The stately brick and stone buildings along Bennett Avenue quickly became home to casinos large and small. But Cripple Creek hasn't exactly struck the mother lode when it comes to gambling, thanks to its relative isolation, lack of large hotels, and distance from Front Range cities. It is a little more than an hour's drive west of Colorado Springs on Colorado 24 and 67.

Bennett Avenue, the main drag, is speckled with casinos and small bars offering the familiar slot machines and black jack and poker tables. But plenty of gift shops, coffee shops, and regular small-town businesses help Cripple Creek retain its authentic character.The band of wild, free-roaming burros which have been the town's trademark for decades still roam the streets, casually munching on lawns or weeds or occasional feed from friends.

You can see how riches were made the old-fashioned way via a tour of the nearby Molly Kathleen Mine, which closed in the 1960s, or take a ride on the Cripple Creek–Victor Narrow Gauge Railroad to savor a true taste of turn-of-the-19th century life in Cripple Creek *(see page 304.)*

Downtown Cripple Creek.
(following pages) Albert Bierstadt's "Sunset in the Rockies," 1866. (Museum of Western Art)

■ BRECKENRIDGE

Breckenridge, located 70 miles west of Denver, on Colorado 9 was a stable producer of gold until 1948. Since the town never died dead dead, many of the original buildings were torn down or modernized. Today, "modern Victorians" line the streets, and the main drag says more about skiing than history. You have to get back into the back streets to find the town's nineteenth-century roots. *(To ski Breckenridge, see page 239.)*

Large-scale hydraulic mining and dredging of the Blue River (running between the ski hill and the town) and its tributaries kept Breckenridge a gold town. It also transformed the Blue's once verdant banks into miles of piles of sterile rocks stretching like a white scar along the bottom of an otherwise green mountain valley.

The local historical society has preserved a sluicing and hydraulic operation and a dredge boat—the wooden monster that did the biggest damage. The animal sits a couple of miles out of town in a stagnant lake surrounded by bare river rock. Over 100 feet long and about 30 feet wide, this Buckcyrus Erie model and dozens like it chewed through the Blue River and its banks like a giant cockroach through a loaf of bread.

It took a while, but 45 years after the gold dredges were put out to pasture, Breckenridge got its river back. The stretch of Blue River that bisects town is no longer a dry pile of rocks with a river running under it. A massive reclamation effort by the town essentially rebuilt the river, from the bottom up. The rocks were hauled away, a natural riverbed was recreated, and now the Blue River once again sparkles in the sunlight as it courses through town. The revitalized river is flanked by pedestrian paths, little "pocket parks," and a variety of other public and private riverside attractions ranging from restaurants to a performing arts space.

■ SILVER BOOMS AND BUSTS

Although Nevada may have had the Comstock Lode, thanks to Leadville, Aspen, Creede, Telluride, Ouray, Lake City, Silverton, and the dozens of camps around Gunnison and Crested Butte, Colorado became the nation's Silver State, and was damn proud of it. The silver boom quickly forced Colorado into the national political spotlight because decisions made in Washington hit the Silver State right in the pocketbook.

Silver's demise came as quickly as its rise. The Coinage Act of 1873—called The "Crime of '73" by Coloradoans and fought with learned and passionate debate—put the nation on the gold standard and stopped automatic federal purchase of silver. The federal government kept buying some silver at set prices, but

These 30 silver bars from the Black Hawk smelters fetched $45,000 before the silver crash. (Colorado Historical Society)

its policy was rudderless and dependent on the political winds in Washington. A good gust was provided by the Sherman Silver Purchase Act of 1890, which drove prices up, but silver's sails drooped when India quit coining silver in 1893, sinking a steady international customer.

The Panic of 1893 finally did the dirty deed. Wall Street money men blamed silver for the economic destruction and convinced Congress and President Grover Cleveland to repeal the Sherman Silver Purchase Act, effectively killing King Silver and the royalties that propped up once prosperous towns.

■ LEADVILLE: MATCHLESS AND UNSINKABLE

Leadville was Colorado's silver king. Scattered strikes were struck as early as 1870, but by 1877 it was boom time. Thousands descended on Leadville, and between 1879 and 1889, the town produced $82 million worth of silver. It seemed "Cloud City" was set to become one of the state's biggest and most prosperous towns.

All of the day's nationally known figures made sure to stop in town if they found themselves in Colorado. Feminist Susan B. Anthony gave a speech to the miners about women's suffrage which quieted Billy Nye's saloon, the biggest building in town in 1877, and raised over $100 for the cause.

Leadville residents, in a display of civic pride running nakedly amok, boasted that their red light district was the best in the nation. That debate aside, at its booming peak Leadville, with its rich mines, solid brick Victorian buildings, and magnificent opera house, was giving Denver a run for its money as *the* most important Colorado city.

The town itself rests on the first fairly flat spot available at the head of sprawling Arkansas Valley. The surrounding hillsides, stripped of all timber during the boom, are once again covered with pine trees, but they don't hide the scattered mine remains, diggings, and tailings of all sizes and shapes. To reach Leadville from Denver take I-70 west to Exit 195 and go south on Colorado 24.

Leadville's **Harrison Avenue** provides a glimpse of silver promise and poverty. Tabor Opera House hosted everyone from Harry Houdini to John Phillip Sousa. Even the long-haired, somewhat eccentric poet Oscar Wilde lectured there on the ethics of art. (His most vivid Leadville memory was a sign above the piano in Pap's saloon that read, "Please do not shoot the pianist. He is doing his best." That little pearl, according to Wilde, was art criticism at its rational best.)

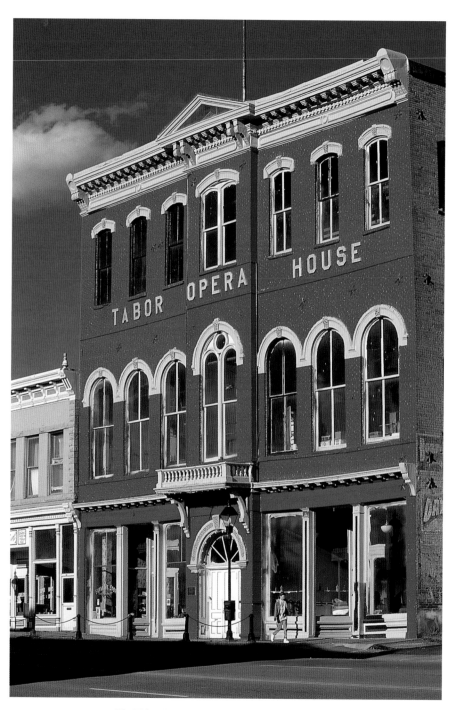

The Tabor Opera House was Leadville's cultural jewel.

What to do in Leadville

Tabor Opera House. Peer at the original, time-tattered velvet seats, with box seats for the silver barons, balcony for the masses, huge stage, and opulent entry. Here a rough and ready populace listened to everyone from composer John Phillip Sousa to author Oscar Wilde. *308 Harrison Avenue (south end); (719) 486-1147.*

Tabor Grand Hotel, a massive chunk of stonework, stands empty, a monument to Horace Tabor's grand dreams and lost fortune. *On the north end of Harrison Avenue. (Also see page 108.)*

Matchless Mine is where the once-rich and beautiful "Baby Doe" Tabor—third in a notorious love triangle *(see page 108)* —died waiting for the next boom. *One mile east of town on Seventh Street; (719) 486-3900.*

❖

Heading south you'll pass "String Town," now a collection of innocent looking homes and businesses, but once the area set aside for the many working girls who began their shift when the miners ended theirs.

Healy House Museum of the **Colorado Historical Society** brings to life what it meant to be a Victorian lady or gentle-man. The dainty main house was home to refined, unmarried school teachers, while the hunting cabin was where the married men congregated to drink whiskey and talk about money and women. *912 Harrison Avenue; (719) 486-0487.*

Mining Hall of Fame displays mining techniques ranging from gold panning to hand-drilling and blasting up to modern 20th-century procedures and equipment. *120 W. Ninth Street; (719) 486-1229.*

Climax Mine

Around the turn of the 20th century, zinc, copper, and gold were discovered in the old Leadville silver mines, keeping Leadville alive as a mining town. The most important new find was the huge deposit of molybdenum discovered in 1918 near the top of Fremont Pass. The mine has produced 1.9 billion tons of molybdenum, and during World War II it produced about 72 percent of the world's supply.

Unfortunately, the Climax Mine has dumped billions of tons of mill tailings into what used to be Tenmile Valley but today is a huge sludge pile completely filling the valley and making reclamation impossible. There is, however, a program underway to cover over the tailings.

Pits and tailings are representative of the debris leftover from Leadville's glory days.

■ LEADVILLE'S COLORFUL CHARACTERS

Denver may have been Colorado's biggest city in the 1880s, but it never rivaled Leadville in rags-to-riches stories, colorful characters, and pitiful demises.

Probably most familiar to Coloradoans is Charles Boettcher, who arrived in 1879 and started a booming hardware business that he parlayed into a diverse financial empire eventually based in Denver. The family's fortunes increased, and its members have played a prominent role in the city's business, philanthropic, and civic affairs ever since. The Boettcher Foundation and the Boettcher Concert Hall are just part of the legacy of a man who started selling nuts and bolts in Leadville.

Merchandising was also the beginning of the good fortune(s) of H. A. W. (Horace) Tabor and his wife Augusta, who arrived in 1860 to open stores in Leadville

and surrounding mining camps. In 1877, Tabor "grubstaked" George Hook and August Rische in return for one third of whatever they found. What they found was the Little Pittsburgh Mine's 30-foot-thick vein of silver, which made the mine a multi-million-dollar producer and Tabor a rich man. He kept investing in mining properties, allegedly buying the Matchless Mine with about $100,000 in pocket change. The mine produced a booming $1,000,000 a year during its 14-year life.

While Tabor was becoming one of Leadville's richest men and civic stars (thanks to his bankrolling of the Tabor Opera House and other generous acts), he

Leadville's 1896 Ice Palace melted away, like the silver boom. (Colorado Historical Society)

was also becoming an adulterer with the beautiful divorcée Elizabeth "Baby Doe" McCourt. A scandalous divorce from the upright Augusta (that would have delighted today's tabloids) followed, and Baby Doe became the second Mrs. Tabor.

The silver crash hit the Tabors hard, and although Horace did manage to become a U.S. Senator, he died virtually penniless in 1899. He told Baby Doe to never give up the Matchless because one day it would again make millions. She honored his request and for 36 years lived in a small shack at the mine. She would trudge to town for supplies and return to the mine, waiting for the silver boom that would never come. In the winter of 1935 she was found frozen to death in her little cabin.

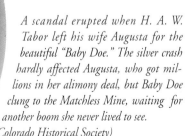

A scandal erupted when H. A. W. Tabor left his wife Augusta for the beautiful "Baby Doe." The silver crash hardly affected Augusta, who got millions in her alimony deal, but Baby Doe clung to the Matchless Mine, waiting for another boom she never lived to see. (Colorado Historical Society)

The hundred-year-old Silver Dollar Saloon, built in Leadville in the 1880s.

■ SOUTH PARK

Gold and silver prospectors poured into the mountains along the South Platte River, just east of the Continental Divide, but didn't find many good prospects. So the towns of the region known as South Park were left to develop, slowly, as small farming and ranching towns. Today the area boasts some of the most spectacular scenery in the state, hot springs, and plenty of wide open spaces. Though not far from Denver, its towns remain unsullied by the tourist-driven goldrush and retain a small-town charm that has been squeezed out of the more easily accessible Rocky Mountain tourist stops. You can drive for hours and see far more cows than condos as you make your way into South Park on Highway 285 from Denver, US 50 from Pueblo, or Colorado 24 from Leadville.

Away from the major travel arteries, such towns as Fairplay, Baily, Buena Vista, Poncha Springs, and Salida still maintain life on the main street. For many, this is the "real" Colorado, the pre-tourist-rush Colorado, the wide-open, undeveloped Colorado of uncluttered river valleys ringed by snow-capped peaks.

Granted, summer brings a nice crop of rafters and anglers who ply the Arkansas and South Platte rivers, which cut through the area, and climbers, mountain bikers, and hikers clambering over the region's impressive array of 14,000-foot peaks. But that's just a short burst of activity that doesn't disrupt or distort the relaxed feel and unpretentious essence of this swath of "pure" Colorado high country.

■ ASPEN

In 1879, in the dead of winter, some intrepid souls strapped on primitive skis (called snowshoes in those days), headed due west out of Leadville, crossed the Continental Divide, and skied down into what would become Aspen. They found what they wanted: huge silver deposits, especially on Smuggler Mountain. Indeed, the largest single silver nugget ever mined, weighing over two tons, was mined in Aspen.

In no time Aspen was racing Leadville for silver and cultural supremacy. In 1883 Jerome B. Wheeler—first president of Macy's Department Store in New York—arrived, bought up mining claims, and built smelters and the stunning Wheeler Opera House.

By 1892, Aspen had 12,000 residents, making it the state's third largest city, behind Leadville and Denver, and it soon started boasting that it was surpassing Leadville in silver output. What a difference a year makes! Almost immediately after repeal of the Sherman Silver Purchase Act, most of the Aspen's mines shut down and over 2,000 miners lost their jobs. Even Jerome Wheeler, the town's high-flying knight-in-silver-armor, became a penniless stable boy with a broken shovel.

By 1930, only 700 hardy souls remained, but thanks to refinement of those original snowshoes that brought prospectors over waist-deep snow into the valley, Aspen would boom again as an international ski resort *(see page 234)*. Located 162 miles west of Denver—a distance that lengthens in the winter when Independence Pass closes—Aspen has developed into a destination resort that is worth the trouble of getting there.

WHAT TO DO AND SEE IN ASPEN

Winter Skiing. One of the best and most famous ski areas in the United States, Aspen is known for its 76 trails, its efficient gondolas and lifts, and its proximity to excellent hotels and dining. *(For a more complete description of Aspen skiing, see the "Skiing" chapter, page 234.)*

Summer Ski Lift Rides. Summer in Aspen has its allure, beginning with its setting. As you enter town, Aspen Mountain starts to loom upward to become a monolith swathed with grass-covered ski trails cutting through dark green pines. A summer ride up the lifts gives you a panoramic view of the town and valley, and you don't even need a parka, although a light jacket is a good idea. In the fall, the aspens and oaks turn the mountains into a pallet of vivid color.

Golfing, Hiking, and Biking. Visitors will find numerous 18-hole courses in Aspen and Snowmass Village. More aggressive outdoor recreationists, might want to visit the Maroon Bells–Snowmass Wilderness Area and numerous hiking/biking trails just minutes from town.

Historic Buildings. The Hotel Jerome at 330 Main Street and the Wheeler Opera House at 320 E. Hyman Avenue, both recently restored to their turn-of-the-19th-century charm, still stand out as shining reminders of the town's silver days.

Shopping. Try downtown's Cooper Street and Hyman Avenue malls.

Intellectual Pursuits. Between the Aspen Institute, the International Design Conference, the Aspen Center for Physics, and the Given Biomedical Institute, not a week goes by without an esteemed orator or a panel of experts delving into the most pressing political, artistic, scientific, and philosophical questions of the day.

■ **FESTIVALS AND EVENTS**
Aspen Filmfest and its smaller offspring, **Shortsfest**, shines the spotlight on cinema, not just the movies. Shortsfest's offerings provoke more thought in 15 minutes than any 15 full-length summer blockbusters. Filmfest features screenings of independent and foreign films that will probably not be coming soon to a multiplex near you.

Aspen Music Festival and School *(also see page 122)* is the best known summertime attraction here, but dance, theater, film, jazz, and other live music are also on the cultural calendar. Thanks to the historic Wheeler Opera House and the Harris Concert Hall, completed in 1993, music is not confined to summer. *(970) 925-3254.*

Aspen's Winterskol *(also see page 120)* is a week of midwinter revelry, and takes place over the course of five days in January. Fireworks, parades, ski races, and an impressive torchlight descent down Aspen Mountain. *(970) 925-1940.*

Jazz Aspen at Snowmass presents a summer-long stream of top name performers, culminating in the Labor Day Festival, a multi-day jam session featuring both the old pros and the young lions following in their footsteps. Venues vary from open-air concerts in Snowmass Village to intimate sets performed in Aspen clubs and bars. *(970) 920-5770.*

DanceAspen fills the town's stages with performances by some of the most prestigious dance companies in the nation, and the world. Performances include an eclectic mix of classical ballet, modern dance, and cutting-edge combinations of everything the world of dance has to offer. *(970) 925-7718.*

Theatre in the Park is a revolving round of plays presented throughout the summer on a tent-covered stage in Rio Grande Park. *(970) 925-9313.*

Aside from the fabulous skiing and a myriad of special events, Aspen also plays host to a multitude of celebrities. You never know if, while wandering through downtown's Cooper Street Mall or dining at one of the dozens of outstanding restaurants, you might not catch Jack Nicholson joking around or Don Johnson forgetting about "Nash Bridges" by dropping cash and riches. The sound of gunfire may mean the gonzo journalist Hunter Thompson (right) is making a run into town from his enclave in Woody Creek. Actress Jill St. John-Wagner (above) might be seen hanging out at the Aspen Center of Environmental Studies. An interesting congregation of folks and fun, in other words.

(following pages) Aspen is situated in the Roaring Fork Valley amidst some of the West's most spectacular scenery.

(top) Aspen mayor John Bennett and friends sample some wine at the annual Aspen Food and Wine Festival. (bottom) Negotiating a reindeer permit, Aspen-style.

(opposite) Another popular summer event is the Balloon Festival.

■ ASPEN'S WINTERSKOL

Because January is generally the coldest month on the slopes, Aspen decided to warm things up with a five-day celebration called Winterskol. And damn-the-weather, full-fun-ahead is the general theme of this yearly event, which started fairly innocently as a way for the locals to catch their breath and celebrate a bit after the holiday rush. Today, Winterskol has become a venerable tradition, having started in 1950, and an event with enough color and dazzle to attract and entertain visitors from around the world.

Did I mention dazzle and color? How's this strike you: a full-blown fireworks extravaganza fired from Aspen Mountain and visible from the whole town followed by a dramatic twisting, turning, torchlight descent down the face of Aspen Mountain. Another nighttime diversion is the famed Bartender's Drink Contest. Anything goes, and usually does, into the concoctions prepared by the town's masters of mixology. Daylight brings all manner of ski races to the town's ski areas; in any given year there's some mix of professional races, races to benefit charities, local and amateur races and celebrity slides down the slopes.

You've got to love the parade, which features a cacophony of homemade contraptions expressing the eclectic intellectual interests of the locals on issues universal and mundane.

All the skiing events, fun, and dazzle mean if you've only five days to spend soaking in the Aspen experience, Winterskol week was made for you. *(For more on Aspen as a ski resort, see* "SKIING," *page 234.)*

(right and opposite) The cliché works: a winter wonderland and spectacular fireworks— the latter illuminating Aspen during Winterskol.

■ ASPEN MUSIC FESTIVAL

Aspen Music Festival and School brings together some of the world's most talented young classical musicians and mixes them with established, experienced players on summer sabbatical from their usual chairs at first-rate orchestras from across the country. The combination is inspiring and explosive. The young people learn from the professionals, and the professionals, in turn, are rejuvenated and inspired by their young charges. The result fills Aspen with a finely tuned consonance of classical music. Most days the huge music tent reverberates with spirited symphonic sound, containing a unique blend of exuberance and experience. Renowned musicians hold master classes in the **Harris Concert Hall.** Brass and string quartets set up shop in the downtown mall, fill the mountain air with well-honed harmonies, and alternately lullaby or bombard passers-by with their combined talent and verve. The historic **Wheeler Opera House** hosts operas, ranging from the classical to the comical, in addition to a wide variety of performances which prove that the old girl's outstanding acoustics are just one of its many Victorian marvels.

Another marvel of the festival is that you don't have to own a tuxedo to attend many of the events. You're Out West, remember, so the tidy, casual look will do just fine.

Inside the carefully restored Wheeler Opera House.

Snowmass Lake in the Maroon Bells/Snowmass Wilderness Area north of Aspen and Marble.

■ MARBLE

Just a couple of ridges west was the next logical leap for the silver prospectors spilling out of Aspen in the early 1880s. While digging around they found some silver, and they stumbled on a huge deposit of pure white marble. But so what? No one knew how to mine it, mill it, or ship it.

Marble (the town) came alive in 1885 when a Welsh marble man opened the quarry. Those first chunks of marble were used in the Colorado State Capitol, but hauling marble with 40-mule pack trains wasn't exactly cheap or easy, so the quarry remained a nickel-and-dime operation.

That changed in 1906 when Col. Channing F. Meek came into town, bought the quarry, and incorporated the Colorado Yule Marble Company. In 1914, the quarry supplied over $1,000,000 worth of marble for the Lincoln Memorial in Washington D.C., a fact proudly touted in the firm's 1915 price list. Back then you could secure an ornamental vase ($16), fruit stand ($7), or Water Kiss Fountain ($250) made from the cuttings of the "beautiful Statuary Golden Vein Colorado-Yule Marble used in the Lincoln Memorial." In 1930, Marble received the

This is some good graz'n pardner.

contract to supply the marble for the Tomb of the Unknown Soldier in Arlington National Cemetery in Washington, D.C. It took 75 men more than a year to carve out the 124-ton block of marble (the largest single piece ever quarried), which was then squared at the mill.

Although now a small-scale operation compared to its glory days, the Yule Marble Quarry disgorges tons of marble a year. The town is about 40 miles south of Glenwood Springs off Colorado 133.

■ ROCKY MOUNTAIN NATIONAL PARK

North of the mining towns of Colorado's central Rockies, and just northwest of the city of Boulder, is Rocky Mountain National Park, which preserves in all its pristine beauty the flora and fauna of the Rockies, as they were before settlers began pouring into Colorado from the east during the 1800s.

Trail Ridge Road, one of the highest paved roads in the nation, runs through the park, and will deliver a view of the top of the Rockies that cannot be matched. As you quickly climb above timberline, you'll find yourself surrounded by 18 mountain peaks over 13,000 feet high. The best way to start the trip is at the start:

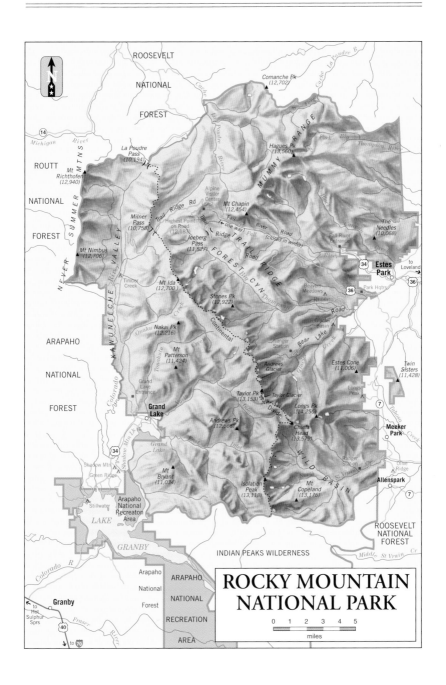

ROCKY MOUNTAIN NATIONAL PARK

0 1 2 3 4 5

miles

the headwaters of the Colorado River, which is just a trickle coming down the western side of the Continental Divide.

Granby, east of Kremmling on US 40 and north of Interstate 70, is the park's western gateway overlooking the Colorado River. As you go north on Trail Ridge Road, you'll pass through Arapaho National Recreation Area, by Lake Granby, and Grand Lake before hitting the town of **Grand Lake.** As you might imagine, there are ample high-country camping, hiking, boating, and fishing opportunities amidst the forests, glades, and lakes in the area.

Then it's uphill as you mount a charge to the top of Trail Ridge Road. Before you sound the bugle, though, you'd better make sure the road is clear of snow, which sometimes doesn't occur until June. By about October, you might not get too far either, thanks to the snowy stuff, so this is definitely a summertime undertaking. That short season means you can also expect crowds, as well as possibly getting stuck behind a tour bus. But those are small prices to pay for the rewards awaiting.

The 410 square miles of park contain abundant wildlife, 700 species of wild-

Edna Mills is the daughter of writer/conservationist Enos Mills (in photograph she is holding) who fought for the creation of Rocky Mountain National Park. Tourists may visit his former cabin-studio (in background) south of Estes Park.

flowers, and 150 secluded alpine lakes. Topping things off is a 13-mile stretch far above timberline that's home to alpine tundra resembling the tundra near the Arctic Circle. A word of caution here. Don't stray from the paved paths onto this fragile flora. Your footprint can do serious damage. Do, however, take some time to explore the tiny blossoms that spring out. They seem to be more vivid than any in the state.

Once you peak out and start down the eastern side of the divide, you'll witness the transformation from tundra to tree-covered mountain valleys to mellow meadows. All along the road are numerous pull-outs with informational signs describing the ecology and naming distant, snowcapped peaks.

Wildflowers bloom by a bubbling creek high in Rocky Mountain National Park.

The **Alpine Visitor Center** and the **Moraine Park Museum** provide more information via knowledgeable park rangers. The park contains 350 miles of trails that provide access for campers, anglers, mountain bikers, and wildlife watchers; for information call (970) 586-1206.

Estes Park (which is a town, not a park) and civilization in all its glory await at the end of the 50-mile jaunt. The town entices visitors with a melange of services and offers everything from souvenir coffee mugs to restaurants to condos.

The **Stanley Hotel** sits on a hillside above the frantic activity, secure in its glistening white facade and historic roots. Built in 1901 by F. O. Stanley, inventor of the Stanley Steamer, the hotel is a reminder of the days when touring Rocky Mountain National Park was clearly a genteel undertaking.

■ GLENWOOD SPRINGS

Historically a hot spot, Glenwood Springs, almost due west of Denver on I-70 and north of Aspen and Marble, didn't have any gold or silver, but it did have something that turned it into an internationally known resort. Glenwood steamed to the head of Colorado resorts thanks to **Glenwood Hot Springs Pool and Lodge** and the palatial **Hotel Colorado,** both built in the late 1880s. The Denver & Rio Grande Railroad quickly began promoting the "Spa in the Rockies," and soon everyone who was anyone, from gangsters to gunslingers to the cream of society to U.S. Presidents, made Glenwood a stop on their trip through Colorado.

The town's most famous visitor was **Teddy Roosevelt,** who set up a western White House in the Hotel Colorado in 1905 and from which he went on a bear hunt in the nearby White River National Land Reserve. While he was out in the wilds he kept in touch with the White House via a telegraph line to the hotel and a messenger who rode out on his horse every day to try to find the President. *(For more on this trip and the origin of "teddy bears," see page 213.)*

One of Glenwood's more infamous visitors was the gunslinger and gambler **Dr. John "Doc" Holliday,** who died and was buried in town on November 8, 1887. Holliday—a Georgian with a dental degree from Johns Hopkins University—was one of the West's most notorious gunmen, thanks to his friendship with Wyatt Earp. In 1881 Doc, Wyatt, and the rest of the Earp family were in Tombstone, Arizona, where they took part in one of the West's most famous events, "the gunfight at the OK Corral." By the time the shooting stopped, the Earps, with help from Doc's sawed-off shotgun, had summarily slaughtered the Clanton clan.

But Doc's fame and proficiency with a firearm couldn't stop the tuberculosis that was slowly killing him, or his taste for whiskey while playing cards. Unglamorous scrapes with the law involving dead men and fleeced gamblers became his calling cards. When he arrived in Glenwood Springs after such trouble in Denver and Leadville, he worked at local saloons, overseeing the faro box or playing for the house at the gaming tables. Illness forced him to retire to the hotel bed where he died at the age of 35. He was buried in Linwood Cemetery on a hill above town. In the 1960s, the town erected a monument over **Doc Holliday's Grave.** The tools of Doc's trade—six-shooters and playing cards—are etched in stone above his epitaph, "He Died in Bed."

■ GLENWOOD SPRINGS TODAY

Today, the railroad (AMTRAK in this case) still promotes Glenwood as a Rocky Mountain spa. Just outside Glenwood Springs is the world's largest natural hot springs pool, which measures over 300 feet long with hot springs water at 89 degrees in the big pool and a hot-tub-like 103 degrees in the therapy pool. Vapor caves are next, actual caves full of, well, vapors, just like a natural sauna.

The city's downtown is a cluster of turn-of-the-20th-century brick buildings, and its residential neighborhoods display an arresting mix of modern split-level homes right next to Victorian gingerbreads. The Colorado River tumbles out of the magnificent Glenwood Canyon to meet the Roaring Fork River right in town, and the White River National Forest attracts hikers, birdwatchers, and hunters.

Its strategic location between Vail, 60 miles to the east, and Aspen, 40 miles to the southeast, also makes Glenwood a regional shopping and supply town, where Aspenites and Vailites can come to get their car fixed for a reasonable price or buy underwear that doesn't cost as much as a new pair of shoes. This central location,

Cutting under the Continental Divide via the Eisenhower Tunnel.

plus a huge hot tub, attracts skiers who like the fact that they can buy lift tickets at the nearby ski hills without having to take out a second mortgage.

Whether you're coming or going from Glenwood Springs on Interstate 70, you will be treated to a natural wonder called Glenwood Canyon, featuring about 15 miles worth of sheer granite walls shooting 2,000 feet straight up and dotted with trees, cornices, startling rock formations, and on and on. Another wonder, this one man-made, is the state-of-the-art, environmentally sensitive, four-lane highway squeezed through the narrow canyon bottom: cantilevered sections of roadway, bridges crisscrossing the river, and every other trick in the highway builder's book include easy access for rafters to the Colorado River and a bike/hike trail along the river.

(opposite and above) The "healing waters" of the Glenwood Hot Springs Pool. They are open 7 a.m.–10 p.m. year round, rain or snow.

ALFERD [SIC] THE CANNIBAL

If you happen to be strolling along the boardwalk sidewalks in **Lake City**, and you see the following community announcement, "Annual Alferd Packer Community Dinner: MEAT PROVIDED," you've arrived at a special time. Here's the story of Alferd:

Los Pinos Indian Agency, south of Gunnison, wasn't used to many white visitors arriving at springtime on foot, especially in 1874. By all accounts that winter had been a doozie, complete with deep snows, chilling winds, few deer or elk, and general nastiness. Just walking to the Agency, about half way between Saguache and Lake City in the middle of the **San Juan Mountains**, from about anywhere was quite a feat.

That's why the Los Pinos folks were a bit suspicious when Alferd Packer arrived that April asking for whiskey, not food. In such nasty weather it would have taken him weeks, if not longer, to make it to the Agency, yet he didn't look, well, even a little bit puny. Instead, Packer looked pretty healthy, if not rosy-cheeked.

When the springtime prospecting rush arrived, suspicions about Packer's winter paunch started popping up, especially when miners on the Lake Fork of the Gunnison River a few miles below Lake San Cristobal came upon the bodies of five men. Not uncommon in those days, but these bodies were different: the flesh had been carefully carved from their bones. At Los Pinos they remembered Packer's rosy cheeks and his amazing capacity to survive a San Juan winter. Not surprisingly, the day's primitive grapevine linked the five men to Packer.

Suspicions led to questions which led to some information and then some excuses from Packer. Packer said he and five other prospectors from Utah set out in January from present-day Delta for the Los Pinos Indian Agency. Ute Chief Ouray warned them not to go.

The snow was too deep, they hadn't brought enough food, there was no game, they were starving. They started eating their boots. Then they started eating each other.

First Packer said his feet froze and the others left him behind. Then he said one man died of natural causes and was eaten by the rest, so it became a case of kill and eat or become tomorrow's cold cuts, as it were.

Packer was jailed in Saguache, but escaped and remained at large for nine years. Finally captured in Wyoming, he was brought back to Lake City in 1883 for trial. After finding Packer guilty of murder and cannibalism, Judge M. B. Gerry uttered (according to the poem by Mrs. Stella Pavich, titled "Packer the Cannibal") the following sentence and rationale thereof:

There was seven Democrats in Hinsdale County!
But you, you voracious, man-eating sonofabitch,
You ate five of them, therefore I sentence you
To be hanged by the neck, until you're dead, dead!
As a warning against reducing the Democratic population
of this State and Nation.

By the skin of his nose, Packer missed the noose. The killings had taken place on Ute land when Colorado was a territory, thus Packer was charged under territorial laws. In between the killings and the first trial, Colorado became a state, so he was tried under state laws, which was a no-no. (Lawyers, don't you love 'em?) Anyway, at his second trial, in 1886 in Gunnison, the proper legalities were observed and Packer was sentenced to 40 years in prison. Packer's case had drawn considerable attention and supporters who believed his side of the story. In 1901, the governor paroled Packer; he died in April 1907, and he's buried in Littleton.

Such a story couldn't rest in peace, though. In one of the best excuses ever conceived for taking a scientific summer field trip, a group of scientists literally dug up the Packer case in 1989. Forensic expert James Starrs gathered a gang of anthropologists, forensic experts of several stripes, and a geophysicist/engineer, and set out for a summer dig in the San Juans.

The team located the five bodies on a bluff above the Lake Fork River and found skulls that had probably been crushed when the men were asleep, signs some of the men had tried to defend themselves, and bones chipped as if they had been coolly butchered. Such "scientific" evidence proved that Judge Gerry was right to proclaim Packer a "voracious" man eater who did considerable damage to Hinsdale County's Democratic Party. That political damage has been permanent, because from statehood onward Hinsdale County has been a Republican bastion. And can you blame it?

Alferd (Alfie) Packer; not a man to
"do lunch with."
(Museum of Western Art)

SAN JUAN MOUNTAINS

THE GREAT SAN JUAN MOUNTAINS OF SOUTHERN COLORADO are not only chock full of minerals, from gold and silver to zinc and copper, but they are also rugged and isolated—so isolated they are being considered as one of the few places in the Lower 48 states appropriate for re-introduction of the grizzly bear. The region became one of the state's top mining districts right out of the chute, so to speak, and its mines kept producing into the 1990s. Today, there are still prospectors in the San Juans, but they use chemistry, computer-programmed geologic tracking, commodity-market hedging, and core samples instead of picks and mules, as they scour the area for the next mother lode.

Meanwhile, the area's isolated, historic towns and ski resorts are busy mining a mother lode of skiers, mountain bikers, and scenery seekers.

■ GUNNISON

Resting at the northern edge of the San Juan mining country, Crested Butte and Gunnison are separated from the Aspen/Marble area by massive mountains that were almost completely impassable in the 1880s. They're still barely passable today via rugged roads over sheer mountain passes. Colorado 133 out of Carbondale carries you to the cutoff for Crested Butte over Kebler Pass—but only in the summer. In the winter you have to keep going, turn off at Hotchkiss on Colorado 92 and take a stunning ride around the Black Canyon of the Gunnison River before hitting US 50 and then Gunnison.

Gunnison was once the supply hub for scattered mining camps (now turned ghost towns) in the nearby mountains. Set out on the "Scenic Ghost Route," described below, and you'll find them.

■ SCENIC GHOST ROUTE

Want to run over some silver miners turned ghosts and spot the houses of ill repute they frequented after a hard day's work? Head north from Gunnison on Colorado 135 until you hit the small town of **Almont**, turn right on County Road 742, and follow the Taylor River Valley to **Taylor Park Reservoir**. Now, take Road

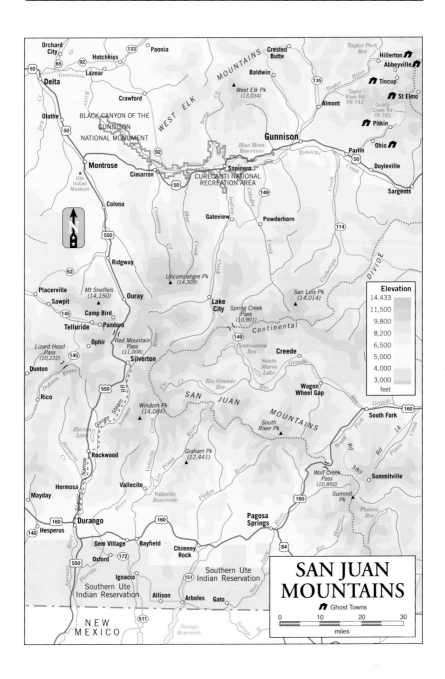

SAN JUAN
MOUNTAINS

Ghost Towns

0   10   20   30
miles

Elevation

14,433
11,500
9,800
8,200
6,500
5,000
4,000
3,000
feet

765 to our first ghostly stop—**Hillerton**, which in 1880 had 1,500 residents, a bank, and booming mines. Stay on 765 and you'll find **Abbeyville**, which was a silver town in the 1880s; then from 1900 to 1912 dredges on local creeks recovered 20,000 ounces of gold.

As you proceed on 765, you'll find **Tincup**, to which by 1900 most of Hillerton's and Abbeyville buildings had been moved. (The first mobile homes in the nation? Sure, let's add that one to Colorado's list of firsts.) You might run into someone besides a ghost because Tincup is alive today. Begun in 1880, by 1882 it had 20 saloons, four hotels, numerous stores, and ladies named Big Minnie, Sagebrush Annie, Santa Fe Moll, and (my personal favorite) Pass Out. Gold was mined in Tincup until 1917, then things went downhill until the town and its original buildings were revived and restored as a summer resort community.

You'll then have to lug over Cumberland Pass, a mere 12,200 feet, which is the highest unpaved auto road in the nation. (Yeah, we like to brag about how high our roads are here in Colorado.) At the summit you will be rewarded with views of the Bon Ton and Blistered Horn mines. Then it's on to Quartz, which started as a silver town but, because it had a rail spur from the Denver and South Park Railroad, continued to prosper as a lumbering center until 1934 when the train left town, followed quickly by everyone else.

Pitkin, the next stop, was the first incorporated town on the Western Slope, but its life was brief. The Alpine Tunnel brought the South Park Railroad to town in 1882, but when the area's biggest silver vein played out after 75 feet of mining, things got pretty grim. Many of the old buildings remain, however, and the old red school house contains a historical exhibit of Pitkin's fast past.

Ohio City had luck on its side, because its mines disgorged both gold and silver, so when the Silver Panic of 1893 hit, the town continued as a gold camp. The Raymond mines have been producing gold, off and on, up to today and the town has a small number of year-round residents who mix in nicely with the solitude, surrounding mountain scenery, and ghosts.

Parlin, the final stop, isn't really a ghost town, but it sure is old. It started as a stage station in 1880, and then both the Denver & Rio Grande and Denver & South Park railroads used it as a supply station and stopover. Today, it is fully functioning as a supply center for area ranchers.

As you continue down County Road 765 you'll hit US 50 and be only 12 miles east of Gunnison, where this whole ghostly trip started.

Fall color in the remote and magnificent San Juan Mountains.

■ CREEDE

Deep in the heart of the San Juans lies the last great silver town, Creede. Its mines weren't tapped until 1889, but for the next four years it became the boomtown of boomtowns, where millions were made and the riff almost outnumbered the raff. Creede also hosted such sure-shooting legends as a marshall named Bat Masterson, Bob Ford (who killed Jesse James), and Calamity Jane and her pal, Poker Alice. The city never slept, turning out 80 million tons of silver during its short life.

A long slumber began with repeal of the Silver Act in 1893. Then five separate fires and some mud slides pretty much destroyed the tangible reminders of its glorious past. Today, Creede has become a regular small town buried deep in the San Juans that doesn't mind the occasional tourist, but whose real attraction is a slow, somewhat isolated lifestyle in the middle of the Colorado Rockies. It's about 100 miles south of Gunnison on Colorado 149. If you visit, try getting tickets for a performance at the **Creede Repertory Theatre.** *(719) 658-2540.*

■ OURAY

Ouray, on the western side of the mountains, is squeezed into a stunning canyon from which it seems there is no escape. Ouray's present mix of hot-spring spas, Victorian buildings, and modern conveniences belies its mining past. The Camp Bird Mines and others in the surrounding mountains produced gold on and off starting in 1893. Those mineral-laden mountains are now crawling with Jeeps full of sightseers, hikers, mountain bikers, and rock and ice climbers.

Ask for directions to the spectacular **Box Canyon Falls.** This involves a short walk up Box Canyon, until it becomes very, very narrow, then a quick step back to avoid being given a massive shower bath by the falls.

For a spectacular drive through the San Juans, take the **Million Dollar Highway**, a vertiginous stretch of US 550 and the start of a 236-mile scenic loop from Ouray through Durango, Silverton, Cortez, and Telluride. *(See page 146 for route instructions.)*

Exploring an ice cave in Box Canyon, one of the San Juans' treasures.

■ SILVERTON

This little Victorian hamlet is set on top of the San Juan mining town pile. It's in a magnificent, isolated valley, which enjoys, oh, about 80 days of summer and summer tourists a year, delivered directly to town via the **Durango & Silverton Narrow Gauge Railroad.** The town's expansive and ornate **Town Hall** recalls Silverton's rich mining history, which lasted for 100 years, thanks to the prolific production of the Sunnyside Mine. From Silverton you can only go down, but it's a great ride regardless of which side you decide to descend.

■ DURANGO

If you drop off the hill south of Silverton, this is where you end up. You can take the trek by car on US 550 and wind through the rusted remains of many an old mine and mill, as well as the *un*rusted **Purgatory Ski Area;** or you can settle in on the restored **Durango & Silverton Narrow Gauge Railroad,** an authentic steampowered locomotive that makes daily runs during the summer. A towering plume of steam will tip you off to the train's whereabouts. *(See page 304.)*

Durango is an interesting old town that keeps itself new. Because of its location,

(above) This ain't no "dime-store cowboy."
(opposite) The Durango & Silverton Narrow Gauge Railroad clears the tracks.

Racing Rails and Roads to Silver

When silver began to outpace gold as king of Colorado's mineral court, silver mines and mining camps started popping up throughout the state quicker than they could be marked on a map. Unlike the gold country, which was relatively close to Denver and the Front Range, silver strikes were made in generally inaccessible high country in the central and southwest Rockies. The coming of a railroad or even a wagon road could thus turn a simple silver mining camp into a booming city and the road builders into millionaires. Thus, conditions were ripe for more than one high-stakes railroad race and several extraordinary displays of high-country road building.

Leadville was the first jewel lusted after by more than one railroader. Coming from the south, both the Rio Grande and the Santa Fe laid tracks right up to the mouth of the narrow Royal Gorge. Before rail crews decided with fist and sledge which track would be the only one to fit through the canyon, a deal was struck. The Rio Grande paid for the privilege to build into Leadville, and reached town in 1880. One railroad wasn't enough to serve Leadville, however, so the Denver and South Park line kept plugging away and reached town four years later.

The Rio Grande was involved in two other races, and won both. It was the first to hit **Gunnison** in 1881 and beat the Colorado Midland to Aspen in 1887. The Colorado Midland, though, was a gutsy little line. Starting in Colorado Springs, it ran through South Park and topped the 11,500-foot Hagerman Pass (which was replaced in 1890 by the Busk Ivanhoe Tunnel) on the way to Aspen.

While most attention focused on Leadville and Aspen, **Otto Mears** attacked the rugged **San Juan Mountains**, whose gold and silver would be no more than piles of shiny curiosities if they couldn't be shipped out of the isolated valleys. The jagged peaks didn't deter Mears, an immigrant Russian Jew, who set out to connect the isolated mining camps with a series of toll roads. In all, Mears built over 300 miles of toll roads in the San Juans, linking the area to the outside world and earning the sobriquet "The Pathfinder of the Southwest." Many of Mears's original roads later became rail lines and his work is still evident today. His road from **Ouray** to **Silverton** is now part of the famed "Million Dollar Highway."

But the days of home-owned railroads were doomed by one man—eastern financier **Jay Gould**. Gould was insatiable. He already held significant interests in the Missouri Pacific, the Rio Grande, the Union Pacific, and the Denver Pacific, and he had operating agreements with the Santa Fe and Rock Island lines. He also bought the Denver and South Park, the Kansas and Pacific, and the Colorado Central. Thus, not only did faceless corporations come to dominate Colorado mining, but Gould, one of the slickest and most ruthless operators in capitalism's heyday, came to control most of the state's railroads, which were its lifelines. The result was predictable. When the once booming silver towns went silent, the screech of the steam whistle, the clackety-clack of iron wheels on iron rails, and the steady chugging of a steam locomotive also receded into silence, all victims of a bust that would have to wait for the intervening decades to provide the historical perspective that supplied the incentive and willingness to fire up the engine, blow the whistle, and let the steel wheels roll once again. *(See "Historic Railroads," pages 304–306 for a list of the state's historic steam-powered train rides.)*

Toll station on Otto Mears's Bear Creek Road from Ouray to Silverton. (Colorado Historical Society)

it became the supply center for the San Juan mining camps and for the surrounding Indian reservations, as well as for the area's farms and ranches. With **Mesa Verde National Park** about an hour's drive to the west on Colorado 160 and all the old silver mining towns, camps, and roads to the north, Durango is a good spot to set up camp during a San Juan stay.

As you stroll down to the historic **Strater Hotel** to catch a little honky-tonk piano or a melodrama, you'll pass blue-collar bars where you can rub elbows with real cowboys and Indians, scope out a broad selection of restaurants or ice cream shops catering to both visitors and locals, and find a funky postcard or curio shop.

■ TELLURIDE

The problem here wasn't good gold, of which the area had plenty, but that it occupied the bottom of a sheer box canyon with just a rough road in or out. Thus, it languished until Rio Grande Southern Railroad chugged to town in 1890, touching off gold boom days.

Bad labor relations and isolation combined to stifle Telluride by 1930, but "To-Hell-You-Ride" was brought back to life in 1953 when the Idarado Mining

(above) Telluride tucked into its sheer box canyon. (opposite) Bridal Veil Falls cascades from the canyon wall east of Telluride.

Company bought old gold mining claims and began mining gold, zinc, and silver—which it did until 1978.

It still takes a bit to get to Telluride, even though it looks like it's just an inch west of Ouray on the map. Don't be fooled. It's a rough inch.

The classic **New Sheridan Hotel** is the centerpiece of the neat line of Victorian buildings along Telluride's main drag today. **Bridal Veil Falls** at the head of the canyon is a dramatic sight, as are the almost automatic rainbows that appear to reach from one mountaintop to the other at any hint of moisture. These falls were utilized to create the first practical method of air conditioning. Furthermore, Telluride was the first electrified town in the world.

Most summer weekends you'll find something going on, more specifically film, dance, and music festivals, the latter ranging from folk music to bluegrass to jazz. *(See "Festivals and Events," beginning on page 291, for details.)*

■ SAN JUAN SKYWAY

If you're refilling your stash of cold ones in **Ouray,** you might not want to glance up Red Mountain. If you do, you might think there is no way in the world to drive to the top of that hill without cardiac or carburetor arrest. Calm your beating

Several peaks within the rugged San Juan Mountain Range top 14,000 feet.

heart. It's just an 11,000-foot mountain pass that was born over 100 years ago when Otto Mears cut and carved a wagon road up the same hill. Not too many travelers have fallen off it since.

Mears's gutsy road-building feat laid the base for US 550, more commonly referred to as the **Million Dollar Highway,** which is just the beginning of the **San Juan Skyway,** a loop of state roads that takes you to almost every delight southwest Colorado has to offer. If you really want to take advantage of this trip you're going to have to give it a couple of days, but once you get rolling you'll see taking a day or two on "the most beautiful drive in the nation" will more than make up for missing the tour at New Mexico's White Sands Missile Range.

Don't be alarmed if your car doesn't exactly roar up Red Mountain Pass; this is one steep puppy, so just take your time. There's plenty to look at anyway. Once you peak out, you'll drop, slightly, into the Victorian mining town of **Silverton.** *(See page 140.)*

As you head south toward Durango the roadside is littered with ghost towns, old silver mine buildings, and tailings. Still, you'll be traveling through Colorado high country at its finest, and topping two mountains passes over 10,000 feet before reaching **Durango.** This historic town mixes late 19th-century charm with doses of progress, making for a real town that also happens to host tourists.

Now, turn west on Colorado 160, into Indian country, both past and present.

Moonlit night in Silverton.

To the south is the Southern Ute Mountain Indian Reservation and just past Mancos is the entrance to **Mesa Verde National Park.** Scanning the seemingly endless mesa you'll understand why it took so long for white men to discover the park's magnificent cliff dwellings and other archaeological wonders *(also see page 180)*. Farther west, you hit **Cortez,** the largest town in the region and the center of today's Indian culture and politics. Straight north on Colorado 145, then four miles north of **Dolores** is the **Anasazi Heritage Center,** a trove of ancient Indian artifacts and information about the Escalante-Dominguez Expedition of 1776 *(page 179)*. Over Lizard Head Pass is **Telluride.** Nestled in a box canyon with ski hills on the right, towering mountains on the left, and bridal veil falls in front, you can't find a more picturesque mountain town.

You're actually due south of Ouray right now, but to get there you'll have to take Colorado 145 to Placerville, then hit Colorado 62 to Ridgeways. Right past town is US 550, which will take you back to **Ouray.** Oh, one final tip. If you do take the entire loop, stop in Ouray when you're finished and spend some time in one of the town's natural hot springs pools or spas.

■ SUMMITVILLE

The ghosts going bump in the night in the once-booming gold-rush town of Summitville don't have to rely on the same old ghost stories to entertain themselves. Summitville, due south of Del Norte and just east of Wolf Creek Pass at over 10,850 feet, experienced its first boom from 1872 to 1874, but the area's gold didn't pick up and leave like the prospectors, so the town has experienced a number of gold-driven rebirths that has kept the ghosts hopping in and out of the old miners' cabins.

In its first boom, Summitville was the state's third largest gold producer. About 50 mines on South Mountain disgorged 257,000 ounces of the shiny stuff. Pretty impressive, until you consider the 245,000 ounces of gold produced in a mere six years beginning in 1986, when a Canadian firm reopened the mine.

But gone were yesteryear's gold pan, pick and shovel, sluice box, or hydraulic hoses. Also gone were the nuggets or flakes of gold easily spotted by the naked eye. Modern miners search for microscopic flecks of gold. Instead of crushing or smelting gold ore, the mine sorted the microscopic gold from the dirt using a weak mix of cyanide and water held in large processing ponds called leeching fields.

Just a leisurely ride in the San Juans.

Like the miners of old, those at the Summitville operation made hay while they could. Unlike the old timers, when the high-tech miners moved on, they left a gaping wound in the earth that leaked a watery toxic stew into the nearby ground. Then a new mining crew went to work: the cleaners. After several years of lawsuits, threats, and bureaucratic back-and-forth, reclamation crews spent another couple of years cleaning up the mess by rearranging the disturbed landscape and putting the toxic genie back in the bottle.

And the ghosts roaming the tattered, weather-beaten old buildings in Summitville chuckled a bit, then had the place to themselves once again.

Summitville's George Popovich still prospects for the mother lode.

W E S T E R N   S L O P E
F R O M   D I N O S A U R   B O N E S   T O   P E A C H E S

IT WAS A HOMEMADE T-SHIRT, BUT ITS MESSAGE CAME THROUGH loud and clear. The design featured the red international "NO" symbol, a carton of milk, a slice of toast popping out of a toaster, and the words, "U.S. National Hang Gliding Championships Dinosaur, Colorado," an event which, at least as far as the T-shirt wearer was concerned, automatically disqualified the milquetoast crowd.

Dinosaur is the definition of a small town. It boats a slim batch of modest homes, a city hall, and a scattering of motels and cafes on streets that cut and jut in random order. Fresh paint and street signs don't overwhelm a visitor, so you have to feel your way around, but it's a short feel.

Dinosaur's isolation and steady winds are why it takes its turn hosting hang gliding confabs and has become a regular stop for hard core hang gliders and para-sailors. The sky fliers routinely hop off Cliff Ridge, confident they can ride the wind for up to 100 miles in any direction, knowing chances are slim they'll land in a shopping mall parking lot or atop a suburban rooftop.

But if a hang glider hit one hell of an updraft that sent him circling around northwest Colorado, he would be treated to a variety of sights far more interesting than shopping malls or suburbia. Floating north out of Dinosaur, he could gaze into the gorges made by the Green and Yampa Rivers as they cut through Dinosaur National Monument. As he headed west, he would peer down on mile after mile of untouched brown-hued hillsides splattered with sage and piñon.

Then, abruptly, around Craig, the pine- and spruce-covered western flank of the Rocky Mountains would rise up in greeting. Continuing south, he would cruise over the densely forested, dark green White River National Forest southeast of Meeker. Cutting back to the west he would zip over the Piceance Basin, where the land alternates between blocks of green, irrigated hay fields, and gray-dry chunks of land waiting for water. Amid the rolling hills of spruce and piñon he might spot hundreds, if not thousands, of the deer and elk that make the basin one of the finest places in the state to view wildlife.

Swooping back northward along the Utah border toward Dinosaur and the desolate desert, he'd see again a mottled mixture of reds, grays, and browns underneath until, with his head spinning with images ranging from desert to forest to

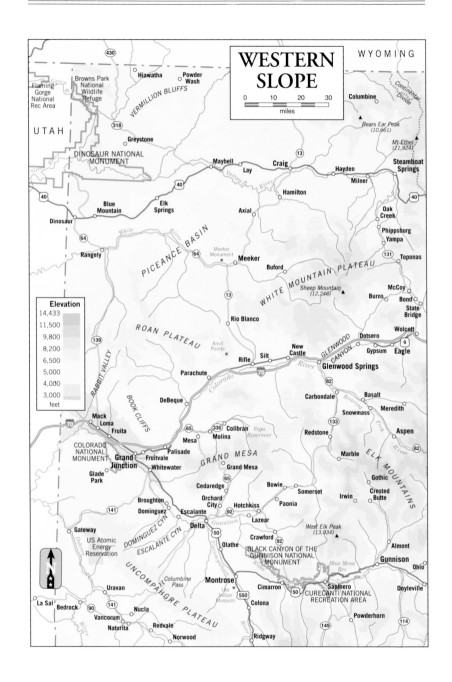

WESTERN SLOPE

0   10   20   30
miles

mountain to pasture, our hang glider once again reaches the isolated burg of Dinosaur.

Dinosaur is the far northwest outpost of Colorado's Western Slope, which can be broken into two distinct regions. The northwest, generally referred to as the Piceance (PEE-aunce) Basin, contains one of the nation's largest storehouses of valuable minerals. This chunk of mostly federally controlled real estate faces Utah on the west, Wyoming on the north, the Rocky Mountains on the east, and bottoms out along Interstate 70 on the south. South of Interstate 70 the mountains still loom to the east with Utah to the west before you head into the San Juan Mountains and southern Colorado.

The basin's natural resources have created a diverse legacy: extensive ranching and farming plus development of oil, coal, uranium, and natural gas, on the one hand; the birth of the wilderness area idea, and two national monuments and a national recreation area on the other; and endless debate over who and what should come first—the miner/oil driller/rancher or the hiker/hunter/camper. Since huge chunks of the basin are federally controlled, most decisions affecting in the region aren't made by the people who happen to live there.

■ DINOSAUR NATIONAL MONUMENT

Whether you head toward Dinosaur National Monument from Steamboat Springs, Meeker, or Grand Junction, it takes hours of two-lane driving to get there. As you meander through this somewhat desolate landscape of red, tan, and white rock, it's hard to imagine that this was once a tropical landscape where giant vegetarian dinosaurs roamed through clumps of conifers, ferns, mosses, and cycads.

The sight of today's huge winged creatures—hang gliders—cruising and cutting into the up and down drafts above the Piceance Basin sky isn't entirely unprecedented. About 140 million years ago a winged dinosaur called the *Rhamphorhynchus* sailed the skies during the Jurassic Period and peered down on the huge walking dinosaurs that have captured the imagination of children and curiosity of scientists ever since. The *Rhamphorhynchus, Brontosaurus,* and herds of other dinos once called the region home, and their fossilized remains are scattered throughout northwest Colorado.

A bona fide race was on after the first dinosaur fossil discoveries were made around 1900, and tourists and paleontologists began to pick up bones and lug them away. The bone boom got going full bore in 1909 when a Carnegie Museum paleontologist arrived and was stunned to see eight tail bones of a *Brontosaurus* sticking out of the ground. Carnegie cash assured that many a museum would become a dinosaur depository. Fifteen years after the first discoveries, over 350 tons of dinosaur bones were dug up and shipped to museums across the country.

The wholesale "grave robbing" came to an end in 1915 when 80 acres of the diggings were designated as Dinosaur National Monument. In 1938 another 326 acres were added.

Therein lies the town of Dinosaur's real claim to fame: it's the gateway to Dinosaur National Monument. (Sort of. Rangely, about 18 miles south of Dinosaur also claims the title, and since it bears some resemblance to a real town, with a community college and a downtown, it's hard to argue the point.) Actually, the gateway and the original portion of the current monument is over 20 miles to the west in, egads, Utah, and features the much publicized **Visitors Center** where real paleontologists chip real bones out of a real dino dig.

■ GREEN AND YAMPA RIVER VALLEYS

Between 1950 and 1955, the nation's eyes focused on Dinosaur National Monument. Those eyes weren't peering in awe at 200-pound dinosaur bones, they were glaring at a proposal to dam the Green and Yampa Rivers.

Thanks to some serious shenanigans that set the tone for the "mainstream" environmental movement from then onward, the dam wasn't built and the Green and Yampa River canyons were preserved. The canyons are located due north of the town of Dinosaur, through juniper and piñon country that contains nary a dinosaur bone but is nevertheless part of the Dinosaur National Monument. That was the deal struck in 1955: Glen Canyon was dammed; the Green and Yampa Rivers became part of the national monument and were permitted to run free.

These two staggeringly abrupt cracks in the earth make you feel fragile in the face of the forces that created them out of windswept desert, especially when you are standing at the edge of the Yampa River Canyon, surrounded by miles of unspoiled desert, or are taking a trail that lets you wander the rim and peer into the deep canyon to watch the snake-like Yampa River slowly and silently twist its way through the bottom. The same feeling of insignificance invades if you are rafting or fishing the Green River and peering up, in between bursts of whitewater, at its towering canyon walls.

Colorado's Age of Dinosaurs

Dinosaur National Monument provides us with a grand view of the Jurassic landscape of 145 million years ago, when the earth's continents were joined together in a single land mass now referred to as "Pangaea." As you look about you at the subtle greys and browns of the desert, try to imagine the brilliant green ferns, conifers, and mosses which once grew here, and the behemoth dinosaurs that wandered among them. One of these was *Apatosaurus* (a.k.a., *Brontosaurus*), a long-necked and long-tailed vegetarian—measuring over 70 feet in length and tipping the scales at 35 tons. Because *Apatosaurus's* brain was smaller than ours, though given the job of directing a body as big as 18 station wagons, some people assumed it was dull-witted and spent most of its time sloshing around in swamps. Yet, now we know from studying rock strata in such places as Dinosaur National Monument that *Apatosaurus* galloped around in herds, probably with its young in the middle, kicking up dust and trampling trees. The smell must have been awful, but they may have been fairly smart. After all, *Apatosaurus* belongs to one of the most successful groups of animals ever to live on the earth.

Other smaller dinosaurs shared Jurassic Park with these monsters, among them the comely *Stegosaurus* ("roofed reptile"), known for the bony knobs and bumps all over its body, the upright plates on its back and its tail spikes. These animals grew to 20 feet in length and weighed about one-and-a-half tons. Early researchers thought that the back plates served as a defensive weapon, but more recently scientists have suggested that they served as solar panels and radiators regulating *Stegosaurus's* body temperature.

Roaming around with these oversized vegetarians were meat-eating carnosaurs, who packed their weight behind large heads, powerful necks, stout hind limbs, and small forearms. These included *Allosaurus* ("strange reptile") and *Ceratosaurus* ("horned reptile"). Adult *Allosaurus* was close to 40 feet long with a skull that reached nearly three feet in length; it had sharp, recurved daggers for teeth—serrated on both sides—lining its jaws. Possibly, it sped around Jurassic Park on its long, powerful hind limbs and grabbed its prey in the claws on its small, muscular forelimbs. *Allosaurus* probably fed on whip-tailed *Apatosaurus*.

As you climb into your two-ton station wagon to leave Dinosaur National Monument, you may feel vaguely relieved to return to the twentieth century, where the descendants of *Allosaurus* (birds) prey on insects and worms.

—Mark Goodwin, scientist at the U.C. Berkeley Museum of Paleontology

(following pages) Rudolph Zallinger's famous mural of the Jurassic Period gives an imaginative view of a world dominated by dinosaurs. (Peabody Museum, Yale University)

A wild horse stands alone in a Piceance Basin blizzard.

■ WILDLIFE IN THE PICEANCE BASIN

The best way to get a feel for the Piceance Basin is to drive Colorado 64 between Rangely and Meeker. Thousands of animals feel quite comfortable ambling across the land and picking their way through stands of sagebrush, cedar, piñon-juniper, and Douglas fir. Towns and motels are nonexistent, so if you'd like to spend the night along the way, bring a tent and sleeping bag.

There aren't any towns in the middle of the basin because in the 1880s the first white men didn't think the place was worth a damn. There wasn't gold and silver for the taking like there was in Central City or Leadville. Thus, many original mining claims were quickly abandoned and of the basin's 804,500 acres, about 675,000 acres eventually landed in the lap of the Bureau of Land Management (BLM). But centuries ago people lived a pleasant life here, as evidenced by the **Dutch Creek Wickiup Village,** a prehistoric site listed on the National Register of Historic Places. Some 35 other sites may be eligible for the same honor.

As you travel the two-lane road, you'll see timber-covered mountains and rolling hills from which tumble small streams. The streams have been channeled and tamed into irrigation works that created 82,000 acres of farmland and another 400,000 acres of open range. Ranches dot the landscape, as do herds of cattle and sheep. The forested hills are also harvested, in the form of thousands of cords of piñon and juniper firewood and hundreds of thousands of board-feet of Douglas fir for local lumber yards.

It's almost impossible *not* to see wildlife either on the ground or in the sky. The area contains one of the largest migratory mule deer herds in North America—numbering over 25,000 head—along with over 1,200 head of elk. In all, there are over 350 species of wildlife in the basin, including 22 species of raptors, ranging from owls to eagles, and, for good measure, a wild horse herd. Underneath it all are oil, gas, asphalt, nacholite, oil shale, and possibly gold.

■ TREASURE CHEST OR PANDORA'S BOX?

Anyone looking for a single spot that embodies the many-faceted debate over how the West should manage and develop its ample natural resources need look no further than the Piceance Basin.

This corner of northwestern Colorado is a veritable treasure chest of natural resources. For 100 years the urge to unlock this treasure has inspired scams, booms, and busts that make the opening of Pandora's Box seem like a minor mishap.

Beneath the rolling countryside lie the world's largest deposits of oil shale, the largest untapped natural gas fields in the lower 48 states, and over 400 million tons of coal. Huge reserves of gravel, oil, asphalt, and nacholite also rest beneath thousands of acres of timber and grazing lands.

The boom-bust cycle these riches inspired began with an 1872 diamond scam. A pair of swindlers "salted" the land with diamonds, scored $600,000 from a San Francisco bank for their "mine," and unleashed a frenzy of fortune seekers. One look at the alleged diamond territory by a U.S. government geologist quickly ended that boom.

About the same time, as legend has it, settler Mike Callahan arrived on the basin, built a cabin, and fired up his shale-rock fireplace, which immediately caught fire: Hello oil shale, "the rock that burns." And hello to the dogged efforts to transform oil shale rock into oil.

Small shale booms erupted at irregular intervals thereafter, but every boom turned to bust, as the discovery of huge new oil fields ready for drilling made shale seem less worth the bother. Sky-high oil prices in the late 1970s and early 1980s sparked the biggest boom of all, with four major oil companies working on oil shale projects. But as prices dropped again the companies dropped their plans.

Natural gas, too, has had its cycle. In the late 1960s the federal government tried to extract this resource with the help of an underground nuclear bomb. That literal boom was a bust: pools of natural gas failed to form in the void left by the bomb.

Today gas-drilling rigs pop up in the middle of hay fields and forests and on the edges of towns. This latest boom hasn't been welcomed by the area's many new-comers, who have seen their vistas dotted and blotted by drilling rigs, their country roads cluttered with truck traffic, and their quiet nights shattered by the roar of diesel engines.

The latest boom is just another in a long list of "resource issues" facing the Piceance Basin and its various landowners, which include the federal government as major landholder, but also private interests ranging from rancher families to multinational corporations.

The oil and mining companies still covet the wealth under the ground. Loggers covet the forests that cover the ground. Hordes of hunters covet the game animals that roam the forests. Ranchers covet their grazing rights and irrigation water. Environmentalists covet the opportunity to preserve this massive "bioregion" and its full complement of flora and fauna.

The result? A cacophony of voices screaming in the wilderness, espousing divergent views, goals, and priorities.

As the debate rages about managing public lands for the benefit of all, only one clear theme emerges: the Piceance Basin is both a treasure chest and a Pandora's Box, and you can't open one without opening the other.

■ MEEKER: WHERE WILDERNESS WAS BORN

In 1919, a federal employee in Meeker, looking at the pristine beauty of the forests east of the mineral-laden Piceance Basin, decided there should be a way to assure that the public interest come first, foremost, and forever. That radical idea would eventually rock the Western Slope, rattle Colorado, and reshape the nation's public lands.

The man, Arthur Carhart, a Forest Service landscape architect working in the **White River National Forest** east of Meeker, was upset. The tranquil beauty of Trappers Lake was being threatened by plans for summer homes, guest ranches, and "civilization" in general. Carhart's radical idea was that certain places should forever be preserved as wilderness, untouched by man.

Carhart's idea of wilderness areas where homes, roads, mines, farms, and men's other "civilizing" tendencies would be banned was picked up and pushed ahead by nationally known conservationists of the day such as Gifford Pinchot, Bob Marshall, and Aldo Leopold. Thus, just west of one of the state's largest mineral storehouses was launched the idea that vast sections of public land should be set aside for those who wanted to merely look at wild land or tread without trace through it, instead of overwhelming it with technology, stripping off its trees, or tearing into its bowels to search for its hidden riches.

As Aldo Leopold wrote: "We abuse land because we regard it as a commodity belonging to us. When we see land as a community to which we belong, we may begin to use it with love and respect."

In 1964, Carhart's radical idea was codified as the U.S. Wilderness Act, which was fought tooth and nail by most Colorado politicians. Today, although wilderness areas attract a steady stream of tourists, creating more wilderness is still a hot topic because old ideas and old ways die hard, especially in ranching country.

Meeker, which rests between Rifle and Craig on Colorado 13, is a small ranching community which gets some mineral-based glory and grief but is sustained by the surrounding cattle ranchers and sheepmen ("Eat Lamb, 100,000 Coyotes Can't Be Wrong"). Driving through Meeker, with its old brick downtown buildings, mellow, small-town ambiance, and quiet, well-kept residences, it's easy to believe the town spawned the idea of tranquil wilderness. Meeker is also home to the **International Sheep Dog Trials,** and therein rests a clue why it's in the middle of the newest public land debate.

Every year or two, like clockwork, Meeker finds itself in the spotlight over the intertwined issues of livestock grazing on public land and "predator control."

For the ranchers who run sheep and cattle, the ability to turn their herds loose on public land for summer grazing at a nominal fee is regarded as a right. "Predator control" means being able to shoot any coyote, mountain lion, bear, or stray dog that might threaten their herds.

To environmentalists, the low grazing fees are a publicly funded subsidy they liken to "agricultural welfare." They see herds of cows and sheep as damaging to grasslands and streams. And they regard "predator control" as government-sanctioned murder of animals which keep the local ecosystem in balance.

Grisly scenes of dead sheep, poisoned bears, or coyote hides hung on a fence inflame passions on both sides. Well-meaning efforts by federal and state land managers to reach some middle ground are resisted by both sides, which prefer to dig in their heels and stand their ground. The debate, and the killing, continues.

❖

Meeker was originally named after **Nathan C. Meeker** who arrived in the area in 1878 to head the White River Indian Agency and change the Ute Indians from hunters and horse racers to solid Protestant farmers. *(For more about this disastrous enterprise read the "Utes" essay in "Southern Colorado," pages 190–191.)* Today, a simple farm implement is prominently displayed at the **White River Museum** outside of Meeker. It's *the plow.* The plow Nathan Meeker planned to use to turn the Utes' horse track into a corn field. Two miles west of Meeker on Colorado 64 is a plain wooden sign and stone monument that pinpoints the **White River Ute Indian Agency.**

Behind the sign you can see the broad valley that the Utes used to call home and that has been tamed into pasture and farmland. But turning to the east, you can see the hidden valleys, hot springs, and peaceful retreats that the Utes will always remember as "the land of shining mountains."

■ GRAND JUNCTION: PEACHIEST TOWN AROUND

As soon as they were fairly certain the Utes would be removed from the Western Slope, land speculators and farmers went right to work. It is not stretching the truth to say that fruit trees and crops were being planted, mining claims staked, and hot springs turned into spas before the Utes' footprints had disappeared.

Grand Junction was the apt name speedy speculators chose for a grand town to replace the Ute camps at the confluence of the Grand (Colorado) and Gunnison rivers. Nestled between desert plateaus on the west and mountainous, pine-covered mountains to the southeast, and with water readily available, Grand Junction was able to take advantage of every leg upon which the Western Slope economy rests.

Today, this city is the Western Slope's largest town, supplying the region with everything from transmissions to tricycles. Tourism and agriculture are two other props holding up Grand Junction, and in both cases variety provides the spice of economic life.

The city is uniquely situated between an alpine wonderland and the arid, wind-carved beauty of the desert. On the western fringe of the Grand Valley rests the Colorado National Monument, featuring stunning rock formations in a desert-like setting. The eastern side of the valley is defined by the Grand Mesa. A trip to the top of the mesa reveals the full strata of high-country scenery, from sagebrush to piñon and juniper forests to higher elevation aspen and pine, to barren peaks poking above the timberline.

Consuming the fertile floor of the Colorado River Valley between these two natural wonders are orderly acres of orchards and vineyards representing man's efforts to order nature around. In the early spring visitors driving on I-70 can see two seasons at a glance: fruit trees decked with bright flower buds cover the valley floor while the Grand Mesa looms over it crowned by the snows of winter.

As spring passes into summer and fall, the carefully planted rows of fruit trees deliver a bountiful harvest, the most notable of which is the Grand Junction peach. The combination of cool nights and hot days creates a robust, definitive peach bursting with flavor that is craved by connoisseurs and hoarded by Coloradoans, who travel for miles at harvest time to buy peaches by the case.

But there's more than peaches on those trees. Apples, cherries, and plums are also mouth-watering home-grown products. A newcomer to the valley is the grape. More specifically, the wine grape. When growers and vintners started growing wine grapes and announcing the birth of the Colorado wine industry in the early 1980s, the move was looked upon by traditional fruit farmers as either a nice hobby or a waste of time.

They quickly changed their tune. The same growing conditions that produced peachy peaches also produce distinctive wine grapes. Innovative wine makers took it from there, and Colorado wines have progressed from a regional oddity to a credible contender in the American wine market. More than a few Grand Junction winers proudly display prizes garnered in wine competitions, and the future looks bright for the valley's latest agricultural undertaking.

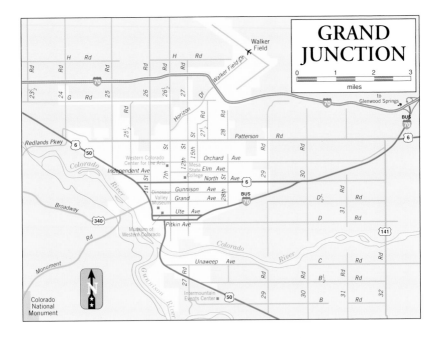

Grand Junction itself is an interesting mix of what's old, brick, and stable, and what's new, gleaming, and hopeful. Coming off Interstate 70, you'll be greeted by the gleam in the form of a strip of new motels, office buildings, and commercial space sparked by nearby Walker Field Airport. The airport's modern glass and polished chrome design is a solid benefit of the 1980's shale boom, since the oil companies were soaked for most of the bill.

Downtown—with its trees and flowers, serpentine lanes, pedestrian-friendly stoplights and crosswalks, and solid brick stability—looks new, but that's because it's been working on renewing itself for a long time. In 1962 Grand Junction became the second city in the nation to take a chance on reviving its downtown by creating a more relaxing, "shopper-oriented" atmosphere featuring ample parking and locally owned shops.

Community effort has helped add two new highlights to downtown. First is the renovated **Avalon Theatre**. The former vaudeville house turned movie house turned urban eyesore has been spruced up and remodeled to become the city's premiere performance space. *645 Main Street; (970) 242-2188.* And years of work have transformed an abandoned industrial zone on the banks of the Colorado and Gunnison rivers into a family friendly stretch of urban greenway called **Confluence Park.**

Of particular interest downtown is the **Dinosaur Valley Museum,** a special exhibition of the Museum of Western Colorado, whose other exhibits include a great gun collection—from muzzleloaders on up—and loads of other Western Slope lore. Dinosaur Valley features half-size replicas of several dinosaurs, which move, stomp, and roar, a working paleontology lab, and other educational exhibits. *362 Main Street; (970) 241-9210.*

Since Grand Junction sits astride Interstate 70, making it easy to find and get to, regardless of the weather, it's a good launching pad from which to set out on targeted trips to the region's attractions.

Gayla and Jackie Hawks are a mother-daughter barrel-racing team from the Grand Junction area.

■ A TASTE OF THE WESTERN SLOPE

Come harvest time, getting a taste of the Western Slope is as easy as falling off a log. Roadside fruit stands start to sprout along highways and county roads throughout the Grand Valley in midsummer. Roadside vendors run the gamut from a couple of kids with a cooler full of cherries (the rural equivalent of the street-corner lemonade stand) to little plywood shacks to full-blown markets with rows of just-picked fruits and vegetables

Palisade, just west of Grand Junction, offers up peaches, plums and apples. A trip up the North Fork Valley between Delta and Paonia along Colorado 92 yields prize Paonia cherries, more peaches and apples, and vegetables from zucchini to squash.

The king of the vegetable kingdom, however is Olathe sweet corn. You'll never be satisfied with regular ears of corn after one bite of Olathe sweet corn, guaranteed. Its kernels are big and juicy and bursting with a full-bodied, sweet taste that takes your taste buds way beyond any previous corn-related experience.

■ GRAND MESA

The nation's highest flat-topped mountain, Grand Mesa is just to the east of Grand Junction. Hunters, fishermen, campers, and nature lovers stream to the forest and its hundreds of streams and over 300 lakes via Colorado 65, plus county and four-wheel-drive roads. Colorado National Monument, which can be reached off Interstate 70 from either Fruita or Grand Junction, is a dramatic dose of desert wind carving, jolting color juxtapositions, and unanticipated arches.

A good introduction to the monument is the 23-mile Rim Rock Drive. The road's tunnels are punched through the same red sandstone the wind has carved into arches and gentle curving formations. The red of the rock is accentuated by stands of bright green juniper and piñon trees, some seeming to grow right out of the rock. Lonely sandstone spires stand sentinel atop steep canyons dropping 2,000 feet that afford a quick view of the Colorado River valley below as the road twists and turns back around and upon itself.

■ RABBIT VALLEY DINOSAUR DIGS

You don't have to take a long drive through uninhabited country to Dinosaur National Monument to satisfy your children's fascination with dinosaurs (or yours—come on, admit it). Today, right off Interstate 70 near Grand Junction where the Western Slope's northern and southern halves meet, you can avail yourself of guided tours and supervised digs just minutes from civilization.

Located 24 miles west of Grand Junction in the middle of dusty desert-like landscape, Rabbit Valley gives you a chance to take an unsupervised stroll or guided tour through actual, scientific dino digs. Also of interest to dinosaur buffs are the self-guided tours through **Riggs Hill** and **Dinosaur Hill** near the town of **Fruita**.

Across the interstate from Fruita is the **Devil's Canyon Science and Learning Center.** The 26,000 square foot building is filled with robotic dinosaurs that move (and even spit) and over 20 interactive educational activities, ranging from a dino digging pit to a simulated earthquake. *550 Crossroads Court, Fruita; (970) 858-7282.*

■ DELTA AND MONTROSE

Driving south of Grand Junction on US 50, you may get the feeling you're lost in the middle of the desert. If you dote on the desert and have some extra time, turn west on Colorado 141 at Whitewater to get a taste of the type of slickrock desert country that appeals to mountain bikers, dirt bikers, or backpackers seeking desert solitaire. The highway eventually runs into and follows the **Dolores River,** which is fed by a number of small streams pouring out of an isolated chunk of the Uncompahgre National Forest to the east. Desert, river, and forest all in one bundle, in other words.

Eventually, 141 takes you to the old uranium towns of **Nulca** and **Naturita,** where you can choose to head east to the San Juan Mountains, and if your desert thirst hasn't been quenched, continue south along the Utah border all the way to Cortez.

For those who think a desert is as exciting as a kitty box and choose to stay on US 50 out of Grand Junction, that particular stretch of desert will quickly give

URANIUM: THE UNFORGETTABLE BOOM

When the Ute Indians created war paint from a yellowish rock found throughout Colorado's Western Slope, they could not have imagined what the white men who displaced them would create from that same rock. The rocks that supplied the Utes with yellow pigment was a form of uranium ore, and the atomic bombs that destroyed Hiroshima and Nagasaki owed their existence, in part, to Colorado uranium.

Between the Utes, the atomic bomb, and the uranium boom, Colorado can claim another atomic link. In the middle of the Rockies along the banks of the Colorado River is a little town named Radium. It was here that famed French chemist Madame Marie Curie came before the turn of the century to collect uranium samples for her pioneering radiation experiments. Her work allowed physicists to create the theories upon which the atomic bomb was based.

As World War II raged and the Manhattan Project sped toward creation of atomic bombs, attention focused on Colorado's uranium country. The area's mill tailings were reworked for their uranium, and over 70 percent of the Manhattan Project's domestic uranium came from Uravan and neighboring Vancorum.

After the shooting war stopped, the Cold War really heated up the uranium business. Prospectors were everywhere and so was uranium. Over 100 uranium companies set up shop in Grand Junction, and the boom was on. By 1955, Colorado led the nation in uranium and vanadium production, with over 400 mines feeding over a dozen processing plants.

While uranium towns like Uravan prospered, workers took no special precautions against radiation exposure because little was known of its long-term effects. Mill tailings—which everyone assumed didn't contain enough uranium to be a problem—were blown about by the wind and used as fill dirt and in concrete in hundreds of Western Slope buildings.

The residents of Uravan, like thousands of other Coloradoans who had worked the uranium mines and mills, had an unwelcome surprise coming. First, the uranium and vanadium market slowly shrunk, forcing many plants and mines to close. Vanadium was still processed at several mills into the 1980s. Then, it became clear that uranium exposure could cause cancers and other deadly side effects. In addition, it turned out that even slight amounts of uranium, such as those in the tailings piles, emitted radon gas, which could cause lung cancer. By the 1990s, the federal government agreed to compensate workers whose health had been affected by job-related uranium exposure.

The cooling and then the end of the Cold War spelled the doom of the uranium industry on the Western Slope.

But the yellow ore had one last boom left to bestow. In the late 1980s, the federal government decided huge pilings of uranium mill tailings resting in the middle of towns and along riverbanks were unsightly at best, a health hazard at worst.

Bulldozers and dump trucks came rolling back to uranium country, this time to complete a $366 million effort to cover up, seal off, destroy, or hide all the leftover traces of the state's uranium industry by tearing down old processing mills and hauling off or stabilizing 25 million cubic yards of radioactive waste. This final atomic boom, which lasted about 10 years, is now over, and represents the final chapter of the Western Slope's red hot, heartbreaking love affair with uranium.

way to some of the state's most productive farmland. The key to its productivity is the **Gunnison River,** which you wouldn't know existed except for the roadside markers pointing out its beautiful canyons. Among the most magnificent are **Escalante and Dominquez canyons,** named after Franciscan priests who tromped through western Colorado in 1776 and claimed the whole place for God and Spain.

Of course, the Spaniards didn't tell the Ute Indians that their home wasn't theirs anymore. It took settlers from the east another 100 years to accomplish that task. Being forced to leave the mountains they had roamed for generations brought the Utes bitterness, anger, shame, and pain. Many of the newer settlers couldn't have cared less or were delighted to be rid of the natives.

Occasionally, time heals emotional voids and provides perspective. Today, Delta and Montrose have asked the Utes back, honored them with a museum, and preserved some of their more powerful symbols.

Delta, located at the junction of the Gunnison and Uncompagre rivers about 40 miles south of Grand Junction on US 50, is a casual farming community that also delivers a real taste of Ute tradition.

A small sign near the entrance to Delta points travelers toward the **Ute Council Tree,** a Colorado historic landmark. Because of its central location, this huge cottonwood (85 feet tall and seven feet in diameter) was a meeting place for several Ute bands whose leaders would gather to discuss common affairs. As time passed, these centered more and more on the pros and cons of staying to fight the whites, or ceding territory in return for peace and promises that some part of the Western Slope would remain theirs.

The Ute Council Tree sits in between two houses at the end of a small lane lined by homes. So much for the promises in a string of early treaties that declared the Western Slope would be Ute land "for as long as the grasses grow."

Today the once-stately tree is showing its age. Its branches are battered, some look almost dead, and the huge trunk is starting to split. But while that powerful symbol withers, cooperation between the Utes and the people of the Western Slope is growing. Under a landmark agreement, the U.S. Forest Service allows Ute elders to once again roam their former homeland to identify and preserve ancient Ute holy sites, historic trails, and burial grounds. The Utes are working to inventory the tangible remnants of their former lives in the millions of acres of national forests stretching from Durango to Meeker.

In the town of Delta, one sign points the way between a McDonald's and a Kentucky Fried Chicken to "Fort Uncompagre." The fort provides a summer setting for colorful Ute culture during summertime productions of "Thunder Mountain Lives Tonight!" Ute Indian dancers in full regalia bring back to life their tribe's ceremonial and traditional dances.

Delta also proudly proclaims itself "the city of murals." A quick trip down Main Street, with its stolid, lived-in feel, proves the point. Colorful scenes of the

Ute Indian scouts crossing the Los Piños River. (photo by H. S. Poley courtesy Denver Public Library, Western History Department)

Ute Chief Ouray stressed negotiations, not battle. Neither saved his people's independence. (Denver Public Library, Western History Department)

Henry Farney evokes the Indians' nomadic life in this 1902 oil on canvas.

region's historical roots, natural wonders, and agricultural bounty greet the eye at almost every corner.

The muralists have incorporated Indians, mountains, peaches, apples, and pears in their various works of art. You can see the inspiration for the murals everywhere you look, from the massive Grand Mesa to the east to the desert just beyond the horizon to the west. In every direction are the orchards, farms, and ranches that are the region's economic backbone and create a resilient population whose pride and ties to the land can't be broken by gyrating commodities markets or an occasional killer frost.

A comprehensive view of Ute life is available in the Colorado Historical Society's **Ute Indian Museum,** located two miles south of Montrose. The museum occupies the former farm of famous Ute Chief Ouray, and his equally famous wife Chipeta, who is buried there. Ute beadwork, ceremonial objects, and clothing are on display, as well as photos dating from the 1880s and an explanation of Ute religious and ceremonial life. *17253 Chipeta Drive, Montrose; (970) 249-3098.*

■ BLACK CANYON OF THE GUNNISON AND BLUE MESA RESERVOIR

The **Black Canyon of the Gunnison National Monument** and **Blue Mesa Reservoir** stretch almost the full length of US 50 from Montrose to Gunnison. The canyon's black, jagged, granite walls towering thousands of feet above the Gunnison

River make the Black Canyon both spectacularly beautiful and almost inaccessible from the rim, but a great place to raft or fish. Here, the river is deeper for its width than any other river in North America—almost one half mile straight down. The canyon is the also the highest vertical climbing face in Colorado. Look up and you may see climbers on it. But that wild canyon and fish-filled river are just part of the fun. Blue Mesa Reservoir, the largest puddle in Colorado, also offers great boating and fishing. *(For more information, see* "GREAT OUTDOORS," *page 203.)*

The huge reservoir ending abruptly at an awesome wild canyon captures in a nutshell the great water questions that have been debated since the attempt to dam the Green and Yampa rivers near Dinosaur: Are all rivers to be managed for irrigation, growth, and hydroelectric power? Is a wild river a wasted resource?

Agriculture has sustained the area from day one and won't go away. Logging is another mainstay, and there always seems to be another plan cropping up about increasing the "harvest" from surrounding national forests to feed sawmills and fireplaces. But recreation and tourism are also vital to the Colorado economy.

The final question still being debated is how to accommodate and generate wealth from everyone, be they farmers, lumberjacks, and miners, or hunters, fishermen, and campers?

■ HERDING SNAKES

Trying to preserve some sort of consensus abut how best to use and preserve the Western Slope's natural resources is an exercise akin to herding snakes. Everyone is heading in their own chosen direction. That means that although the so-called New West and remnants of the Old West are on different paths, they can't avoid colliding on a regular basis.

The New West ideal, in a nutshell, is a West whose economic lifeblood is in its natural beauty and its ability to combine a rural lifestyle with modern convenience. Newcomers drawn by those attractions will keep the economy moving, as will the free-spending, non-polluting tourists for whom the natural world can be presented as a huge theme park.

The computer and communications technology have allowed individuals and companies to leave the urban jungle and head for the high country. Some of these newcomers, however, view the area's forests as a natural playground and wildlife as ornaments. They rail against efforts that would sully said bucolic surroundings, but they also don't like it when nature imposes upon them. Thus, there's a cry for compensation when deer and elk invade a newcomer's 35-acre "ranchette" and treat the garden like a salad bar. Newcomers even complain about "agricultural odors." We're talking cow poop, folks, and yes, cows do poop a lot, and yes, it does smell, despite the wishes of those who prefer a sanitized version of rural life.

But there's a flip side to the New West coin. Grappling with industrial-strength tourism, the region's resorts and communities are focusing on decidedly urban issues such as public transit, traffic gridlock, growth control, and subsidized housing for the working class.

Environmentalists jump into the fray concerning what happens on public lands. All the big issues are being aired out: protecting endangered species, expanding wilderness areas, protecting wetlands, curtailing logging, and reining in grazing on public lands.

But the Old West, relying on the individual and believing that nature's bounty is worth something only when it is converted to cold cash, isn't giving up without a fight. "You can't eat scenery," is a common snarl from loggers, who see trees as stands of money ready for the harvest.

Hunters see wildlife as potential pot roasts, and towns see hunting season as a time to make a killing at the cash register. Farmers and rangers alike still want irrigation water, and if it takes a dam or two to keep this high-country desert green and growing, so be it. Grazing cows and sheep on public forests? Been doing it for generations and won't stop just because the "tree huggers" think cow pies dirty up a creek. Got it? The defiant attitude that "this is my land and I'll do what I damn well please with it" still holds sway in many a small town, where land use planning and zoning laws are seen as illegitimate infringements on individual freedom.

■ BOUND TOGETHER

On the surface, it appears the herd of snakes will never march in the same direction. But several threads bind everyone on the Western Slope together.

First is the land itself. Towering mountains, sweeping forests, fertile cropland, and wild rivers invoke respect and awe from old-timers and newcomers alike. Land is sacred and if you don't take care of it, it won't provide cash from crops or tourists.

Second, everyone is realizing that everyone is partly right about everything. Acres of tidily tended ranches and farms provide the scenic rural greenbelts that attract newcomers. Forests are living organisms that need to be literally pruned of dead wood to thrive. Too many deer and elk can overgraze the wildlands as quickly as too many cows and sheep, thus hunting is a valid "wildlife management tool."

Finally, it doesn't take long to become attached to the hearty lifestyle and people of the Western Slope. Newcomers respectfully ask for, and old-timers gladly impart, their considerable wisdom about how to treat the land and its animals. Grudging respect is afforded those who decide to sacrifice the comforts of the city to scratch out a living in a beautiful place where living the kind of life you love is more important than just making a good living.

Common ground is not in such short supply as one might suppose.

Close quarters in the early mining days called for compromise, a term still being defined on today's Western Slope. (Colorado Historical Society)

SOUTHERN COLORADO
INDIAN / SPANISH / HISPANIC

IN SOME FLASH OF UNINTENDED INTELLIGENCE OR semi-conscious consistency, the U.S. Congress made the right move when it created a single congressional district including the Western Slope and southern Colorado.

Both areas have much in common: a dependence on natural resources, stunning scenery, and isolated communities that don't take much of a hankering to outsiders telling them what to do. Once you drop south out of the San Juan Mountains or head west from Salida, a change starts to take place that sets southern Colorado apart.

Around Cortez and the Four Corners region the desert starts to take on the bone-dry, reddish, windswept look and feel found in Utah and New Mexico. Farther east are forested mesas and very few towns. If enough water is available, green hay fields thrive and feed the area's cattle and sheep. Where there's no water, the land is gritty and covered with sagebrush. The triangular San Luis Valley, of south-central Colorado, is one of the largest level basins in the state's mountainous regions. Ringed by mountains, its streams keep the area lush by Colorado standards.

In a bizarre twist of nature, at the northeast end of the valley is **Great Sand Dunes National Monument,** a veritable white ski hill made of sand and tucked between the green fields of the valley and the towering peaks the **Sangre de Cristo Mountains,** maybe even more inspiring than anything up north.

But it's more than the scenery that sets southern Colorado apart. It's also the history: ancient Anasazi cultures and cliff dwellings, the Spanish conquest, and the arrival of traders and settlers in the 1800s who came by horse and covered wagon. In today's southern Colorado there's also a unique ambience. It's a slower pace, an old-fashioned grace, and the pleasure one feels in visiting an area steeped in time, rather than racing furiously toward the future. If anything, southern Colorado tends to look south to Santa Fe for inspiration, rather than north to Denver, and since the **Ute Indian Reservations** straddle and dip into New Mexico, perhaps the whole area's in the wrong state. Certainly, the area retains and heartily embraces its Indian, Mexican, and Spanish roots.

Four Corners: a desolate dot where four state boundaries meet.

■ FOUR CORNERS, CORTEZ, AND THE ANASAZI

No one knows if it is a map-maker's joke, a fluke, or just something that happened, but barely a mile off US 160 is the only place in the nation where **the borders of four states meet.** Once only a circular bronze plaque set in concrete informed you that, if you got down on all fours, you could be in Colorado, Utah, New Mexico, and Arizona all at the same time. Today the plaque is circled by plywood booths filled with Ute, Navaho, Apache, and other Native American artwork, crafts, artifacts, and rugs. If you are traveling west into Colorado, it's worth a stop to touch all the states and to see what real Indian arts and crafts made by real Indians look like, and cost.

Looking into Colorado, past the surrounding desert, you can see the outline of the San Juan Mountains. As you continue into Colorado on 160 toward those mountains, you enter the **Ute Mountain Indian Reservation. Towaoc,** nestled

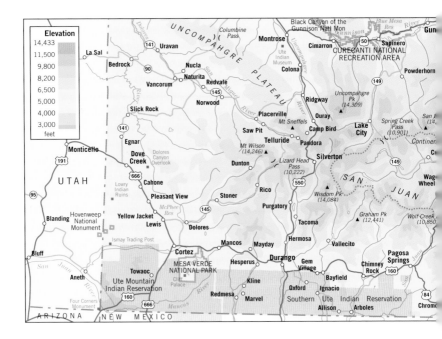

against the hills off US 160, is the only substantial town on the reservation. Towaoc's **Ute Mountain Tribal Park** features a pottery showroom, visits to ancient Anasazi dwellings, and guided hikes into the backcountry; *(970) 565-3751.*

A certain question starts to crop in your mind as you start to leave the reservation. For miles previously, the land has been barren, desert-like, with just a sprinkling of native shrubs and bushes. But as you leave the reservation, verdant hay fields, pastures, and ranch land spring to life. The reason for this has to do with the availability of water.

Cortez, the largest town in the region, is also a depository of current Southwest Indian art and culture, thanks to its many art and craft galleries featuring work from Ute, Navajo, Apache, and other Native American artisans. The town and surrounding area are excellent places to get a feel for Anasazi culture. The **Anasazi Heritage Center,** located nine miles north of Cortez in **Dolores,** houses educational and participatory exhibits on the Anasazi. It is also the storehouse for two

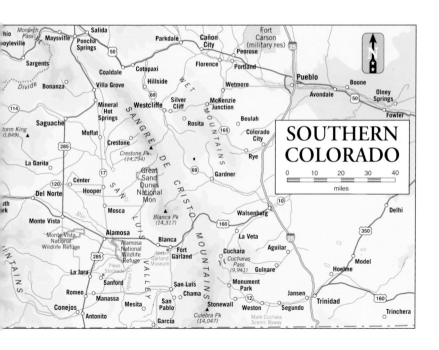

million artifacts that would have, without some arm-twisting, been drowned by the McPhee Reservoir, farther north. *27501 Highway 184, Dolores; (970) 882-4811.*

Crow Canyon Archaeological Center, four miles outside of Cortez, offers lectures and tours of current diggings. The center stresses "do-it-yourself" archaeology by showing and telling amateur diggers where and how to dig for artifacts. *For information and directions call (970) 565-8975.*

Hovenweep National Monument is located just west of Cortez, through desert country reminiscent of dozens of generic car commercials. Tall towers still guard some of the deserted ruins (Hovenweep is Ute for "Deserted Valley"). The ruins were saved from savaging thanks in part to their inaccessibility (even today, you can only drive to one set of ruins) and partly because it was designated a national monument in 1923. *From Cortez take McElmo Canyon Road; or from US 666 take County Road 9 at Pleasant View; (970) 529-4461.*

Lowry Pueblo, built around A.D. 1000 and uncovered in 1928, features the largest ceremonial room, or *kiva,* discovered to date and is more accessible, thanks to its 1965 restoration and designation as a national historic landmark in 1967. (The Visitor Center is just across the border in Utah.) *From US 666, take County Road 9 at Pleasant View; (970) 247-4082.*

A hard-core Anasazi buff would need several days to hit all these sights, and Cortez is accommodating to such folks. It hasn't been glamorized and offers a relaxing small-town atmosphere for visitors.

■ MESA VERDE

The entrance to Mesa Verde is just ten miles east of Cortez on US 160; then you've got miles of park to explore and, in the Cliff Palace, some of the most enthralling ruins of an ancient civilization to be seen anywhere in the world. The National Park Service **Far View Visitors Center** provides background information and directions, and is the only food stop on the way—so pack a lunch or pack your wallet if you want to eat. *Inside the park, about 15 miles from the entrance; (970) 529-4543.*

After the Visitor Center, it's an uninterrupted drive through piñon-covered hills and mesas where long ago (and almost unbelievably) corn, beans, and squash were once grown. No streams are now visible, nor are there any remnants of irrigation works. In the mesa area, you will see numerous half-ruined pit houses and other structures that belonged to ancestors of the later cliff-dwelling Anasazi, whose dwellings you're on your way to see.

After driving those miles, most people seem to come to the conclusion that the Anasazi chose this spot to live in for purposes of defense or because it was easy to hide in. It would have taken some serious seeking to find these folks just to make a little war and plunder their pottery.

■ ANASAZI HISTORY

A rudimentary Anasazi culture first got underway about the time the Western World went from B.C. to A.D. This first Anasazi group is now called the "Basket-makers" and for about 450 years they eked out a meager existence, foraging for desert plants, hunting with spears, and making baskets. Eventually this culture evolved into what is now called the "Modified Basketmaker Period" (450 to 750), identified by the use of the bow and arrow, pottery, beans, corn, and underground pit houses. Then came the houses and communal buildings erected from stone and adobe built from 750 to 1100.

Which is another way of saying that the people who moved into the cliffs didn't just pop from behind some sagebrush with all their spiritual and cultural refinement. Rather, they were taking advantage of centuries of history and experience. And they used every shard of it in such monuments to their culture and skill as the Cliff Palace.

■ CLIFF PALACE

When the Ute Indians first migrated into this area, they looked at the Anasazi ruins, decided they were haunted, and afterwards avoided them. Indian tribes farther south in New Mexico also had seen evidence of the vanished culture as they'd migrated through southern Colorado into New Mexico. They were the ones who first referred to these ancient people as "Anasazi," or "enemy ancestors."

No one thought much about the ruins at Mesa Verde after that for a long, long time, not until the winter of 1888 when two cowboys out looking for stray cows way the hell in the middle of nowhere suddenly stopped in their tracks in a state of shock. What Richard Wetherill and Charlie Mason had caught sight of was an intact, abandoned stone city fit for 400 people. It's not recorded if they found the

(following pages) The stunning Cliff Palace at Mesa Verde National Park remains an architectural triumph and retains an air of mystery.

cows, but the world quickly learned what they did find—the **Cliff Palace**—a complex of about 200 individual homes, 23 underground ceremonial *kivas,* and towers rising as high as four stories.

The world came to see what the cowboys found, and every clod in a pith helmet came away with something, be it a stone or pottery shard, from the surrounding area's estimated 800 cliff dwellings. Congress got off its duff in 1906 to stop the random looting and created **Mesa Verde National Park,** the first national park designed to preserve archaeological treasures.

Tucked underneath huge overhangs, built from A.D. 1100 to 1300, then abandoned almost as soon as they were completed, the cliff-dwellings still stun and mystify. Some of the stone-crafted dwellings, such as the Cliff Palace, could accommodate up to 400 people. The masonry walls were not just rocks and mortar slapped together, but were crafted with care, plastered, and in some cases decorated. The fact that many of these buildings are still standing 700 years later is testimony to the masons' skill.

The mystery of Mesa Verde seems to resolve itself into two basic questions: Why did these people come here, and why, after barely 100 years, did they start to leave the Club Med of the day? Every Southwestern archaeologist in khaki shorts tries to answer those questions, and most visitors arrive at their own conclusions after a tour.

The pros speculate the dwellers departed for one or more of these reasons: drought, over-intensive farming which ruined the land, or in order to flee from nomadic raiders.

Same goes for the move to the cliffs: fear of attack, trying to protect the water feeding the state's first irrigation systems, or just stumbling on the caves' natural protection and building from there.

■ SPANISH EXPLORERS

The Catholic kingdom of Spain entered the New World to reap both riches and souls. By 1521, with the aid of guns, horses, and armor, Mexico had become a Spanish colony, and its silver and gold mines began their prodigious production, via the natives' slave labor. But like every gold- or silver-crazed prospector, the Spaniards lusted after the big bonanza, the quick strike somewhere over the next

KIVAS, CROSS, AND CRESTONE

There's a voice in the wilderness crying,
A call from the ways untrod:
Prepare in the desert a highway,
A highway for our God!
The valleys shall be exalted,
the lofty hills brought low;
Make straight all the crooked places,
Where the Lord our God may go!
—Isaiah 40:1-11

From *kivas* to Catholicism to Crestone, southern Colorado has witnessed and been a testimony to an unrelenting faith in powers greater than what mere mortals possess.

For centuries the Pueblo peoples turned to their *kivas,* to seek in solitude the power of their gods and spirits. Starting as a rude hole in the ground, the *kiva* evolved into a standardized, circular pit that provided symbolic structure to honor

The cliff-dwellers went into underground kivas for ritual ceremonies.

nature's four elements—wind, water, fire, earth—or other supernatural elements in the ceremonial life.

The *kivas* are silent now, but a sensitive traveler can descend into one *kiva* at **Mesa Verde**, for instance, and still get just a tingle, a tremor of feeling that something special, unexplainable, but still powerful can occur when people slow their hurried pace and listen to the earth around them, the earth that still sustains them, the earth that they will eventually be buried under.

The Spanish conquerors who brought the Catholic faith and its churches to

This rare photograph captures penitentes flagellating themselves in 1896. (Museum of New Mexico).

southern Colorado also brought a unique off-shoot of Catholicism: the **Penitentes.** Begun in the 13th century to honor St. Francis of Assisi, the Penitente societies, which died out everywhere in Europe except in Spain, met in *moradas,* or lodges, and practiced self-torture as part of their devotions. From the early 1800s on, these exclusively male societies filled a void in the isolated towns of northern New Mexico and southern Colorado, many of which had no priests or others willing to undertake charitable work and maintain a sense of spiritual community.

Penitentes obeyed the tenants of the Catholic Church except during Holy Week. Then, dressed in black hoods and white breechclothes, they would publicly perform a painfully honest re-enactment of Christ's capture, trial, and crucifixion. The re-enactment included self-flagellation with whips or cactus, carrying a heavy wooden cross, and actually having one member tied to the cross until he fainted.

The societies and their grisly ceremonies were eventually banned by the Church, but that just made the Penitentes secret societies instead of open ones. Hundreds of Penitentes continued their unique devotions well into the 1900s, and some portions of the groups' ritual self-torture are still practiced today. Also, many of their *moradas* remain scattered throughout southern Colorado.

In **Crestone,** located at the top of the San Luis Valley on the edge of the San Isabel National Forest, earthly calls of another nature beckon to those of a new age and to the spirit of a new breed of believer. This little summer hide-away has become the focus of many New Age spiritualists.

The area, allegedly sacred to the Indians, is supposed to be the center of some cosmic earth wart where all manner and variety of earthly, unearthly, spiritual, and transcendental planes, energy sources, and general action converge, coagulate, reincarnate, cross-mutate, and co-mingle. Doubters dub it a reincarnation of the Age of Aquarius; skeptics wait for the new spirituality of Crestone to start enduring the test of time. Believers come to rest, refresh themselves in the natural surroundings, listen to the vibrations from earth, wind, and trees, and soak in powers unknown but felt all the same. (Some also buy real estate, but that's another story.)

No one knows why this southern Colorado has been and still is home to such a sustained sprouting of spiritual outburst. The He/She/It who provokes such shows of faith isn't saying. Maybe if you climb into a *kiva,* feel the passion of a Penitente, or commune with a Crestoner you will receive a glimmer of the grace that fuels such faithful fire.

ridge or just north of the next river where gold was resting in piles for the taking. In their case they thought that bonanza was the legendary "Seven Cities of Gold," or "Cibola." Throughout the 1600s and 1700s, expeditions—some going as far north as Colorado—set out from Spanish territory to find cities built of gold.

The most famous Spanish explorers to reach Colorado were two Franciscan priests, Silvestre Escalante and Francisco Dominquez. In 1776, when the newly formed United States of America began its battle for independence, the Franciscans set out on a trek that would make winter at Valley Forge seem like a Boy Scout weenie roast, complete with hot chocolate.

Embarking from Santa Fe, they headed northwest, hit and bounced around the San Juan Mountains until they came to the Dolores River, followed it to the Gunnison River, then onward to the White River, stopping here and there to pray a bit and officially claim all they tromped over for God and Spain. They then headed due west into Utah in an effort to find a trail to California, until heavy snows and inhospitable desert forced them back to Santa Fe.

What the desert-dwelling Native Americans thought about being "discovered" by Spanish explorers is unrecorded, but they may have thought they'd just discovered something: a new breed of pale and pretty peculiar men. What kind of fool would come to the desert wearing heavy clothing, a helmet on his head, and armor over his clothes that turned him into a miniature sweat-drenched pottery kiln?

The new breed's "big dogs" and "booming sticks," however, did get the natives' attention, and although they themselves became expert horsemen and riflemen, a combination of warfare with Europeans and exposure to their diseases would cause the ultimate destruction of their culture and genocide of their people.

By the late 1700s, southern Colorado was just a hop, stagger, and donkey ride from Santa Fe, in relative terms, and was claimed and settled quickly in the Spanish era, thanks to land grants direct from the King of Spain himself. Thus, the area retains some of Colorado's deepest Spanish/Mexican roots and an identification with New Mexico and Mexico, which in turn made it the final link in a chain that started hundreds of years earlier when the Spanish "discovered" the New World.

■ SOUTHERN UTE INDIAN RESERVATION

As you travel along US 160 you can see the mineral-laden mountains to the north that the Spaniards didn't explore thoroughly, but which white prospectors swarmed all over. Their persistence led to huge mineral discoveries around Durango, Silverton, and Lake City and also prompted the removal of Ute Indians from those mountains.

South of US 160 as it makes it way from Durango to Pagosa Springs is the **Southern Ute Indian Reservation.** The tribe is headquartered in **Ignacio,** about 20 miles southeast of Durango on Colorado 172. Amid rolling hills and ranch land is the **Piño Nuche Pu-ra-sa Tourist and Community Center,** which features a motel, restaurant, arts and crafts shop, museum, and guided trips into Ute country during the summer and hunting season.

It would seem, what with all the Ute cultural centers, the national park, and historic sites and preservation actions taking place from Cortez to Ignacio, that the federal government was right on top of things in southern Colorado.

Nice try.

Through the years it always seemed the same white men who gloried in the myth of the rugged individualist always got the government goodies first, with the leftovers blowing south to the reservations that, in the 1880s, the whites thought consisted of worthless land. After a century of reservation life, broken promises, and patience, members of the Ute Mountain and Southern Ute tribes are still fighting a two-front battle.

First is the fight for respect; second, the struggle for the right to help mold their own destiny by shaping decisions about how and when to develop the natural resources—water, coal, natural gas—modern prospectors found in abundance on the "worthless" land.

As for respect, the following story gives the general picture.

The painting was a melodramatic 1880s effort depicting a "bloodthirsty savage" scalping a hapless white man. No one knew where it came from, why it was chosen, or how long it had actually been hanging in the Bureau of Indian Affairs' "Treaty Room," in Washington D.C.; but after a "suggestion" that it be removed, by then congressman (and Native American) from Colorado Ben Nighthorse Campbell, the offensive painting was replaced with other art.

Campbell, now a U.S. senator, is proof it doesn't hurt to have a Native American from a Colorado reservation stomping around Washington in cowboy boots and bolo tie reminding his colleagues about places like Towaoc, and that when treaty-makers talk about "as long as the sun shall shine and the grasses grow," that's a very long time.

UTES: EXIT FROM THE LAND OF SHINING MOUNTAINS

The Ute Indians who roamed Colorado could always rely on one thing: safe haven in the mountains and valleys they called "the land of shining mountains." Ute bands roamed from the Great Plains into Utah and on the borders of present-day Arizona, New Mexico, and southern Colorado. Whether seeking refuge from other raiders or a quick escape after a raid of their own, the mobile Utes could lose their pursuers in the mountains they knew so well.

Before the Spanish brought horses into North America, the Utes scratched out a living much like the Paiutes, Navaho, and Apaches, with whom they shared their far-ranging domain. They relied on small-game hunting and gathering desert and mountain plants for subsistence.

Physically, the Utes were a stocky, powerfully built people with dark, bronze-colored skin. They would move their camps into the high country for summer hunting, but retreat to gentler climes to wait out winters. Their women's bead-work was, and still is, intricate, colorful, and refined into art itself.

The Utes also developed a rich ceremonial and spiritual life. They "knew" the bear and how to coax him from hibernation with the Bear Dance that signalled the beginning of spring. The Sun Dance, initiated in the middle of summer, was to ensure good hunting.

The Utes were also a playful people, and many of their dances—the Circle Dance, Coyote Dance, Tea Dance—were strictly social in nature. Social, but more serious, were the melodies from handmade flutes that a man used to attract his true love. All sorts of games occupied idle time, including stick dice, archery, ring spearing, juggling, wrestling, and foot races. Horse racing was without question the most popular sport and, unfortunately, contributed to the ultimate removal of the Utes from Colorado.

Spaniards spotted the Utes as early as the 1600s, and eventually arrived at an uneasy peace with them. The Spanish also provided the Utes with the horse, although that certainly wasn't their intention. The Utes became one of the first tribes with extensive herds, thus greatly increasing their mobility and heightening the respect given them by other tribes.

The Utes had few squabbles with the mountain men who arrived from the east in the 1830s. Many married Ute women and appreciated the Utes' knowledge of the land and how to live off it. But things changed when gold was discovered in the

1860s. The gold and silver seekers wanted control of the land, and the farmers who followed saw potentially productive land being "wasted." As Colorado became first a territory and then a state, the drive to drive the Utes off their land intensified.

That drive was accomplished with a series of treaties. The Utes ceded the San Luis Valley (in southern Colorado) in 1863, were moved west of the Continental Divide in 1868, and gave up their claim to other mineral-rich land in 1873. Thus, west-central and northwest Colorado became their home. Its advantages were plentiful game, natural mineral hot springs with their spiritual and healing powers and, for a while, lax federal supervision.

That paternalistic neglect, however, came to an end in 1878 when Nathan C. Meeker arrived to head the White River Ute Indian Agency. Meeker had worked for Horace "Go West Young Man" Greeley, before coming Colorado to lead the utopian Union Colony on the eastern plains. Unfortunately, things got a little more "western" than Meeker probably had in mind.

He quickly decided hunting, fishing, racing ponies, and generally enjoying life just wouldn't do for Utes. In modern jargon, he had no respect for the Ute's unique cultural or belief systems. Instead of free-roaming Indians, he wanted sedentary, Christian farmers. The culture clash made conflict inevitable.

When he suggested a good place to start the "civilizing" process was to forget about racing ponies and plow up the race track, the Indians refused in a manner Meeker thought a little surly. He called for some troops. To the Utes, troops equalled massacre, so they ambushed the troops, killed and mutilated Meeker and all the men at the agency, kidnapped Meeker's wife and daughters, held them for a week, and then released them unharmed.

The politicians and public were outraged; the newspapers went nuts; and soon the women's kidnapping became a lurid tail of horror at the hands of the redman.

"The Utes must go," became the cry of the day.

And go they did, under Army escort, burning forests as they went, to reservations in Utah and southern Colorado on a trek they called the "Trip of Sorrow."

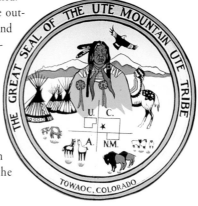

When it comes to having some say in their own destiny, the Utes are still trying to hold the government to one of its oldest promises. This promise was made in 1902 when the government decided to build the Animas–La Plata dam and diversion project to provide water for (among others) Utes. But as the new century approaches, not one shovel full of dirt for Animas–La Plata has been moved.

The Utes, who long ago lost their faith in the government experts, are now bringing their own lawyers, accountants, environmental experts, and congressman to the table and could forge a compromise allowing dirt to move on the project before the 100th birthday of the federal promise.

Flute playing was an important Ute courting ritual. (Center of Southwest Studies, Fort Lewis College, Durango, Colorado)

The Ute's accountants and lawyers are also matching wits with the terrible two-some of the federal government and the oil companies. Just because much of the Four Corners region looks barren, there's no reason to think it is underneath; in fact, it's loaded with coal (which could be developed with Animas–La Plata water) and natural gas.

■ SAN LUIS VALLEY

As you keep driving east on US 160, climb over the Continental Divide, and loop around the Rio Grande National Forest, you drop into another mysterious section of southern Colorado: the San Luis Valley. With its northern outpost of Saguache, the triangular valley stretches out 50 miles in width and runs all the way to the border of New Mexico, making it one of the world's largest valley basins. The northwest border is formed by the San Juan, La Garita, and Conjeos-Brazos mountains, from which the Rio Grande River has its humble beginnings. The water from the Rio Grande and other mountain streams, along with centuries-old Spanish land grants and immigrants, created the conditions for a farming culture that has a long and deep taproot. With sufficient water to feed the valley's hay and potato farms and generations of farming families working the land, the valley has long been a green little emerald encircled by mountains. On the southeast side, the inspiring Sangre de Cristo Mountains put an abrupt end to the flat valley floor. At sunrise or sunset, the sky turns a vibrant red against and around the range's peaks, making it easy to understand why "blood of Christ" became the obvious choice when it came time to name the range.

In the valley itself, the small, isolated towns that have been influenced by the Indian, Spaniard, and white man are not only steeped in history, but radiate a friendliness and open-mindedness unequaled anywhere else in the state. The scenery is breathtaking as well, and the forests provide many nature-oriented diversions. The **Cumbres and Toltec Scenic Railway**, running from Antonito to Chama, New Mexico, provides as authentic a narrow-gauge railroad trip as any in the state and the mountain scenery is unbeatable all along the route. Just the train ride makes it worth a trip through the area. *(See "Historic Railroads," page 304.)*

Alamosa, where US 160, US 285, and the Rio Grande meet, is the largest town in the valley, home to Adams State College, and the gateway to the **Great Sand**

Life springs eternal, even on the great dunes of the San Luis Valley.

Dunes National Monument, 30 miles to the north. This huge pile of sand sandwiched between flat farmland and mountain splendor is a geological wonder and quite a playground—you can even ski on it. *Take US 160 east from Alamosa; at Blanca turn onto Colorado 150 and go north; (719) 378-2312.*

The town of **Manassa**, off Interstate 285 on 142 south of Alamosa, might be worth a visit for boxing aficionados, as it has a small museum dedicated to the great boxer, Jack Dempsey, also known as the "Manassa Mauler." East of Manassa, on Colorado 159, lies the town of **San Luis**, which, in 1851, became Colorado's first "officially" incorporated town. It also has the second oldest "common" land— land open for use by all residents —in the United States, with Boston's puny little square being the first. Residents are now engaged in building a religious shrine for special Holy Week celebrations. (See "Religious Tradition," following.)

The San Luis Valley's abundant natural hot springs are as soothing as the famous springs in Glenwood, Ouray, or Steamboat, but they remain, for the most part, under-promoted and basically undeveloped. The surrounding mountains get hundreds of inches of pure Colorado champagne powder perfect for skiing, and do contain small ski areas, but no mega-resorts typical of the central mountains.

■ SAN LUIS HISTORY

After the Mexican War of 1846, the United States gained the territory of New Mexico, which included the San Luis Valley, its people, ranches, communities, and a culture which had been doing quite nicely all by itself for decades, thank you. But trouble with raiding Indians forced the government to pay attention, and in 1852, little Fort Massachusetts was built in the hills above the San Luis Valley. It was abandoned six years later because it was too vulnerable to Indian attack.

That logic set well with the Utes, but not with the valley's white settlers. **Fort Garland** was built in 1858, and its strategic location at the head of the San Luis Valley and accommodations for over 100 soldiers provided a bit stronger sense of security. Assigning legendary frontiersman **Kit Carson** to command the fort in 1866 helped morale a bit, too. The fort is now restored to its past glory as a living museum. *On US 160, 25 miles east of Alamosa; (719) 379-3512.*

Kit Carson

■ **RELIGIOUS TRADITION**

The San Luis Valley did not draw its strength or morale from muskets and men alone. For centuries the area's strength has also come from its common culture, a mixture of Spanish and Mexican, which took root long before the United States, New Mexico, or Colorado existed. Faith in the time-tested credos of Catholicism also became a cornerstone upon which much of south-central Colorado was built and that continues to infuse new life into the people of the area.

The Spanish explorers brought Catholic priests on their expeditions in an effort to at least lay claim to any lost souls they might encounter. For 300 years those priests found northern New Mexico and southern Colorado a fertile ground for soul searching (even if the Indians didn't think much of it). The San Luis Valley was no exception. It is home to the state's oldest Catholic church, **Our Lady of Guadalupe,** located in **Conejos,** and officially dedicated by the bishop of Santa Fe in 1863.

The church was the centerpiece of life in small, isolated towns. Priests and sisters cared for the sick, taught the children, and sheltered the poor and homeless. If priests or nuns weren't available, the Penitentes, who were more widely known for their self-flagellation ceremonies during Holy Week, would step in to fill the void.

An early Catholic church and mission. (Colorado Historical Society)

Today, the town of **San Luis** is hoping that a unique, newly created path through the Holy Week observances will not only be a spiritual experience for all Christians, but a positive economic experience for the small town.

On a nearby mesa, the town's 800 residents have carved a 1.4-mile gravel trail that twists through the trees and cuts through the rocks. The trail will be lined with 15 bronze sculptures representing the **Stations of the Cross**. The two-thirds of life-size sculptures make the whole project look more like a shrine than a piece of religious art.

The shrine/artwork will serve several purposes. It will provide the area's devoted residents a unique Holy Week celebration. The scale of the effort is also sure to bring pilgrims, the curious, and those seeking a little different Holy Week experience or spiritual renewal than can be had in an urban pew.

Those pilgrims and visitors should prove a boon for the small, isolated town and its artists and merchants. Although any such economic spin-offs will be gladly accepted, the oldest town in Colorado will endure regardless, since it seems to have learned another lesson quite well:

> *By your endurance you will gain your lives.*
> —Luke 21:19

■ TRINIDAD: WAR IN THE MINES

The beginning of the twentieth century saw unions and miners in the gold and coal mines agitating about hours, conditions, wages, scabs, use of the state militia, and union representation. Violence was common on both sides. The Western Federation of Miners (WFM) won recognition in Telluride in 1901, but that success was hard to repeat. In 1903, Cripple Creek became a battlefield and when a WFM agitator blew up a trainload of scabs, killing 13, the public turned against the union. By 1904, the strike was over, the public anti-union, and the miners still complaining statewide.

But the biggest collision between the workers and their corporate bosses, and one that retains a place in union history, took place in 1914. It pitted coal miners and the United Mine Workers (UMW) against coal mine owners and Rockefeller's CF&I. The miners wanted an eight-hour day, better wages and safety controls, and the ability to choose their own housing. The miners were urged on by a personal visit by Mary Harris, better known as the famous socialist organizer, "Mother Jones."

The strike in the Trinidad coal fields became official in September 1913. The owners tried to keep the mines open with non-union workers; the strikers tried to keep the strikebreakers out. Union men and their families set up tent cities near the mines and lived off union strike funds. Tension heightened through the winter. The mine operators called for the state militia, which was promptly dispatched.

A scuffle between the militia and miners on April 20, 1914, was the spark that touched off the explosion at Ludlow Station, 18 miles south of Trinidad. The militia tried to move the 900 miners and their families from their tent city, killing five miners and one militiaman. Afterward the bodies of two women and 11 children were found in the burned remains of the tent city, thus the action became known as the "**Ludlow Massacre**" (which is marked with a monument about 15 miles north of Trinidad off US 25).

Ten days of outright war erupted and was only quelled when President Woodrow

WILLA CATHER'S COLORADO

*I*n Mexican Town lived all the humbler citizens, the people who voted but did not run for office. The houses were little story-and-a-half cottages, with none of the fussy architectural efforts that marked those on Sylvester Street. They nestled modestly behind their cottonwoods and Virginia creeper; their occupants had no social pretensions to keep up. There were no half-glass front doors with doorbells, or formidable parlors behind closed shutters. Here the old women washed in the back yard, and the men sat in the front doorway and smoked their pipes. The people on Sylvester Street scarcely knew that this part of the town existed. Thea liked to explore these quiet, shady streets, where the people never tried to have lawns or to grow elms and pine trees, but let the native timber have its way and spread in luxuriance. She had many friends there, old women who gave her yellow rose or a spray of trumpet vine.

Dr. Archie took up a black leather case, put on his hat, and they went down to the dark stairs into the street. The summer moon hung full in the sky. For the time being, it was the great fact in the world. Beyond the edge of the town the plain was

Wilson dispatched the U.S. Army to the area. That settled the violence, and negotiations ended the strike in December 1914. It was only a partial victory for the union, since the UMW wasn't recognized as the miners' future representative. Instead, a "company union" was created that was supposed to represent the working man. That plan was applauded at the time as a great compromise, but such "company unions" are one reason that even today in Colorado coal country you're likely to see a baseball cap that states, "Guns, God, and Guts Made the UMW."

Visitors to Trinidad today will find a quiet town, with many well-kept 19th-century buildings and lovely parks. In the center of town is **Kit Carson Park** where a larger than life bronze statue of Kit and his horse ride forever toward the Mountain Branch of the Santa Fe Trail. The Colorado Historical Society operates the **Trinidad History Museum** downtown, which includes the 1870, two-story **Baca House**, the 1882 brick **Bloom House**, and the fascinating **Santa Fe Trail Museum**; *300 East Main Street; (719) 846-7217.*

so white that every clump of sage stood out distinct from the sand, and the dunes looked like a shining lake. The doctor took off his straw hat and carried it in his hand as they walked toward Mexican Town across the sand.

North of Pueblo, Mexican settlements were rare in Colorado then. This one had come about accidentally. Spanish Johnny was the first Mexican who came to Moonstone. He was a painter and decorator, and had been working in Trinidad, when Ray Kennedy told him there was a "boom" on in Moonstone, and a good many new buildings were going up. A year after Johnny settled in Moonstone, his cousin, Famos Serreños, came to work in the brickyard; then Serreños' cousins came to help him. During the strike, the master mechanic put a gang of Mexicans to work in the roundhouse. The Mexicans had arrived so quietly, with their blankets and musical instruments, that before Moonstone was awake to the fact, there was a Mexican quarter; a dozen families or more.

As Thea and the doctor approached the 'dobe houses, they heard a guitar, and a rich barytone voice—that of Famos Serreños—singing "La Golandrina." All the Mexican houses had neat little yards, with tamarisk hedges and flowers, and walks bordered with shells or whitewashed stones. Johnny's house was dark. His wife, Mrs. Tellamantez, was sitting on the doorstep, combing her long, blue-black hair.

continues

(Mexican women are like the Spartans; when they are in trouble, in love, under stress of any kind, they comb and comb their hair.) She rose without embarrassment or apology, comb in hand, and greeted the doctor.

"Good-evening; will you go in?" she asked in a low, musical voice. "He is in the back room. I will make a light." She followed them indoors, lit a candle and handed it to the doctor, pointing toward the bedroom. Then she went back and sat down on her doorstep.

Dr. Archie and Thea went into the bedroom, which was dark and quiet. There was a bed in the corner, and a man was lying on the clean sheets. On the table beside him was a glass pitcher, half-full of water. Spanish Johnny looked younger than his wife, and when he was in health he was very handsome: slender, gold-colored, with wavy black hair, a round, smooth throat, white teeth, and burning black eyes. His profile was strong and severe, like an Indian's. What was termed his "wildness" showed itself only in his feverish eyes and in the color that burned on his tawny cheeks. That night he was a coppery green, and his eyes were like black holes. He opened them when the doctor held the candle before his face.

"*Mi testa!*" he muttered, "*mi testa,* doctor. *La fiebre!*" Seeing the doctor's companion

at the foot of the bed, he attempted a smile. *"Muchacha!"* he exclaimed deprecatingly.

Dr. Archie stuck a thermometer into his mouth. "Now, Thea, you can run outside and wait for me."

Thea slipped noiselessly through the dark house and joined Mrs. Tellamantez. The somber Mexican woman did not seem inclined to talk, but her nod was friendly. Thea sat down on the warm sand, her back to the moon, facing Mrs. Tellamantez on her doorstep, and began to count the moonflowers on the vine that ran over the house. Mrs. Tellamantez was always considered a very homely woman. Her face was of a strongly marked type not sympathetic to Americans. Such long, oval faces, with a full chin, a large, mobile mouth, a high nose, are not uncommon in Spain. Mrs. Tellamantez could not write her name, and could read but little. Her strong nature lived upon itself. She was chiefly known in Moonstone for her forbearance with her incorrigible husband.

Nobody knew exactly what was the matter with Johnny, and everybody liked him. His popularity would have been unusual for a white man, for a Mexican it was unprecedented. His talents were his undoing. He had a high, uncertain tenor voice, and he played the mandolin with exceptional skill. Periodically he went crazy. There was no other way to explain his behavior. He was a clever workman, and, when he worked, as regular and faithful as a burro. Then some night he would fall in with a crowd at the saloon and begin to sing. He would go on until he had no voice left, until he wheezed and rasped. Then he would play his mandolin furiously, and drink until his eyes sank back into his head. At last, when he was put out of the saloon at closing time, and could get nobody to listen to him, he would run away—along the railroad track, straight across the desert. He always managed to get aboard a freight somewhere. Once beyond Denver, he played his way southward from saloon to saloon until he got across the border. He never wrote to his wife; but she would soon begin to get newspapers from La Junta, Albuquerque, Chihuahua, with marked paragraphs announcing that Juan Tellamantez and his wonderful mandolin could be heard at the Jack Rabbit Grill, or the Pearl of Cadiz Saloon. Mrs. Tellamantez waited and wept and combed her hair. When he was completely wrung out and burned up,—all but destroyed,—her Juan always came back to her to be taken care of,—once with an ugly knife wound in the neck, once with a finger missing from his right hand,—but he played just as well with three fingers as he had with four.

—Willa Cather
The Song of the Lark, 1915

(opposite) From stirrups to sombreros, Spanish and Mexican influences came north from Santa Fe into southern Colorado (Colorado Historical Society)

■ HIGHWAY OF LEGENDS

If you've come into the San Luis Valley from the south, arriving at Trinidad on Interstate 25, take the Highway of Legends (Colorado 12) on a drive through desert, mountain, and plain. Beginning at Trinidad, it loops around to the west through the towns of Segundo, and Monument Park, over Cucharas Pass to Cuchara in the San Isabel National Forest, then on to La Veta before arriving at Walsenburg farther north on Interstate 25. (Needless to say, the drive is equally delightful if you're driving from Walsenburg south to Trinidad.)

GREAT OUTDOORS

COLORADO'S EXPANSIVE WILDLANDS, FROM DESERT TO MOUNTAIN TO PLAIN, offer almost too much to do, to see, to hear:

- The splash of color as a pheasant bursts from a row of yellow-dead corn and shoots into the sky like a miniature helicopter.

- The solitude of an untouched mountain valley in full summer bloom where the only sounds are the faint rattle of aspen leaves, feet crunching on the narrow path, and barely audible mumbles about finally finding God's country left the way He designed it.

- The crackling and small pops of a campfire and its glowing coals which send a small circle of light just a little way into the surrounding wall of pine trees, beyond which is nothing but quiet darkness.

- The grunts and gulps of thin air needed to make a conquering yelp at the top of a 14,000-foot peak.

- The slight swish of fishing line as it slices the air and lands with a gentle plop in the middle of a rippling mountain trout stream as the wind whisks through the neighboring willows.

- The sensation of softly treading through fall foliage in search of elusive deer and elk.

- The quiet lapping of a seemingly gentle river against raft and paddles that suddenly have to battle a torrent of tossing turns and shouted instructions as the water turns as white as the knuckles on the paddles.

- The sweet sweat from mountain bikers or cross-country skiers as they muscle their way over trails through forest and desert.

Flaming Gorge
Reservoir

WYOMING

MEDICINE BOW RANGE

Browns Park
Nat'l Wildlife Refuge

VERMILLION BLUFFS

ELKHEAD MTS

Mt Zirkel
12,180

Mt Ethel
11,924

Rocky Mountain
National Park

Dinosaur
Nat'l Monument

DANFORTH HILLS

Pagoda Peak
11,120

Longs

Lake Granby

Arapaho
Nat'l Rec Area

BOOK PLATEAU

THE FLAT TOPS

Eagle Creek

ROAN CLIFFS

70

UTAH

Green

Colorado

River

Grand
Junction

Aspen

Divide

Mt
1

GRAND MESA

Snowmass Mt
14,092

Maroon Peak
14,156

SAWATCH RANGE

Mt Elbert
(14,433 higest
point in Colorado)

Colorado
Nat'l Monument

Gunnison

UNCOMPAHGRE PLATEAU

BLACK MESA

BLACK CANYON OF THE GUNNISON

Mt Harvard
14,414

Mt Yale
14,194

Mt Princeton
14,197

San Miguel

Black Canyon of
the Gunnison
Nat'l Monument

Curecanti
Nat'l Rec Area

River

Mt Qura
13,971

Sheep Mt
13,168

San Luis Peak
14,014

LA GARITA MTS

Flagstaff
12,072

Uncompahgre
Peak
14,309

Continental

SAN JUAN MOUNTAINS

Dolores

SAN MIGUEL MTS

Mt Wilson
14,246

Sunlight Peak
14,059

River

LA PLATA MTS

Sleeping Ute Mt
9,977

Hesperus Mt
13,232

Durango

Montezuma Peak
13,150

Rio Gran

Mesa Verde
Nat'l Park

San Juan

River

ARIZONA

NEW MEXICO

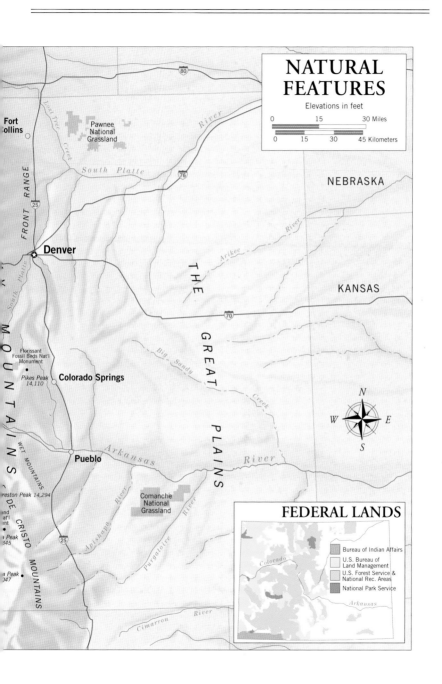

NATURAL FEATURES

Elevations in feet

0	15	30 Miles
0	15	30	45 Kilometers

Fort
Collins

Pawnee
National
Grassland

Lost Tree Creek

River

South Platte

80

76

NEBRASKA

FRONT RANGE

25

Denver

River

Arikee

THE

South Platte

KANSAS

70

MOUNTAINS

Florissant
Fossil Beds Nat'l
Monument

Big Sandy

GREAT

Pikes Peak
14,110

Colorado Springs

Creek

N

W   E

S

WET MOUNTAINS

PLAINS

Arkansas

Pueblo

River

reston Peak 14,294

and
at'l
ent

DE

Apishapa River

Comanche
National
Grassland

Purgatoire River

a Peak
345

25

CRISTO

a Peak
047

MOUNTAINS

Cimarron

River

FEDERAL LANDS

Colorado

Arkansas

	Bureau of Indian Affairs
	U.S. Bureau of Land Management
	U.S. Forest Service & National Rec. Areas
	National Park Service

■ RESERVOIR FISHING AND BOATING

Every sizeable Colorado stream or lake with ready access is ready for fishing. The Division of Wildlife (DOW) maintains a string of fish hatcheries which allows it to keep fresh loads of fish frolicking in wild waters. A slight dose of whirling disease (which comes from a bacterial parasite that deforms and kills small, fingerling trout) has complicated the fish stocking job and, in some cases, cut down the number of fish stocked in various areas. Although the DOW is still supplanting existing stocks of fish with "stockers," it is also altering its regulations, sometimes on a stream-by-stream or lake-by-lake basis, concerning bag limits or catch-and-release rules. That means you just have to check with the DOW for the latest regulations before heading out. Luckily, plenty of fish of every variety still lurk in the state's lakes and streams, so you don't have to worry much about whether you'll fish on your trip, you just have to decide what kind of fish you want to catch and how you want to catch it.

Lake fishing has its followers, and it's easy to see why. Just bring your gear, a camp chair, and a cooler of beer, then cast your line, settle down, reel 'em in, go back to camp, and start lying.

All of the lakes listed below can accommodate some sort of floating craft from which to ply rod and reel, but there are two monster reservoirs that give you a chance to run your motor out of gas: Blue Mesa and Dillon Reservoirs. Check them out of driving's your thing.

Blue Mesa Reservoir. East of Gunnison, Blue Mesa is the biggest body of water in the state and, come winter time, it also becomes the biggest ice cube in the state. As with the other lakes mentioned, those with the proper gear (some say lack of intelligence being the most important) can brave the below-zero temperatures, dig holes in the ice, set up a camp chair or ice fishing shack, unscrew the thermos of hot chocolate or other anti-freeze, and begin.

Dillon Reservoir. Saddled between Dillon and Frisco on Interstate 70, Dillon Reservoir offers all manner of motor- and sail-propelled boating.

Grand Mesa. There are hundreds of lakes on the Grand Mesa just west of Grand Junction.

Horsetooth Reservoir. Just west of Fort Collins is Horsetooth Reservoir, with miles of shoreline and mountain views that might make you want to leave your camp chair and cooler. Well . . . on second thought.

John Martin Reservoir. On the plains bordering US 50 outside Las Animas, John Martin Reservoir has a long shoreline.

Pueblo. Pueblo Reservoir is almost within the city limits.

Spinney Mountain Reservoir. A couple hours of beautiful mountain driving time to Hartsel from either Cañon City or Col-

orado Springs will deliver you to the middle of Middle Park and Spinney Mountain Reservoir, which yields some of the biggest fish in the state with appalling consistency.

Steamboat Lake. Nestled up north right under Hahns Peak, and Lake Granby, at the edge of Rocky Mountain National Park.

Vallecito Reservoir. A good-sized pond surrounded by pines and San Juan scenery west of Durango.

Colorado fly fishing.

■ STREAM FISHING

This brings out anglers of a different cast, so to speak. These folks actually prowl up and down a riverbank, fighting through cottonwood stands, willows, and oak brush to find the right ripple, the gentle swell, the slow rolling flat spot that could harbor the rainbow or brown trout they seek.

Gold-medal trout streams, on the other hand, were set aside for those who eschew such feeding frenzies and prefer the craft involved in tempting trout with merely a fly or lure, and the respect for your prey integral to the catch-and-release concept, which places the fish fight above the fish fry. The catch-and-release policies in place on these gold medal waters have had the added benefit of sparing them any trauma associated with whirling disease, which only strikes baby fish. Since the streams are home to populations of full grown trout, they continue to offer outstanding fishing featuring stout trout which have matured over the years into hefty, "better take a picture of this one or no one will believe how big it is" behemoths.

Having said that, what all these rivers have in common—and most other gold medal waters do, too—is that less restrictive fishing is nearby, meaning you can drop the fly-fishing fans off, go a couple of miles, break out the marshmallows and camp chairs, and partake of regular river regulations. Thus, all types of fishing fans can hook up and figure out a way to wade into the type of water that suits them without having to break up families, end long-standing friendships, and otherwise turn the bait bunch against the fly and lure lovers.

Portions of ten rivers in the state have received the gold medal designation, and they're scattered all over the place; this is a regional sampling of gold medalists.

Colorado River. Before it becomes a wide slug of water, the Colorado River starts out as a pretty innocuous creek in Grand County, and about nine miles of that Colorado River is golden between Kremmling and Hot Sulphur Springs along US 40.

Frying Pan River. You can hook two gold medal streams in one day by visiting the Frying Pan River, golden from Ruedi Reservoir downstream through a narrow, red-rock canyon until it hits **Basalt** and the **Roaring Fork River,** which gets gold as it comes out of Aspen along Colorado 82 and continues onward to Glenwood Springs.

Gunnison River. Tumbling out of Black Canyon and shifting gears into a gold medal fishing playground, the Gunnison rolls and twists its way down to the North Fork.

North Platte River. Just west of Walden and accessible by Colorado 14 from east or west, the North Platte runs golden all the way to Wyoming.

South Platte. Down south a bit, a number of stretches of the South Platte are gold medal material as the river makes its way from reservoir to reservoir. A favorite with Front Range urbanites: within an hour or so you can go from being in a traffic jam to being knee-deep in great fishing.

Rio Grande. In the San Luis Valley, the Rio Grande is designated gold medal from where the South Fork hits to a couple of miles beyond.

For general information about Colorado fishing, call (303) 297-1192.

■ WHITEWATER RAFTING

Any river that runs high enough to float a good-sized log will probably also be hosting some sort of raft, kayak, or canoe. All the rivers mentioned under "Fishing and Boating" are regularly rafted and generally floated (and fished while floating, too) by individuals or by rafting companies that provide the raft, guide (complete with bad jokes), paddles, or any combination thereof. The following rivers go beyond just a quiet little float. They offer either wet and wild whitewater rapids or serene scenery—or both—which makes a memorable trip.

Green River. In the northeast corner of the state, the Green River offers a great view of Dinosaur National Monument from the bottom up. It's hard to believe there is a runnable river anywhere near this high desert country. Once you get onto the river and peer up the surrounding sheer dusty canyon walls, you forget the mesas and sink deep into the feeling of being surrounded by an amazing act of nature. You will have to go through federal floating permit hassles, but the trip is worth it.

Colorado River. For most of its run through Colorado, the Colorado River is pretty docile, if not downright mellow. There is one section, though, that gives you a good splash and stuns with startling scenery: where the Colorado follows Interstate 70 and cuts through Glenwood Canyon, a granite-lined, tree-sparkled slash in the earth that reaches about 2,000 feet above the river, with a surprise—possibly a Rocky Mountain bighorn sheep or startling peak view—around every twisting bend.

Gunnison River. You need to trust your guide or be a serious river rat to run the Gunnison River through the Black Canyon National Monument. Yes, the towering canyon walls are black granite, and yes, you can lose yourself, your boat, and your booties as the river crashes down one of the steeper drops in the state. This is not a rookie's river. You can only get down to it or up out of it at a few points. Again, federal regulations rule, but getting the right to float is the easy part, getting it floated is the challenge.

The Crystal River. Between Marble and Carbondale, the Crystal River rolls along as a docile little creek alongside Highway 133 for ten months of the year. When spring runoff hits, however, the Crystal becomes one of the state's most exhilarating and challenging kayaking trips. It's fast, narrow,

and full of whitewater that is more than enough of a skills test for the best boaters.

South Platte River. The small town of Fairplay, located just over an hour away from Denver on State Highway 285, turns into rafting central every summer, thanks to the South Platte River. The South Platte winds its way in a grand loop, heading south, then east, then north, and offers miles of rafting and scenery. Other put-ins along the South Platte include Hartsel, Lake George, and Deckers, all strung out along the river on Highways 24 and 67.

Rafting many of Colorado's rivers can be thrilling enough, and kayaking can be downright exciting.

The Arkansas River. Just over the Continental Divide from the South Platte, the Arkansas also offers great whitewater and mountain scenery. Trips can start from Buena Vista, on Highway 24, to Salida. From Salida, the river follows US Highway 50 through stunning canyon country all the way to the Royal Gorge, just outside of Cañon City.

■ WHEELS IN THE HILLS

There are all kinds of ways to get into the backcountry. Some are as easy as driving to work, some require a little more effort than shoveling snow off the sidewalk, and some are downright difficult. Let's start with the easy stuff.

Thanks to ranching, logging, and mining, four-wheel-drive and off-road vehicle roads lace, traverse, and loop through almost every national forest in Colorado. Here comes the broken record again. Since it's not like these roads get regular

Most of Colorado's towns are mountain-bike friendly.

road-grader service, go to the local Forest Service or BLM office, get a map, find out which are still passable, and get going. During the winter, these same thoroughfares become great **snowmobile** or **cross-country skiing routes** as well.

The best time of year for vehicle sightseeing has to be fall, when the aspen turn golden, the oak brush become copper, and the cottonwoods convert into canopies of color, all set off by the dark green of the interspersed stands of evergreens or red rock mountainsides.

Another tip about off-road access concerns the state's 21 designated wilderness areas. You can't drive a motorized vehicle or mountain bike into a wilderness area, but in many cases you can cruise right up to the edge of the wilds and at least look in from the comfort of your rig, or maybe even open the door and take a few steps in.

National parks and monuments also offer some easy driving/hiking duty. Most have trails that allow you to get out of the car for a couple of hours and tramp around. You can either just get a glimpse of the scenery (**Dinosaur**) or take a stroll with an educational bent (**Mesa Verde, Rocky Mountain**).

■ MOUNTAIN BIKES

Mountain bike riders also enjoy the state's trails: if you can drive it, horse it, or hike it, you can probably bike it. Anticipating the mountain bike boom, Colorado pedaled into the craze ahead of the crowd. Volunteers and donations helped create two unique mountain bike trail systems.

Kokopelli's Trail starts out with a taste of the best sandy desert biking experience and, for dessert, lands you in the alpine high country. The original trail was a 128-mile trek from Loma, near Grand Junction on the Western Slope, to Moab, Utah. Success spawned offshoots, more volunteers, and opportunities to tie into half a dozen other existing trails. Western Colorado and eastern Utah now offer over 1,000 miles of trails ready for knobby tires and tireless pedalers.

The Colorado Trail, on the other hand, will take you through the middle of the Rocky Mountains from Durango to Denver. You'll have to skirt some wilderness areas, and some sections are definitely not for amateurs, but with a map you can figure out how to take advantage of the trail for a quick ride or an all-out enduro.

A mountain bike trek doesn't have to be an expedition, or even a dirt track experience in the high county, for that matter. If you and your bike find yourselves taking a break along the Front Range there are plenty of urban bike trails that allow you to unlimber the bike and limber up the legs before you hit the high country.

Denver, Boulder, and Pueblo all have extensive trail systems in their city limits that take bikers along riverbanks and through parks.

The state's mountain towns and resorts are also "bicycle friendly." In most resorts, mountain bikes are the preferred method of travel for getting around town. Trail systems run along major roads and highways so you can get from here to there on your bike.

If you like long road rides, check out the trails along I-70 through the mountains. The trip up and down Vail Pass is exhilarating and pedaling through Glenwood Canyon is breathtaking.

Oh, and remember those big hills that you ski down in the winter? Next time ask about the portions of the ski hill that are open to mountain bikes in the summer. In many cases, you can experience the thrill of coursing down a ski run atop two wheels instead of carving down the mountain strapped into a board and boot combination.

For those who insist mountain bikes should be ridden on trails in the mountains, here are a few suggested trails.

Animas Mountain Trail. Starts at the intersection of Second and Fourth avenues in Durango, and takes a moderately difficult route up the mountainside to a scenic viewpoint overlooking the Animas River Valley.

Bear Creek to Methodist Mountain. A tough, 20-mile loop from Salida and back. Take County Road 108 out of town and peak out at around 9,000 feet above sea level before returning to Salida along the banks of Bear Creek and US 50.

Bear Creek Road. A marked county road takes you on a gradual climb out of the middle of Telluride for two miles, with a lovely waterfall for your reward. Want steeper? Try the 2.5-mile loop **Judd Wibe Trail**, which meanders around Cornet Creek and delivers beautiful views—and sore legs.

Boy Scout Trail. This trail in Glenwood Springs is aptly named: if you go, be prepared. The trail starts at the top of Eighth

Street, just up the hill from downtown, and is a technically difficult jaunt to the top of Lookout Mountain.

Hunter Creek Trail. This trail, just outside of Aspen, is a local favorite. You can start up Smuggler Road and cut over into the Hunter Creek Valley, a sprawling expanse of national forest land that makes you forget the high-dollar glitter of Aspen.

Lenhardy Cutoff. This route sends you on a smooth ride into the Buena Vista back country on County Road 371, which takes off from town. Not tough enough? Try the advanced Buena Vista to Mt. Princeton loop. Take County Road 306 out of town to County Road 345, find the trail markers for the Colorado Trail, and get ready to climb over 2,000 vertical feet before going back to town on County Road 321.

Peaks Trail. Linking Frisco to Breckenridge, this moderate climb though the hills starts at the intersection of Main Street and I-70 in Frisco and delivers you to the base of the Breckenridge Ski Area.

Tabeguache Trail. This one gives you a taste of high desert biking. The trail starts a couple of miles up the road to

the Colorado National Monument then, after some difficult pedaling, leads you all the way to Montrose through the desert scrub country.

So, what are you waiting for? Grab your helmet and water bottle and hit the road.

Washout Road This more relaxed trip starts north of Poncha Springs at the intersection of Colorado 285 and County Road 140, thens turn up County Road 250 until you hit Forest Service Road 5630, which is Washout Road, and which leads you back to 285.

Off the road and down a creek.

■ FOOT, HORSEBACK, OR SKIS

Wilderness areas are the domain of the backpacker, horse camper, angler, and cross-country skier. You don't have to undertake a five-day outdoor expedition to enjoy a little wilderness wonderment, either. You can travel for an hour or so and watch all traces of civilization vanish with each step in some of the state's lesser-known and less-traveled wildernesses. Or you can partake of the pedestrian-mall wilderness experience, for instance, in the Maroon Bells/Snowmass Wilderness Area outside Aspen. Generally, the closer the wilderness to resorts or towns, the heavier the traffic, so if it's solitude you seek, head for a wilderness area you've never heard of or hasn't been recommended by dozens of guidebooks and outdoor magazines. The unheralded places—**Mt. Bierstadt** (14,060 feet) is a good example. Go to **Georgetown** on Interstate 70, drive past town to **Guanella Pass**, park the car, hop on the trail, and after two hours, three miles, and a 2,500-foot-altitude gain, you are atop a 14'er. "In-shape" and "experienced" are the key words here when tackling such summits, so don't go wandering up any mountain with just a peanut butter and jelly sandwich in your pocket. Get a map, bring food and water, don't go alone, and dress appropriately.

You shouldn't get the impression that finding a good hike is rougher than the hike itself. Winter or summer, we're talking easy duty when it comes to finding a trail. The national forests are laced with hiking trails. Almost without exception, every resort town has created or is creating some sort of hiking/pedestrian "experience" within a stone's throw or quick drive from your motel room.

Cross-country ski trails are the logical result when snow covers all the state's hiking trails and forest roads and trails. Most of the state's ski areas also offer cross-country trails to break the monotony of lift lines and to stretch downhill muscles *(see "SKIING")*.

Any mention of cross-country duty has to include the **Tenth Mountain Hut and Trail System**. Developed by members of the famed Tenth Mountain Division (of World War II), the trail and huts (actually comfy cabins) stretch from Aspen, through the Leadville area—the division's old stomping grounds—onto Vail, offering a number of multi-day treks through some of the most scenic mountains in the state. If you use the huts, you can ski for a day, then relax with a gourmet meal eaten next to a warm wood stove, sleep in a real bed, and get up raring to go again the next day.

■ HIKES WITH KIDS

Colorado's mountains can look imposing a just a bit scary when you have kids in tow. But there are many short, educational, and fun hikes where kids and parents can experience the outdoors together. These are just a sample.

Great Sand Dunes National Monument. *(See page 193 for location.)* You can turn a mountain hike into a day at the beach frolicking in the 55 square miles of wind-swept sand dunes in the monument. Drive a little over a mile past the monument entrance and turn left into a parking lot right next to the sand. Then just let the kids romp. Remember to take plenty of water and sunscreen during the summer.

Hanging Lake Trail. *(Interstate 70 between Glenwood Springs and Vail.)* This is a short, steep trail, just over a mile long. Take your time, because it's more than worth it when you reach the top. Hanging Lake is just what the name implies: a turquoise body of water clinging to the mountainside. The lake is fed by a wonderful waterfall and just behind that is Spouting Rock, where water shoots out of a, what else, rock.

Molas Trail. *(In San Juan Mountains.)* In the heart of the San Juans, drive out of Silverton on Highway 550 to the turn for Molas Lake and Trail, and park in the parking lot. The trail meanders through high mountain meadows and offers amazing views of such high points as the Needle Mountains.

Petroglyph Point Trail. *(In Mesa Verde National Park; fee required.)* This loop trail, almost three miles long, starts about 20 miles inside the park at the museum parking area at Chapin Mesa. The trail circles a canyon and mesa that hold various ruins from the Anasazi Period, including a four-room cliff dwelling and the park's largest collection of petroglyphs (images carved into rock).

Ute Trail Tundra Walk, *(In Rocky Mountain National Park; fee required.)* This trail starts at the top of Trail Ridge Road at the Alpine Visitors Center *(see page 127)* and travels up to four miles. This is high alpine tundra country, and it's as delicate as it is beautiful. The trail exposes hikers to the varieties of grasses, flowers, and trees growing "at the top of world," or at least at almost 11,000 feet above sea level.

■ BIGHORN SHEEP

It's the quintessential Colorado wildlife scene, and one not soon forgotten by those fortunate enough to see it: hundreds of feet above a canyon floor a group of Rocky Mountain bighorn sheep in single-file delicately pick their way up the barren canyon wall. As the rams, ewes, and lambs scale a nearly vertical granite face, they alternate between gentle, precisely placed steps and adventurous, high-energy bounds, which send loose rocks clattering into the canyon below. The bighorns' climb looks impossible because the human eye cannot detect the tiny toe-holds and miniscule ledges which form their uphill trail. When the group tops out, a mature ram happens to stand still for a moment, his sturdy figure and curled horns appearing in silhouette against the skyline.

Such a scene delights every variety of wildlife enthusiast, from hunters to photographers, but few would have the opportunity to see it today if not for man's "meddling" with nature.

Originally plentiful, bighorns, like deer and elk, were decimated by the 1880s, thanks to the influx of hungry miners in every nook and mountainous cranny. By the turn of the century there were no sport-game hunting seasons in the state, and only one surviving bighorn herd, located near Tarryall west of Colorado Springs.

The effort to re-establish bighorns throughout Colorado, begun in 1945, has involved trapping and moving about 1,800 of the Tarryall bighorns to new areas in the state. By 1953, thanks to transplants from the Tarryall herd, the state's bighorn population had risen to about 3,000 animals scattered in enough regions to allow for the first bighorn hunting season since 1887. Today, more than 100 years later, transplants, disease control, and other management techniques have enabled the bighorn population to top the 6,000 mark, and counting.

There are currently nearly 80 different bighorn herds scattered throughout Colorado's high country. These herds range in size from the 20-head group in Waterton Canyon outside Denver to the 300 bighorns roaming the Collegiate Range. Bighorns have also been reintroduced to Rocky Mountain National Park, Dinosaur National Park, Mesa Verde, and the Colorado National Monument.

As the number of bighorns has grown, so has the sale of bighorn hunting licenses, and fees go to support the transplant program.

As with most big-game animals, habitat loss and increasing development pressure are serious threats to Colorado's bighorns. Since the animals usually roam above timberline in generally inaccessible terrain during the summer, man's activities haven't had a significant impact on their summer range. Winter range in the lower elevations, however, is a different story. For example, there once was a herd of bighorns that wintered on the cliffs and amongst the apple orchards of the Vail Valley. As can be expected, as soon as ski runs and condos started going up, most of the bighorns left.

The bighorns' tight-knit social structure also makes them susceptible to devastating outbreaks of disease, such as lungworm and other bacterial infections. One such outbreak decimated the Tarryall herd, which fell from 3,000 animals to 150. Despite the various threats to Colorado's bighorn sheep, a combination of the transplant program, limited hunting, and consistent disease control should allow the state's bighorns to flourish.

These domestic sheep, being herded in the San Juan Mountains, are distant cousins of Colorado's famous bighorns.

TEDDY TO FIGHT BEARS WITH KNIFE

GLENWOOD SPRINGS—President Roosevelt is planning to eclipse his previous reputation for daring and will try to kill every bear he gets in Colorado on his coming trip with a hunting knife, instead of a rifle.

While the story has not been generally credited . . .

Front Page, Denver Post, April 2, 1905

As it turned out, President Theodore Roosevelt did kill some black bears during his 1905 Colorado trip, but not with a hunting knife. His love of big-game hunting was not the only reason for his visit. The forests through which Roosevelt trekked were at that time part of the White River National Land Reserve, created by President Benjamin Harrison in 1891, and Roosevelt wanted to include it in the system of national forests, which remain one of the most appreciated legacies of his presidency.

As the President readied for the hunt, his staff saw to the installation of phone and telegraph lines, turning Glenwood's elegant Hotel Colorado into the "Little White House of the United States."

The President, meanwhile, picked out a nondescript Cayuse pony named Possum, climbed on a well-worn saddle, and said "well, okay" to letting a scruffy hunting terrier named Skip follow along side. Before long he was headed toward a tent camp pitched at 9,000 feet in the forest south of Silt.

One member of Roosevelt's staff was then assigned the task of climbing on a horse every day at the Hotel Colorado, tracking down the President, and keeping him up-to-date on national and international affairs. On May 5, Roosevelt came out of the backcountry for a brief stay in the Hotel Colorado that, thanks to a ragtag cloth bear, became almost as important as his hunting trip.

There are a couple of versions of the teddy bear myth. One has it that Teddy's daughter Alice was admiring the bears brought back by the hunters and decided to name one Teddy. A second version claims that the maids at the Hotel Colorado stitched together a crude little stuffed bear named Teddy and presented it to the president. Anyhow, a little marketing and hype later, the teddy bear was enthroned as an indispensable children's toy, a position it still holds.

When he was finished, Roosevelt took back to Washington the scruffy little dog, Skip, he'd grown fond of on the trip, as well as tales of how he shot his first bear two days into the trip, and how 10 black bear and three lynx were bagged by the rest of his entourage.

■ WHERE TO WATCH WILDLIFE

A full range of Rocky Mountain wildlife can be seen throughout Colorado. Although most species hide from humans by inhabiting the state's millions of acres of national forests and parks, there are a number of places where if you get out of your car, lookin the right direction, and open your eyes, you have a pretty fair chance of seeing wildlife. Below are some of the most accessible areas for watching wildlife.

■ GEORGETOWN
(Rocky Mountains)

Rocky Mountain sheep, the state animal, prance and parade among the rocky cliffs and crags directly above Interstate 70 near Georgetown, about 50 miles west of Denver. The Bighorn Viewing Site (exit 228) is equipped with high-powered telescopes and information about these nimble cliff-dwellers. A herd of about 200 animals can usually be seen all year.

■ JENSEN STATE WILDLIFE AREA
(Western Slope)

Located between Meeker and Craig in northwest Colorado, this wildlife area is home to elk, deer, blue grouse, red-tailed hawks, rabbits, coyotes, grouse, and pheasant, depending on the season. *For more information, call (303) 878-4493.*

■ ROCKY MOUNTAIN ARSENAL
(Western Slope)

For decades the U.S. Army manufactured nerve gases and other high-potency killing devices on a small portion of this huge federal reserve, located just west of Denver International Airport. In 1992, all the land that wasn't part of the munitions manufacturing became a wildlife refuge. The area boasts hundreds of species including deer, bald eagles and other birds, and dozens of other small animals. *(303) 289-0232, ext. 150.*

■ SAN LUIS VALLEY
(Southern Colorado)

Approximately 20,000 sandhill cranes invade the Monte Vista National Wildlife Refuge during their spring migration through the San Luis Valley. A number of endangered whooping cranes usually accompany them. Bus tours and other events mark the event, which usually takes place in February and March. *Call (800) 835-7245 for more information.*

■ SEVERENCE

This town of just over 100 people located about ten miles north of Fort Collins hosts as many as 50,000 snow and Canada geese for the winter. It's pretty easy to spot birds in the adjoining fields and farmlands.

A mule deer buck with felt-covered, summertime antlers.

S   K   I   I   N   G

HERE'S A SURE BET. AFTER A DAY ON THE SLOPES, walk (or limp if it was a real rough day) into the nearest bar. Settle down next to some likely looking locals and ask what contributions their particular ski town made to ski history. Then watch it fly, and I don't mean snow. Ten to one you will be snowed under with colorful tales, bits of truth, a little exaggeration, or downright lies about how this place, or the ridge just down the road, is where it all started.

Out will come stories of miners and their "snowshoes" racing down a slope with a long pole behind them serving as a rudder. Also presented will be a long list of people's names who "really" had the idea first that Colorado's towering mountains were the perfect ski hills. Technologically speaking, there will be reminders of how an ingenious rope/pulley system was used to lug people up an infant ski hill, or how early ski lift towers were built by muscle and guts, or how someone tore the engine out of a Buick and jury-rigged it to primitive cable lifts to create the first modern ski lift.

Listen intently, nod your head a lot, laugh now and then, maybe say you heard some other town claimed a particular first, agree wholeheartedly with the locals about what a load of baloney that is, and you might end up drinking for free all night.

■ EARLY DAYS

So who's telling the truth about the beginning of Colorado's huge, internationally famous ski industry?

Well, almost everyone, actually.

Let's start with God.

Or a messenger of His named Father John Dyer, who strapped on a pair of skis and figured out how to operate them well enough to avoid meeting his maker. By 1864 the Methodist minister delivered the Word and the mail to the hardscrabble mining camps in South Park and the soon-to-be-boomtown of Leadville.

It's hard to refute any story about half-drunk gold or silver miners strapping

(previous pages) These ranchers take hay to their cattle by means of a sleigh and a team of Belgian horses.

barrel staves to their feet and scooting across the snow. It was probably more fun than dancing to the pounding of a pickled pianist with the few well-worn women in town. Many of Colorado's mining camps and towns created ski clubs in the late 1800s.

Primitive skis also came in handy to cowboys, miners, or mail carriers who couldn't let snow deter them from their rounds, even in the late 1800s. Thus, anywhere snow measured belly deep to a tall mule, skis were part of the Colorado gold and silver scene. From then on, though, things get a little harder to nail down because the definition of "developing skiing" takes on meanings ranging from skiing with fellow miners to a vague idea about cutting down a few trees whose bark had been damaged by impact from early skiers, to actually designating entire mountains just for skiing and developing the machinery to get skiers on snow.

So, the following is a cursory glance at the start of recreational skiing in Colorado, but remember, it's not comprehensive enough to base a bar brawl on. Just keep smiling and nodding your head.

The first star of Colorado skiing was Norseman Carl Howelsen, a champion ski jumper who eventually landed in Steamboat Springs. In 1914, Howelsen organized a winter festival (which survives to this day), constructed a ski jump on Howelson Hill, and demonstrated his talents to the awed locals.

About the same time the scene shifted to an unlikely ski town—Denver—and an unusual ski hill—Genesee Mountain. A number of ski clubs decided any trip very far into the mountains was as risky as actually skiing, so they brought the skiing closer to home on Genesee Mountain, just west of town. They cut a skinny little ski run from the trees, built a jump for the adventuresome, and *violá*, Denver became a ski pioneer. Throughout the first twenty years of this century, ski clubs in Boulder and Colorado Springs also trekked to the nearest snow-covered hill and plowed down the thing.

Ironically, the Depression was when skiing really went commercial. Hey, during the Depression spending a Rocky Mountain winter day with sticks strapped to your feet, being dragged up a mountain by a rope, reaching the top—complete with frozen butt—and then heading downhill so you could fall face-first into the snow would be one hell of a good time. Or at least that's what people thought in Aspen, Breckenridge, Steamboat, Wolf Creek Pass, Monarch Pass, Glenwood Springs, Estes Park, Allenspark, Grand Lake, Creede, Cumbres Pass, Berthoud Pass (which featured the state's first rope tow in 1937), Hot Sulphur Springs, and Glen

THE FIRST SKIERS

*S*o far as anyone can find out, skiing came into being in Norway. A cave drawing from about 2000 B.C., near the Arctic Circle in that land, shows a man skiing down hill on twelve-foot skis with a balance pole, knees slightly bent. The oldest surviving pieces of skis are 4,500 years old. The pragmatic purpose of the ski, obviously, was to enable people to move efficiently and quickly through snow-covered country impassable, or nearly so, to the unaided human foot. Skis allowed snowbound country folk to visit neighbors in the dead of winter or to go to the nearest village for company, supplies, a mug of brew, the latest news or, maybe, some romancing with a lusty town wench (women's lib was late coming to the harsh winter climates of Scandinavia). And, more important, skis endowed the wintertime hunter with a mobility as magical as jet airplanes to modern man, a potentially as lethal as the horse to footbound soldiers. However, though people in several parts of our world have been using skis for transportation, sport and, alas, war for more than a hundred years, the human beast is a fun-loving creature who eventually discovered how to turn a cheap, simple tool into an expensive, complex toy.

Skiing emigrated to both Europe and America about 1850, but around 1960 its expansion took off with a rush, changing this sporting activity into a social event with economic and political implications as far removed from moving efficiently through snow as snow is from smog.

—Dick Dorworth
"The Ski. The Tool," *Mountain Gazette,* 1978

Miners, cabin fever, and "snowshoes" got Colorado skiing going downhill. (Colorado Historical Society)

Cove, since they all had some sort of rudimentary ski area operating before World War II.

But those efforts all paled in comparison to what was happening at Winter Park, which was destined to become the state's first truly commercial ski area.

When the Moffatt Tunnel was completed in 1927, the Denver & Rio Grande Railroad ran right past some very enticing ski hills. In 1938, the city of Denver annexed the area and developed the unnamed trails into the Winter Park Ski Area. Using donations, city and federal funds, and volunteers and laborers from Depression-era government agencies, work went quickly. The new T-bar lift was a quantum leap over the old rope tows or boats. By 1941 runs, lifts, buildings, and skiers were all over the place, thanks in part to the famous "ski trains" that delivered skiers right to the slopes.

The Winter Park Ski Train is still operating today; call (303) 296-4754 for information.

Skiers in the late 1940s disembark from the ski train at Winter Park. (Colorado Historical Society)
(opposite) Over 200 inches of snow falls annually in the Colorado Rockies.

■ CHOOSING A SKI RESORT

Skiers today can sample three distinct skiing experiences in Colorado: **mega-resorts**, **historic hideaways**, and **hometown hills**. They can also decide, by their choice of resort, whether seared ahi or tuna salad is more to their taste.

Proximity to the urbanites along the Front Range and Denver made the eastern slope of the Rockies the logical place to build mega-resorts. These resorts run the gamut from full-scale, planned, resort complexes that can accommodate a destination skier flying in from Tulsa, to just a great ski hill and parking lot to accommodate the Denver accountant who moved from Tulsa to be within an hour's drive of great skiing.

Scattered deeper throughout the Rockies and farther from Denver are the historic hideaways, ski resorts that mix their mining heritage with champagne powder to entice destination skiers. Flung far and wide, north to south, and every place in between are the hometown hills. These unpretentious ski areas, usually miles from the nearest town, feel like Mom and Pop operations compared to the big resorts, but once you find them you might fall in love with their simplicity, friendliness, and miles of uncrowded ski runs that give most people a skiing day just as challenging, diverse, and delightful as you'd find anywhere else.

Probably the best way to start planning your ski vacation is with a copy of the *Colorado Ski Country USA* ski guide. The group is a nonprofit skiing promotional outfit and the guide will provide an avalanche of good information about all the ski areas and amenities they offer. Write Colorado Ski Country USA, 1560 Broadway, Suite 1440, Denver, CO 80202; (303) 837-0793. Ticket price ranges are listed in this book as:

> inexpensive = under $35; moderate = $35-$50; expensive = over $50.

■ VAIL: THE ULTIMATE MEGA-RESORT

Irish Baron Lord Gore's hunting party probably peeked into the Vail Valley in the 1850s. All they saw were deer, elk, and buffalo, which they killed in prodigious numbers and left to rot. It would take more discerning eyes and about 110 years to see the valley's potential as not merely a baron of Colorado skiing, but the king of the "planned unit development" approach to ski areas.

The eyes belonged to Earl Eaton, a uranium prospector, and Pete Seibert, a former Tenth Mountain vet, who needed only one peek at the valley's mountains to envision a great ski area. By the late 1950s and early 1960s, ski areas were cropping almost as fast as the gold camps of a century earlier, so the two got crafty. Instead of shouting to the rooftops about this mother lode, they quietly applied for a forest area ski permit, formed the innocent-sounding Trans Montane Rod and Gun Club, and started buying land.

There was nothing at the base of the mountain, so Vail planned and created a historic aura. With Victorian mining towns a dime a dozen, the architects went further back into history and drew up tidy plans based on European resorts: a huge Tyrolean Hause to house skiers.

With plans locating every tree, park bench, and ski rack, the entire resort was built in one year. Vail opened in 1962, with the usual lack of snow that God or someone seems to love to ordain new ski resorts with. Never fear. A Ute medicine man was called, arrived, did his dance, chants, and gyrations, and *voilà*, the snow came. Strange but true.

Vail then set out to become the Rockies' most famous resort, using a mega-promotional campaign that, by some estimates, cost more than the construction of the resort itself. It worked. Then came the clincher: the resignation of President Richard Nixon. Vailites forgot politics and jumped for joy: one of their part-time own, Gerald Ford, was now President. As a Congressman, Ford had vacationed in Vail for years (who cared). Now he was the big cheese and Vail was "Gerry's" Western White House. Basking in the glow didn't describe Vail's reaction. Sending the whole town into a tanning booth and hitting broil is closer.

Vail's success drew corporate attention. Ralston, Quaker Oats, Federated Stores, Sears Roebuck, Gillette Holdings, and other corporate giants have all owned a piece of Vail, which always made it part of corporate skullduggery somewhere else than Vail. Familiar story, different Colorado setting, in other words.

Corporate cash covered every inch of the valley with golf courses, condos, West Vail, East Vail, and made Vail a year-round resort replete with a summertime full of enticing events in a town surrounded by millions of acres of national forest. Repeating such successes is **Beaver Creek**, the exclusive ski mountain and development just down the road. Again, every shrub and condo was placed by design (except for the trailer court you pass on the way to the slopes. Oh well, reality has to rear its ugly head every once in a while, even in Ski-ra-la).

A bit of reality arrived in the late 1980s when the town of Vail discovered a glaring omission: no cemetery, presumably because the planners didn't plan on people preferring permanent plantation in a town with no roots. The roots have grown. The town of Vail, not Vail, Inc., is plotting cemetery placement and who should be planted there, as in only long-time residents or also mere condo owners seeking eternal rest under the snow they loved.

■ VAIL TODAY

You can't miss Vail if you're driving Interstate 70 because the town, with its original Tyrolean-style core, has been supplemented by bigger and newer hotels and commercial areas. The ski runs are right off the road. Indeed, the hardest part of a Vail vacation just may be the two-hour drive from Denver and getting off the highway. Once off, the town and its businesses take over. Park your car in the parking garages and prepare to be shuttled to and fro, from and around. You can ride from motel to ski lift to restaurant to shopping areas and back again day and night.

The place works. The snow gets plowed. The trash gets dumped. The shuttles run on time. It's clean. The lifts are fast and plentiful. The people are friendly.

Then there's the snow: standard issue Colorado white gold, especially in the back bowls, which covers more runs than you can cover in a three-day weekend. Vail/Beaver Creek remains the first, and still probably one of the best, of the planned ski resorts.

✦ Vail Mountain

Box 7, Vail, CO 81658; (800) 525-2257 or (970) 845-2500; snow report (970) 476-4888. 100 miles west of Denver on I-70.

Terrain: 174 trails on 4644 acres: Front side: 32% beginner, 36% intermediate, 32% advanced; Backside bowls: intermediate and expert *only.*

Lifts: one gondola, nine high-speed quad chairs, one fixed-grip quad chair, three triple chairs, six double chairs, six surface lifts.

Snowmaking: 347 acres.

Vertical drop: 3300 feet (991 m).

Ticket prices: expensive.

Facilities: rental equipment and lessons; child care; disabled skiing, call (970) 479-3264.

Dining: 14 restaurants ranging from full service to delis to hot dog shacks strewn across the mountain and at base facilities.

Olympic medalist Billy Kidd plows through powder at Steamboat Springs.

Accommodations: Vail central reservations, (800) 525-2257

Cross-country skiing: 30 kilometers of groomed trails. Ticket prices vary.

◆ **Beaver Creek**

Box 915, Beaver Creek, CO 81620; (800) 525-2257 or (970) 845-2500 reservations; snow report (970) 476-4888.

Terrain: 146 trails, 1,625 acres; 23% beginner, 43% intermediate, 34% advanced.

Lifts: three high-speed quads, four triple chairs, four double chairs.

Snowmaking: 550 acres.

Vertical drop: 4,040 feet (1,018 m).

Ticket prices: expensive.

Facilities: rental equipment and lessons; child care; snowcat excursions.

Dining: five restaurants, ranging from cafeteria to gourmet, on the mountain and at base lodges.

Accommodations: *See* Vail, *above.*

Cross-country skiing: 30 kilometers of groomed trails on Beaver Creek Mountain. Ticket prices vary.

■ ASPEN

In 1938 Elizabeth Paepke visited Aspen and fell in love with the charming, if somewhat dilapidated, old buildings that survived the silver boom. People were being hauled up Ajax Mountain in a boat tow. Famed Swiss mountaineer Andre Roche had designed "the Roche," a 3,000-foot (914-m) tow on the face of Ajax Mountain. It hosted a number of regional and national ski races in the late 1930s and early 1940s.

The war put everything on hold, but in 1945 Elizabeth brought her husband Walter to Aspen. He looked at the ski hill and Victorian town and decided this was the place for a world-class resort. Unlike other skiing visionaries, Paepke had the money, education, and drive to make it happen. He started buying land, gave away paint to spruce up the town, and tapped Pfeifer and Herbert Bayer, to turn his plans into reality.

Thanks to his Container Corporation of America—which revolutionized the cardboard box business—Paepke was a wealthy man. But he still needed some investors, and they came gladly. Others soon signed on: motel man Conrad Hilton, Paul Nitze—Paepke's brother-in-law and later Secretary of the Navy—and D. R. C. (Darcy) Brown—a local who retained extensive family holdings in the area. The Forest Service quickly finished the paperwork, two lifts were built, Ajax was renamed Aspen Mountain, and in 1946 the locals held the first Roche Cup on their new ski hill.

The January 11, 1947, grand opening included the U.S. Army Band, the governor, the Tenth Mountain Division Color Guard, dozens of notables, and no snow in Aspen. Luckily, at 11,300 feet (3,444 m) where the lifts topped out, there was plenty of snow and the celebration was a success.

In 1950, Aspen claimed its place among the world's best ski hills when it hosted the Federation Internationale de Ski biennial world championships. The world's best ski racers descended on Aspen for the event and proclaimed Aspen Mountain one helluva ride. Aspen the ski town was on its way.

But Paepke, with his classical education at Chicago's Latin School and Yale, wanted more than a ski resort. The Athenian ideal of a fit body and cultivated mind was the ultimate goal. Skiing pretty much took care of the body, and in 1949 Paepke went to work on the mind. That year was the 200th birthday of the German poet, philosopher, and statesman, Wolfgang Goethe, and Paepcke planned to celebrate that birthday in Aspen. He invited the world's foremost philosophers and thinkers to town for "contemplation of the noblest works of man," in Paepke's words. He convinced Albert Schweitzer to attend, along with Arthur Rubenstein, Dorothy Maynor, Mortimer Adler, and Dimitri Metropoulos and his Minneapolis Symphony. The event was stimulating, to say the least, and put Aspen on the world's cultural map.

Ski developments and the town kept pace with the intellectual rampage. New runs and lifts were added on Ajax, making it one of, if not the, most challenging ski hills in the nation. The once-deserted streets started to fill, the nineteenth century miners' cottages were restored, businesses and motels opened up, and Aspen's second boom started.

But a mountain that challenges international racers can also scare beginners or casual skiers, so Friedl Pfeifer turned to **Buttermilk Mountain** in the 1960s to create a teaching hill for beginners and those seeking a more casual skiing experience.

"Whip" Jones then built **Aspen Highlands,** which took on the aura of an unpretentious, home-town ski hill. Finally, the Aspen Ski Corp. made the big jump to Snowmass Valley south of town and built a brand new ski area with modern lifts, challenging runs, and a complete ski village that existed only to serve the skier.

Even though many of the state's ski areas have tried to duplicate the Aspen example, there still remains just one Aspen, because no other ski area has all the Aspen elements—a Victorian mining town history, pioneering ski efforts, fantastic ski terrain, a learning hill, a completely planned ski area and town built just for skiing, and a heady dose of culture, philosophy, and music to stimulate the mind.

■ SKIING ASPEN

Today, get off Interstate 70 at Glenwood and start up Colorado 82's four lanes which turn to two not-so-safe lanes just past Carbondale to reach Aspen. The road is called "Killer 82" because of so many car/car wrecks and car/deer wrecks. Go slow, enjoy the scenery—basically wide-open ranchland squeezed between mountains on both sides—and don't pass; you'll get there soon enough.

Woody Creek, on the left across from the Snowmass Ski Area is interesting. Stuck in the middle of a trailer park full of Aspenites who actually work is the **Woody Creek Tavern,** the earthy and infamous hang-out of gonzo journalist Hunter S. Thompson, who has a spread farther up the road so his target practice with all manner of weapons—from typewriters to submachine guns—won't disturb the neighbors.

You can see the runs on Snowmass Mountain from the highway, with The Burn—a powder-hound, tree-bashing delight on the far left. Past the airport rests

Skiers descend between tall evergreen trees on the Face of Bell on Aspen Mountain.

Buttermilk Mountain and then, when you're on the edge of town, comes a glimpse of Highlands Ski Area.

Your first choice as you hit town is a Y. Bear left to find Intellectual Alley, properly named the Aspen Meadows—home to the Aspen Institute for Humanistic Studies, the International Design Conference, the Aspen Center for Physics, and the Aspen Music Festival, where students ("Practice or Perish") from around the world come for a summer of instruction. This is also the famed West End, full of huge, generally empty, usually lavish, second homes of movie stars, moguls, and idly rich who "need" a home in Aspen. The same breed has covered Red Mountain with similar homes.

Take a right at the Y and then a big bending left and you're on Main Street. This is still Colorado 82, which will eventually lead you over Independence Pass in the summer, but is closed in the winter. The funky old Aspen fades the closer you get to the middle of town—Mill and Main, a corner occupied by the **Hotel Jerome**. Aspen Mountain's famous runs are visible anytime you look up. As you head toward the hill, salons, restaurants and bars, boutiques, and "shoppes," some in nineteenth-century buildings, a few in 1960–70 style leftovers, and some in brand new efforts, are the order of the day, a mix also apparent in the pedestrian mall two blocks from the ski lifts.

If you're staying for a few days or fly in, forget about a car. Bus service is reliable and will deliver you all over town and to all the ski hills. And it's the cheapest ticket you'll buy during your stay, to boot.

✦ **Aspen Mountain**

Aspen Skiing Company, Box 1248, Aspen, CO 81612; (800) 525-6200 or (970) 925-1220; (970) 925-1221 snow report. Off Colorado 82; call for directions.

Terrain: 76 trails on 675 acres: 70% intermediate, 30% advanced.

Snowmaking: 210 acres.

Lifts: one high-speed six-passenger gondola, one quad superchair, two quad chairs, four double lifts.

Vertical drop: 3,267 feet (996 m).

Ticket prices: expensive.

Facilities: rental equipment and lessons. Challenge Aspen offers some of the best services for disabled skiers; contact them at (970) 923-0578 .

Dining: three on-mountain restaurants, at the base, middle, and top.

Accommodations: Aspen central reservations, (800) 2262-7736 or (970) 925-9000.

Cross-country skiing: There are 50 miles (80 km) of cross-country trails, both heading into the backcountry or quick loops in and around the Aspen vicinity. Contact Snowmass Touring Center (970) 923-3148 or Aspen Touring Center (970) 925-2145.

No snowboarding. (Aspen is the only mountain in the state that bans it.)

✦ **Buttermilk Mountain/Tiehack Mountain**

Aspen Skiing Company *(see address and phone numbers above)*.

Terrain: 45 trails on 410 acres: 35% beginner, 65% intermediate.

Snowmaking: 108 acres.

Lifts: five double chairs, one high-speed quad, one surface.

Vertical drop: 2,030 feet (619 m).

Ticket prices: expensive.

Facilities: rental equipment and lessons; child care; Fort Frog for children; activities for the disabled.

Dining: two on-mountain restaurants and one in the base lodge.

Accommodations: *See* Aspen Mountain *above.*

Cross-country skiing: *See* Aspen Mountain *above.*

✦ Snowmass

Aspen Skiing Company *(see address and phone numbers above).*
Terrain: 79 trails, 2,655 acres; 9% beginner; 69% intermediate; 22% expert.
Snowmaking: 130 acres.
Lifts: seven quad SuperChairs, two triple chairs, six double chairs, two platter-pulls.
Vertical drop: 4,406 feet (1,344 m).
Ticket prices: expensive.
Facilities: Rental equipment, lessons; child care; disabled skiing (see Aspen Mountain above).
Dining: four on-mountain restaurants.
Accommodations: in Aspen call the Aspen central reservations at (970) 925-9000; in Snowmass Village, (800) 332-3245.
Cross-country skiing: see Aspen Mountain above.

✦ Aspen Highlands

Aspen Skiing Company *(see address and phone numbers above).*
Terrain: 81 trails, 619 acres, 19% beginner, 29% intermediate, 52% advanced.
Snowmaking: 110 acres.
Lifts: nine double chairs, one poma, two high-speed quads.
Vertical drop: 3,800 feet (1,158 m).
Ticket prices: expensive.
Facilities: Rental equipment and lessons.
Dining: three on-mountain restaurants.
Accommodations: *See* Aspen *and* Snowmass *above.*
Cross-country skiing: *See* Aspen Mountain *above.*

■ MEGA-RESORTS NEAR DENVER

Developers paid attention to Vail and quickly bunched a batch of resorts within easy driving distance (under two hours) of Denver or other large population centers in Colorado. They learned their lessons well. The resorts get their skiers on the hill as quickly and painlessly as possible. Of course, it also helped that the mountains happen to contain some of the best skiable terrain in the U.S. The following resorts are strategically placed to accommodate a day-trip from Denver or a week of skiing fantasies.

■ BRECKENRIDGE

Eighty-five miles (137 km) west of Denver on Interstate 70 and Colorado 9, Breckenridge is a hybrid combining a gold mining past with a planned skiing future. The town mined gold from 1859 to 1948, decayed, and was revived in 1961 by the Breckenridge Ski Area, now one of the biggest in the state with four mountains plus back bowls. It's sort of strange to walk down the main drag—which is lined with restored and "new Victorians" and see the ski runs behind them—and then visit the back streets and historical displays and get a dose of dilapidated nineteenth-century mining history.

✦ Breckenridge Ski Area

Box 1058, Breckenridge, CO 80424; (970) 453-5000 or (800) 789-7669; snow report (970) 453-1643 ext. 7244. On Colorado 9, south from I-70.

Terrain: 135 trails on 2,023 acres; 20% beginner, 31% intermediate, 49% advanced.

Snowmaking: 504 acres.

Lifts: four SuperChair quads, one triple, eight doubles, four surface lifts.

Vertical drop: 3,398 feet (1,036 m).

Ticket prices: moderate.

Facilities: Rental equipment, lessons; child care; Kid's Castle on Peak 8, this section of mountain for kids and a restaurant. Facilities available for disabled skiers: call (970) 453-6422 or (800) 383-2632.

Dining: five on-mountain restaurants, two at the base.

Accommodations: Breckenridge central reservations, (970) 453-2918 in Colorado; nationwide, (800) 221-1091.

Cross-country skiing: 50 kilometers of groomed, double-set trails.

■ COPPER MOUNTAIN

Located 75 miles (120 km) from Denver on Interstate 70, this area is sprouting into a real resort, complete with condos, restaurants, and other amenities at the base of a great ski complex designed to get you out of your car and onto the mountain as quickly as possible.

✦ **Copper Mountain Resort**
Box 3001, Copper Mountain, CO 80443; (800) 458-8386 or (970) 968-2882;
snow report (800) 789-7609. On I-70 about 75 miles west of Denver.
Terrain: 118 trails on 2,433 acres, 350 acres are set aside for guided extreme
skiing: 25% beginner, 40% intermediate, 35% advanced.
Snowmaking: 270 acres.
Lifts: three quad chairs, six triple chairs, six double chairs, four surface lifts.
Vertical drop: 2,601 feet (973m).
Ticket prices: moderate.
Facilities: Rental equipment and lessons; day care; 30-acre portion of Union
Creek set aside for families and children.
Accommodations: Copper Mountain central reservations, (800) 458-8386.
Cross-country skiing: 16 miles (25 km) of groomed trails.

■ **KEYSTONE, NORTH PEAK, ARAPAHOE BASIN, AND OUTBACK**
These are four fine hills lurking just over 70 miles (113 km) from Denver on Interstate 70. You pass through the town of Silverthorne before arriving at the ski
hills and Keystone Village, which is growing out of the village stage by constantly
adding new restaurants, shops, and a variety of condos and places to stay. Keystone
is keyed to the beginner and intermediate, while North Peak and the Outback are
preferred by experts. Arapahoe Basin caters to snowboarders with a half-pipe for
performing acts of aerial derring-do.

✦ **KEYSTONE MOUNTAIN/NORTH PEAK/ARAPAHOE BASIN**
Box 38, Keystone, CO 80435; (800) 541-3176, (970) 468-2316 general information; accommodations/reservations (800) 222-0188; snow report (970)
468-4111. Off I-70 about 70 miles west of Denver. Ticket prices are moderate
and interchangeable at the various slopes.

✦ **Keystone Mountain**
Terrain: 92 trails, 1,755 acres: 32% beginner, 57% intermediate, 11% advanced.
Vertical drop: 2,900 feet (713 m).
Lifts: one gondola, two high speed quad chairs, two triples, six double chairs,
four surface lifts.
Facilities: Night skiing. Rental equipment and lessons; child care.

Dining: three restaurants on Keystone Mountain and numerous others at base.
Accommodations: central reservations for Keystone Village and Silverthorne
(800) 222-0188.
Cross-country skiing: 11 miles (18 km) of groomed and packed trails near the
four resorts, 57 miles (91 km) of backcountry trails. Ticket prices $7.
Snowmaking: 849 acres.

✦ **North Peak**
Terrain: 19 trails, 249 acres: 10% beginner, 37% intermediate, 53% advanced.
Vertical drop: 1,620 feet (494 m).
Lifts: one gondola, one quad, one triple.
Snowmaking: 150 acres.
Dining: two on-mountain restaurants.

✦ **Arapahoe Basin**
Terrain: 61 trails,490 acres: 10% beginner, 50% intermediate, 40% advanced.
Vertical drop: 2,270 feet (692 m).
Lifts: one triple chair, four double chairs.
Dining: one on-mountain restaurant, one at the base.

✦ **The Outback**
Terrain: 17 trails, 899 acres: 67% intermediate, 33% advanced.
Vertical drop: 1,520 feet (456 m)
Lifts: one high-speed quad.
Snowmaking: 100 acres.
Night skiing: Terrain and lifts variable depending on conditions. Ticket prices
vary in the inexpensive range.

■ WINTER PARK/MARY JANE/VASQUEZ RIDGE

Once no more than a ski hill and some railroad workers' shacks, this area was one
of the state's first ski areas. After more than a half-century it's still going downhill,
which in this case is good. Paresenn Bowl has become a favorite for intermediate
skiers yearning for the challenge, but not the terror, of ungroomed fresh powder.
Families can also take advantage of lower lift prices when they ski Mini Mountain
and Galloping Goose. The Ski Train, which has become an institution as well as a
means of transportation, will deliver you to the area's 112 trails and all the resort
trimmings. Call (303) 296-4754 for information.

◆ **Winter Park/Vasquez Ridge**
Box 36, Winter Park, CO 80482; (800) 453-2525 outside Colorado, or
(970) 726-5587. On US 40, north from I-70; about 70 miles from Denver.
Terrain: 121 trails, 2,581 acres: 25% beginner, 51% intermediate, 24%
advanced.
Snowmaking: 280 acres
Lifts: six high-speed quad chairs, five triple chairs, nine double chairs.
Vertical drop: 3060 feet (677 m).
Ticket prices: moderate.
Facilities: Rental equipment and lessons; child care; home to the National
Sports Center for the disabled, the largest facility of its kind in the nation.
Dining: 12 restaurants scattered on the mountains and at base lodges, from
full-service dining to cafeterias and pizza. Bar service.
Accommodations: Winter Park central reservations handles bookings for the
entire Fraser Valley, (800) 453-2525.
Facilities: Snowboarding allowed; facilities available for handicapped skiers.

Winter Park in season.

■ HISTORIC HIDEAWAYS

Scattered throughout the central Rockies are a number of resorts with a historical flavor. With the exception of Crested Butte, detailed below, these towns are described here mainly in terms of skiing. *To read more of their history see* "ROCKY MOUNTAINS," *page 84 and* "SAN JUAN MOUNTAINS," *page 134.*

■ CRESTED BUTTE

Thirty miles (48 km) north of Gunnison, Crested Butte has had its share of gold and silver miners, gunslingers, coal miners, and skiers; and when it comes to Colorado history, Crested Butte has tasted more than a smattering of it all. Although it wasn't a gold or silver boomtown, its location just north of Gunnison made it the logical supply center for the surrounding mining camps.

The town didn't die when the mining camps did; instead, it turned into a mining town itself, thanks to the huge vein of high-grade coal at its back door and the 1881 arrival of the Denver & Rio Grande Railroad. By 1884 Crested Butte had become one of Colorado Fuel and Iron's company towns under the compassionate hand of CF&I owner, John Cleveland Osgood.

Then we have the outlaws. Or the outlaw legends, at least.

First was Butch Cassidy and the Sundance Kid, *sans* Wild Bunch. In 1902, or so the story goes, the pair entered a local saloon, but robbery wasn't on their mind, a few cold beers were. A few were all they got because a batch of men with badges were coming after them. The pair left town, and since they were running, not riding, and didn't get caught, it's safe to say they kept one foot ahead of the law.

The famous James brothers, Frank and Jesse, also were supposed to be short-time visitors, hiding out for a while in Parlin, outside of Crested Butte, and creating no mischief. Creating some mischief, however, was Billy the Kid, who was alleged to have worked in an outlying sawmill, been fired, held up the next passing stage, and continued down the road into legend.

The Big Mine kept Crested Butte an honest-to-goodness Colorado mining town, prosperous if not exactly booming, until 1953. Then it happened. The Big Mine shut down and everyone expected Crested Butte to join the ghost town parade.

Skiing came to the rescue. Rozeman Hill had been hosting skiers since 1951, but it wasn't until 1963 that Crested Butte Mountain opened and created a unique situation when it came to linking a historical town to a ski area: the two weren't linked.

Crested Butte Mountain is not, in fact, at Crested Butte's doorstep. It, and its attendant planned village and amenities, are located a couple of miles north of town. The new ski area was an immediate hit with students from Western State College in Gunnision, and helped create the college's unofficial, and we're talking very unofficial, slogan: "Ski Western State and Pick up A Degree in Your Spare Time."

There's a splash of modern action at the entrance to Crested Butte, but once you make a left and turn on to Elk Avenue and start to explore the back streets, of which there aren't too many, things start to look old and settled, ready for the region's famed harsh winters.

Dashing downhill or traipsing through the trees: Colorado skiing offers it all.

Crested Butte has retained its Victorian charm and the influences left by the southern European immigrants who worked the coal mines. It still feels like a small town that is part Victorian mining town and part real town that has kept up with the modern world. It's not full of condos; not every building has been painted or remodeled to appeal to the second home market; and it didn't pave most of its streets until the 1980s. It just happens to have a great ski mountain right up the road.

◆ **Mt. Crested Butte**
   Box A, Mt. Crested Butte, CO 81225; (800) 544-8448 or (970) 349-2222; snow report (970) 349-2323. On Colorado 135; call for directions.
   Terrain: 85 trails, 1,150 acres, including 550 acres of ungroomed terrain called the "Extreme Limits": 13% beginner, 30% intermediate, 57% advanced.
   Lifts: two high-speed quads, three triple chairs, four doubles, four surface lifts.
   Vertical drop: 2,787 feet (933 m).
   Ticket prices: moderate.
   Facilities: rental equipment and lessons; child care for infants to three-year-olds.
   Dining: three on-mountain restaurants, three at the base.
   Accommodations: either at the ski area or in the town of Crested Butte, call (800) 544-8448.
   Cross-country skiing: 19 miles (30 km) of groomed track.
   Snowmaking: 300 acres

■ SKI COOPER
The famed Tenth Mountain Division trained here, just 10 miles (16 km) from Leadville, king of the silver cities, with its Victorian allures. Ski Cooper has kept up with the times, and now features Chicago Ridge, a 1,800-acre back bowl just for powder junkies (accessible only by snowcat). It's a pretty long 100 miles (160 km) from Denver over Interstate 70, Colorado 91 or US 24.

◆ **Ski Cooper**
   Box 896, Leadville, CO; (719) 486-3684 reservations; snow report (719) 486-2277. On US 24, south from I-70.
   Terrain: 26 trails, 365 acres: 30% beginner, 70% intermediate.
   Lifts: one triple chair, one double chair, two surface lifts.
   Vertical drop: 1,200 feet (366 m).
   Facilities: rental equipment and lessons; child care.
   Ticket prices: inexpensive.

Dining: cafeteria at the base lodge.

Accommodations: closest accommodations are in Leadville, (800) 933-3901 or (719) 486-3900.

Cross-country skiing: 24 km of groomed track; snowcat tours to Chicago Ridge and other backcountry powder hot spots.

■ STEAMBOAT SPRINGS

Way up in the north-central part of the state about 160 miles (260 km) from Denver via Interstate 70 and US 40, Steamboat was a skiing pioneer, but its main business was as a regional retail center for local ranchers and coal miners. The skiing boom didn't destroy those roots, it just led to the present mixture of skiers and real cowboys the town loves to tout. If you want to be cool, ski in a cowboy hat.

✦ **Steamboat**

2305 Mt. Werner Circle, Steamboat Springs, CO 80487; (800) 922-2722 or (970) 879-4074; snow report (970) 879-7300. On US 40, north from I-70.

Terrain: 135 trails, 2,939 acres: 15% beginner, 54% intermediate, 31% advanced.

Skiers with lit torches gracefully slide down a mountain during the Winter Carnival in Steamboat Springs.

Snowmaking: 400 acres.

Lifts: one gondola, three quad chairs, six triple chairs, seven double chairs, three surface lifts.

Vertical drop: 3,600 feet (1,097 m).

Ticket prices: moderate.

Facilities: Rental equipment and lessons; child care; instruction for physically and developmentally disabled, call (970) 879-6111, ext. 531.

Dining: six restaurants ranging from cafeteria to barbecue to gourmet on the mountain and at the base.

Accommodations: call Steamboat central reservations: (800) 922-2722.

Cross-country skiing: 19 miles (30 km) of groomed trails, call for rates

✦ **Howelsen Hill**
Box 775088, Steamboat Springs, CO 80477; (970) 879-2043. On US 40, north from I-70.

Terrain: 15 trails, 100 acres, 100% intermediate.

Lifts: two surface, one double.

Vertical drop: 440 feet (134 m).

Ticket prices: inexpensive.

Dining: snack bar at base lodge.

Accommodations: see Steamboat.

Facilities: Night skiing. Bobsled track 4,200 feet (1277 m) open day and night. Five- and 90-meter ski jumps. Cross-country skiing on 6 miles (10 km) of groomed trails, 2.5 km open at night, free.

■ **TELLURIDE**
This picturesque town in the San Juan Mountains boomed long enough to get a good shot of Victorian-era buildings. The Telluride Ski Area came to town in 1971 and has since expanded to both sides of Coonskin Mountain, with a modern, planned resort on the backside, so you can choose from Victorian gingerbread to chrome and glass accommodations.

✦ **Telluride**
Box 11155, Telluride, CO 81435; (970) 728-4424, general info (970) 728-4431; snow report (970) 728-3614. On Colorado 145; call for directions.

Snowboarder on Telluride Mountain.

Terrain: 64 trails, 1,050 acres; 21% beginner, 47% intermediate, 32% advanced.

Snowmaking: 155 acres.

Lifts: two high-speed quad chairs (including the world's longest), five double chairs, two triple chairs, one poma lift.

Vertical drop: 3522 feet (965 m).

Ticket prices: moderate.

Facilities: rental equipment and lessons; child care; facilities for disabled.

Dining: seven restaurants scattered throughout the area on the mountain and at the base lodges.

Accommodations: Telluride central reservations, (800) 525-3455.

Cross-country skiing: more than 31 miles (50 km) of groomed trails.

Skiing Genessee Mountain in the old days. (Denver Public Library, Western History Department)

■ ABOUT HOMETOWN SKI HILLS

Hometown ski areas range in size from mere hills with a couple of creaky old lifts to fairly good-sized mountains with lifts and amenities just a notch or two below the big hills. They provide good skiing to the people living nearby and those visitors lucky enough to discover the slower-paced, more intimate ski experience that appeals to families, beginners, and those tired of the crowds.

Most people would be surprised to learn that not every Colorado ski area falls into the mega-resort or historic category. Tucked into the mountains here and there are small ski areas with plenty of great skiing, but not the glitz, promotional muscle, history, and massive mountain operations of the "big guys." Visiting them you'll enjoy the following:

- Being able to ski down the hill without carving turns around other skiers and tearing up the slope as if you were a steroid-crazed halfback executing an open-field punt return.

- Not having to keep looking over your shoulder for fear of being run over by someone skiing like a steroid-crazed halfback executing an open-field punt return.

- Lift lines that don't give you a chance to read a whole chapter of *War and Peace* before you head up the hill.

- Lift ticket prices that don't require notes from your banker and your mother.

- Being able to eat and afford some standard, good old American food, like a hamburger, in the base lodge, instead of wandering around a mall to find a fern-infested "grille" where you eat ham à la burger served on a croissant for the price of a good pair of ski poles.

- The feeling that by the end of the day the lift operator is almost family and the rest of the hill's crew does really like having you around and would go out of their way for you.

■ LITTLE HILLS CLOSE TO BIG CITIES

■ ELDORA

The 21-mile (34-km) drive through Boulder Canyon on Colorado 119 is a great drive in itself, then you arrive at Boulder's hometown hill—Eldora—which you can also make in less than an hour from Denver.

✦ **Eldora Mountain Resort**
Box 430, Nederland, CO 80466; reservations (303) 440-8700, from Denver (303) 258-7082; snow report (303) 440-8800. On Colorado 119; call for directions.
Terrain: 43 trails on 386 acres with 16 trails covering 91 acres available for night skiing: 15% beginner, 85% intermediate.
Snowmaking: 180 acres.
Lifts: five double chairs, three surface lifts, one triple chair.
Vertical drop: 1,400 feet (427 m).

Ticket prices: inexpensive.
Facilities: rental equipment and lessons.
Dining: one on-mountain restaurant, one at base lodge.
Accommodations: closest are in town of Eldora, (800) 422-4629.
Cross-country skiing: 28 miles (45 km) of groomed and backcountry trails.

■ LOVELAND BASIN

Just 56 miles (90 km) west of Denver right on Interstate 70 before the Eisenhower Tunnel is one of Colorado's original ski areas, which has expanded its terrain above timberline. The area's devotees routinely cross-country ski into the deep powder bowls above timberline.

✦ Loveland Basin

    Box 899, Georgetown, CO 80444; (303) 569-3203 reservations; from Denver (303) 571-5580.

    Terrain: 70 trails, 1,365 acres; 25% beginner, 48% intermediate, 27% advanced.

    Lifts: one quad chair, two triple chairs, five double chairs, one poma, one Mighty-Mite for the ski school.

    Vertical drop: 2,410 feet (735 m).

    Ticket prices: inexpensive to moderate.

    Facilities: rental equipment and lessons.

    Dining: Two cafeterias and three restaurants at the base area.

    Accommodations: closest are in Georgetown, 12 miles (19 km) away, (800) 225-LOVE.

    Snowmaking: 159 acres.

■ SILVERCREEK

Seventy-eight miles (126 km) from Denver on Interstate 70 and US 40, or just 15 minutes north of Winter Park, SilverCreek emphasizes teaching families how to have fun on skis and gears its tow hills to the student with one of the state's best instructional programs.

✦ SilverCreek Ski Area

    Box 1110, Granby, CO 80446; (800) 448-9458 or (970) 887-3384; (970) 629-1020 Denver direct.

    Terrain: 33 trails, 251 acres: 30% beginner, 50% intermediate, 20% advanced.

(opposite) Ice climbing has become an increasingly popular sport in Colorado. Here a team tackles an icefall in the Telluride area.

Snowmaking: about 100 acres.
Lifts: two triple chairs, one double chair, one poma lift, one surface lift.
Vertical drop: 970 feet (296 m).
Ticket prices: inexpensive.
Facilities: Rental equipment and lessons a specialty; child care.
Dining: cafeteria at the base lodge.
Accommodations: ski-in/ski-out condos, hotel and motel rooms and nearby guest ranches in the surrounding communities of Granby, Winter Park, and Grand Lake, (970) 726-9421 or (800) 462-5253.
Cross-country skiing: 25 miles (40 km) groomed track.

■ LITTLE HILLS SCATTERED ALL OVER THE PLACE

■ ARROWHEAD

Just west of Vail on Interstate 70, Arrowhead is now part of the Vail/Beaver Creek ski area.

✦ **Arrowhead Ski Area**
Box 69, Edwards, CO 81632, (970) 926-3029; for reservations and ticket information, (800) 525-2257.
Terrain: 13 trails, 178 acres: 30% beginner, 50% intermediate, 20% advanced.
Snowmaking: 80 acres.
Lifts: one high-speed quad chair and one tow.
Vertical drop: 1,700 feet (518 m).
Ticket prices: expensive.
Facilities: Rental equipment and lessons.
Dining: one restaurant at the base area and one on the mountain.
Accommodations: At the ski area, call (303) 926-8300, or in Vail/Beaver Creek Valley, call the Vail Resort Association (800) 525-3875.
Back-country skiing: private lessons, and equipment rental available through Paragon Guides, (970) 926-5299.

■ CUCHARA VALLEY

On the east side of San Luis Valley, this resort is only about 75 miles from Pueblo on Interstate 25 and Highway 160. This small ski area is generally geared to beginners and intermediates, although there are a few runs to give an expert a thrill. Lift lines are unheard of.

✦ **Cuchara Ski Valley**
924 Penadero Ave. #3, Cuchara Valley, CO 81055; (719) 742-3163, (800) 227-4436.
Terrain: 25 trails on 230 acres: 25% beginner; 75% intermediate.
Snowmaking: 170 acres.
Lifts: one triple chair, three double chairs.
Vertical drop: 1,562 feet (475 m)
Ticket Prices: inexpensive.
Facilities: Rental equipment and lessons.
Dining: on-mountain restaurant.
Accommodations: limited at the ski area. Closest lodge two miles (3 km) away.

■ MONARCH

Set between Gunnison and Salida on US 50, this resort gets mountains of snow and—thanks to all that soft and dry powder snow, the warm welcome mat that's always out, and the bang for the skiing buck—draws skiers from all over south-central Colorado.

✦ **Monarch Ski Area**
23715 US Hwy. 50, Monarch, CO 81227; (800) 332-3668 reservations; snow report (800) 228-7943; (719) 539-3573.
Terrain: 54 trails, 670 acres: 28% beginner, 46% intermediate, 26% advanced.
Snowmaking: who needs it when you average 350 inches of snow a year?
Lifts: four double chairs.
Vertical drop: 1,000 feet (305 m).
Ticket prices: inexpensive.
Facilities: Equipment rental and lessons; child care.
Dining: cafeteria at the base lodge and a snack bar on the mountain.
Accommodations: The 100-room Monarch Lodge is the only lodge at the ski area, call (800) 332-3668, or call the local chamber of commerce, (719) 539-2068, for information on rooms in Gunnison and Salida.
Cross-country skiing: two miles (3 km) of track skiing. Snowcat skiing: Great Divide Snow Tours, from $20-80 per day.

■ POWDERHORN

Located 35 miles (56 km) from Grand Junction on Interstate 70 and Colorado 65, Powderhorn sits on the flanks of the Grand Mesa, a huge flat-topped mountain, which allows it to receive a steady downpour of light powder. The area draws skiers from across the western slope. Excellent cross-country skiing and snowmobiling can be found in the national forest surrounding the mountain.

✦ **Powderhorn Ski Resort**
Box 370, Mesa, CO 81643; (970) 268-5700.
Terrain: 27 trails, 510 acres: 20% beginner, 80% intermediate.
Snowmaking: 50 acres.
Lifts: one quad, two double chairs, one surface lift.
Vertical drop: 1,650 feet (503 m).
Ticket prices: inexpensive.
Facilities: Rental equipment and lessons. Child care.
Dining: restaurant, bar and cafeteria at the base lodge.
Accommodations: limited lodging at the ski area; call (800) 241-6997 for lodging information in Grand Junction and nearby towns.
Cross-country skiing: 12 km of trails.

■ PURGATORY/DURANGO

Perched in the mountains 50 miles (80 km) north of Durango on US 550, this is the prime ski area and resort for the entire Four Corners region, and has a well earned reputation as a challenging and fun place to ski. It is both a self-contained resort offering lodging, dining, and shopping, as well as a day trip for many in the outlying area.

✦ **Purgatory/Durango Ski Area**
945 Main St., Durango, CO 81301; (800) 525-0892 or (970) 247-8900.
Terrain: 75 trails on 1200 acres: 20% beginner, 50% intermediate, 30% advanced.
Snowmaking: over 245 acres.
Lifts: four triple chairs, five double chairs, one high-speed quad.
Vertical drop: 2,029 feet (618 m).
Ticket prices: moderate.
Facilities: Rental equipment and lessons; child care.
Dining: six restaurants ranging from cafeteria to gourmet at the ski area.

Accommodations: eight condo complexes at the ski area; extensive lodging in Durango, (800) 525-0892.

Cross country skiing: 16 km of groomed trails.

■ SUNLIGHT MOUNTAIN RESORT

About 16 miles (26 km) from Glenwood Springs is my hometown hill, and here's how she works. You take a leisurely drive on a two-lane county road passing a subdivision or two, several ranches, and great mountain scenery. You arrive at the ski area and park. A set of condos is up the hill, a hotel with restaurant and lounge just off to the side. You go to the main lodge, walk up and buy your lift ticket, get on the lift, ride the lift, get off the lift, and start skiing. If you want to dawdle you can get a cup of hot chocolate in the cafeteria or stash something in a locker, or talk shop at the ski shop. Good skiing, no frenzy, light on the wallet, easy duty.

✦ **Ski Sunlight**

10901 County Road 117, Glenwood Springs, CO 81601; (800) 445-7931 or (970) 945-7491. Off I-70; call for directions.

Terrain: 60 trails, 460 acres: 20% beginner, 58% intermediate, 22% advanced.

Snowmaking: 110 acres.

Lifts: one triple chair, two double chairs, one surface lift.

Vertical drop: 2,010 feet (613 m).

Ticket prices: inexpensive.

Facilities: rental equipment and lessons; child care.

Dining: cafeteria at the base lodge.

Accommodations: limited number of condos at the ski area, (800) 445-7931, full range of lodging in Glenwood Springs (800) 221-0098.

Cross-country skiing: 15 miles (24 km) of groomed trails.

■ WOLF CREEK

Set atop the Continental Divide near Wolf Creek Pass between Pagosa Springs and Del Norte on US 160 in the south of the state, this resort gets more snow than any other ski area in Colorado.

✦ **Wolf Creek**

Box 2800, Pagosa Springs, CO 81147; (970) 264-5629.

Terrain: 50 trails, 800 acres: 20% beginner, 80% intermediate.

Lifts: two triple chairs, two double chairs, two surface lifts.

Vertical drop: 1,425 feet (434 m).

Ticket prices: inexpensive.

Facilities: Rental equipment and lessons.

Dining: two cafeterias.

Accommodations: closest lodging is in Pagosa Springs, (970) 264-5629.

■ SKIING ADVENTURES

■ CROSS-COUNTRY HUT SKIING

Spending days in the backcountry on your cross-country skis surrounded by nothing more than the beauty of snow-covered scenery is the prime allure of cross-country hut systems. Colorado is home to two of the best hut systems in the nation, which allow you and a few friends to ski away your days in splendid forested silence with only the sounds of your skis and the winter world around you to interrupt your trek.

✦ **The Alfred A. Braun Hut System**

Colorado's original hut system offers six huts in the Elk Mountains connecting Aspen to Crested Butte. The huts sleep anywhere from seven to 14 skiers. Box 7937, Aspen, CO 81612, (970) 925-5775 for reservations.

Price: $17.50 per person, four person minimum.

✦ **Tenth Mountain Trail**

Commemorating the historic Tenth Mountain Division, this hut system links Aspen to Vail and Leadville with a string of comfortable huts through some of Colorado's most striking mountains and valleys. The huts sleep 16 skiers. Tenth Mountain Division Hut Association, 1280 Ute Ave., Aspen, CO 81612, (970) 925-5775 for reservations.

Price: $22 per person, no minimum.

■ HELICOPTER SKIING

Expert skiers can combine the thrill of cutting fresh tracks through wilderness powder with the ride of a lifetime via chopper skiing.

✦ **Telluride Helitrax**

Guides take you into the heart of the San Juan Mountains stretching in all directions from Telluride.

Telluride Helitrax, Box 1560, Telluride, CO 81435, (970) 728-4904.

Price: Call for prices and reservations.

■ SNOWCAT SKIING

For those who like to get to the wild and uncut, yet stay a little closer to the ground, the solution is to take a snowcat into unscathed skiing terrain.

✦ **Chicago Ridge Snowcat Tours**

Ride into the heart of over 1,600 acres of Chicago Ridge, atop the Continental Divide, and plunge into powder you usually only dream about. The views are worth the ride.

Chicago Ridge Snowcat Tours/Ski Cooper, Box 896, Leadville, CO 80461, (719) 486-2277.

Prices: Call for prices and advanced reservations for full- and half-day rides.

✦ **Great Divide Snow Tours**

Ride into over 600 acres of untouched terrain that boasts some of the deepest and longest-lasting powder in the state.

Great Divide Snow Tours/Monarch Ski Resort, 23715 US Hwy. 50, Monarch, CO 81227, (888) 996-7669, (719) 539-3573.

✦ **Steamboat Powder Cats**

Travel into the woods two miles (3 km) north of the Steamboat ski area for unmatched powder skiing. Intermediate skiers are welcome and a deluxe overnight trip to a charming mountain cabin is also available.

Steamboat Powder Cats, Box 2468, Steamboat Springs, CO 80477, (800) 288-0543, (970) 879-5188.

Prices: Call for prices, reservations required.

Denver's new and expanded International Airport has increased access to Colorado from all over the world. The main terminal's unique architecture has pleased some and confounded others.

PRACTICAL INFORMATION

■ WEATHER

Here's what you can expect concerning general weather trends when traveling through Colorado. **Eastern plains weather** resembles that of the Midwest. Spring is tornado season, but it's also when the plains start to turn green. Fall harvest season is pleasant and temperate; winter is snowy and windy but mild by Midwestern standards. Summer can be hot (80–90°F), but verdant greenery on all sides seems to make travel cooler.

In the **mountains,** summers are made to order, being not too hot in the day (70–80°F) and cool at night (50–40°); however, as soon as the sun goes down so does the mercury, so even in summer bring a jacket. Fall, with its fantastic colors, is a bit unpredictable but not that much cooler than summer. Winter, of course, is cold and snowy, but that's why you'd come to the Rockies in the winter in the first place.

The Western Slope is a high mountain desert, but it's not Death Valley. Summer temperatures can be in the high 90s and occasionally in the 100s, but again as soon as the sun drops the mercury plunges into the 60–70 range) making for comfortable sleeping. Fall and spring are just a bit cooler all the way around, making them preferred seasons for the locals. Winter is milder than in the mountains, but things still freeze and snow still falls, it just melts faster. The **extreme south of the state,** along the border with New Mexico, can generally be counted on to be hotter and drier than the northern regions.

WORDS OF CAUTION

You can't take the weather for granted in the mountains. Always be prepared, regardless of the forecast, time of year, or the assurances of your companions. Bring

WEATHER

along rain or cold-weather gear for even the simplest of outings and be prepared to add or shed layers of clothing as the day progresses.

If you're driving along through the eastern plains in the spring and you see a twister/tornado on the horizon, find a place to hunker down and stay there.

Every couple of winters or so a monster storm settles in and starts snowing so hard and fast you can barely see your hood ornament. Blowing and drifting snow can close the highways crossing the plains and running up and down the Front Range, and Denver International Airport sometimes converts itself into a huge hotel.

TEMPERATURES				
PLACE	JULY		JANUARY	
	°F HI/LOW	°C HI/LOW	°F HI/LOW	°C HI/LOW
Aspen	80/45	27/7	34/8	1/-13
Denver	88/57	31/14	42/15	6/-9
Estes Park	79/46	26/8	38/17	3/-8
Grand Junction	94/64	34/18	36/15	2/-9
Lamar	93/63	34/17	45/14	7/-10
Mesa Verde	88/58	31/14	41/19	5/-7
Pikes Peak	48/34	9/1	9/-4	-13/-20

SNOWFALL / RAINFALL		
PLACE	SNOW	PRECIPITATION
	INCHES	INCHES
Aspen	138	19.4
Denver	60	15.3
Estes Park	37	13.8
Grand Junction	26	8.0
Lamar	26	14.4
Mesa Verde	80	17.4
Pikes Peak	553	29.7

■ ABOUT COLORADO LODGING

In Colorado, you will never be too far from basic accommodations. Towns along every interstate and major highway, or near ski resorts or any sort of tourist attraction house your standard string of Best Westerns, stands of condos, or hotel chains in addition to mom-and-pop operations. Therefore, what follows is a select listing of the more interesting, historic, or unique hostelries scattered throughout the state. *(Also see "Guest Ranches," on page 294.)*

Hotel & Motel Chains

Best Western. (800) 528-1234

Days Inn. (800) 329-7466

Doubletree. (800) 222-8733

Hilton Hotels. (800) 445-8667

Hyatt Hotels & Resorts. (800) 233-1234

ITT Sheraton. (800) 325-3535

La Quinta. (800) 531-5900

Loews Hotels. (800) 223-0888

Marriott Hotels. (800) 228-9290

Quality Inns. (800) 228-5151

Radisson. (800) 333-3333

Ramada Inn. (800) 272-6232

Renaissance Hotels (800) 468-3571

Westin Hotels. (800) 228-3000

■ ABOUT COLORADO RESTAURANTS

Wherever you venture in Colorado—high into the mountains to first-class ski resorts, off-the-beaten-path to the unspoiled little towns scattered around the Eastern Plains, through the fertile farm and ranch land of the Western Slope, or into burgeoning Front Range cities—you'll find ample opportunities to indulge your tastebuds at an endless selection of eateries.

While Colorado restaurants have long enjoyed a reputation for hearty, "mountain-style" cooking ("Rocky Mountain Oysters," anyone?), the past few years have brought a new vitality to Centennial State cuisine, thanks to an influx of high-caliber chefs and restaurateurs. Undaunted by short growing seasons and the challenge of importing hard-to-find ingredients, these culinary pioneers often go to great lengths to get the products they need for their dishes. (Federal Express is enjoying a booming business flying fresh seafood and other goodies in from around the world to appease foodies in areas like Aspen and Vail.) As a result, menus around the state are as likely to feature sophisticated dishes as they're to offer barbecued ribs slathered with sauce.

■ LODGING AND RESTAURANTS BY TOWN

Lodging rates, per person, double occupancy:
$ = up to $50; $$ = $50 to $100; $$$ = $100 to $150; $$$$ = over $150

Restaurant prices, per person, excluding drinks, tax, tips:
$ = less than $10; $$ = $10 to $20; $$$ = over $20

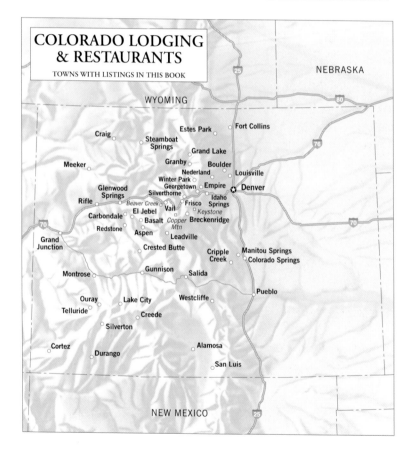

COLORADO LODGING & RESTAURANTS

TOWNS WITH LISTINGS IN THIS BOOK

ALAMOSA
(SOUTHERN)

The Cottonwood Inn. 123 San Juan Ave.; (719) 589-3882 **$$**
Turn-of-the-century antiques and regional artwork make this a bed-and-breakfast browser's delight.

Oscar's. 710 Main St.; (719) 589-9230 **$**
Mexican pottery, paintings, and vigas create a festive setting in which to enjoy heaping plates of chile rellenos, pork grilled with chiles, and "giant" chalupas. The margaritas can be potent.

True Grits Steakhouse. Junction of Hwy. 17 and Hwy. 160; (719) 589-9954 **$$**
Cozy up to a T-bone, sirloin, or New York strip in this rustic eatery and you'll know the wild west is alive and well. Colorado-grown potatoes and homemade sunflower bread are favorites, too.

ASPEN
(ROCKY MOUNTAINS)

Aspen Club Lodge. 709 E. Durant Ave.; (970) 925-6760 **$$$$**
Aspen Club affords a European flavor with down comforters, French doors, and rich, dark colors throughout. Nestled at the base of Aspen Mountain.

Aspen Meadows. 845 Meadows Rd., (970) 925-4240 **$$$$**
Conveniently located next to the music tent and Aspen Institute campus.

Boomerang Lodge. 500 W. Hopkins St.; (970) 925-3416 **$$$**
Small, downtown lodge where the accommodations range from motel-style to southwestern deluxe.

Hearthstone House. 134 E. Hyman Ave.; (970) 925-7632 **$$$$**
For over 30 years regulars have returned to this European-style, 22-room inn, drawn by its warmth, excellent service, and afternoon tea. New owners plan to continue traditions with a few changes.

Hotel Jerome. 330 E. Main St., (970) 920-1000 **$$$$**
An 1889 jewel built during the Aspen silver boom. Each of the 44 spacious rooms are individually decorated with delicate Victorian touches and period furnishings.

The Little Nell. 675 E. Durant Ave.; (970) 920-4600 **$$$$**
Among the grandest of Aspen's luxury accommodations. Every room, uniquely decorated, has marble baths, gas fireplaces, and views of either the town or the mountain. Ski-in, ski-out service, fine restaurant.

Little Red Ski Hause. 118 E. Cooper Ave.; (970) 925-3333 summer: **$**; winter: **$$**
Two blocks from Aspen Mountain. Comparable in decor and decorum to an 1890s' dorm, with 20 rooms, some with private baths. Breakfast is included, and occasionally other meals are offered at a reasonable cost. A good place to meet people if you are vacationing alone.

⊞ ITT Sheraton Luxury Collection.
315 E. Dean St.; (970) 920-3300/
(888) 454-9005 $$$$
Maintaining the former Ritz's signature splendor, the Sheraton embraces a more casual lodge flavor. There are plenty of inviting places to sit and unwind in the lobby, including by the large stone fireplace. Antique grandfather clocks and a magnificent art collection also grace the lobby while the guest rooms feature marble bathrooms and cherrywood furnishings.

SARDY HOUSE HOTEL

⊞ Sardy House. 128 E. Main St.; (970) 920-2525 $$$$
Housed in a red-brick Victorian mansion, this small hotel pampers guests with its whirlpool tubs, terry-cloth robes, cherrywood beds, and candlelit dinners.

⊞ Snowmass Lodge and Club.
0239 Snowmass Club Circle;
(970) 923-5600 $$$$
Elegant rooms and health club in an exquisite setting in Snowmass Village.

✗ Ajax Tavern. 685 E. Durant Ave. at base of gondola; (970)920-9333 $$

An offshoot of Napa Valley's famed Tra Vigne and Mustards Grill, this upscale bistro features California and Mediterranean-influenced dishes. Slide in for a micro-brew or martini on the patio.

✗ Baang Cafe & Bar. 325 E. Main St.; (970) 925-9969 $$
Colorful, geometric decor with copper accents is the knockout backdrop for flavorful "east meets west" (Baang means to tie or bind together in Chinese) cuisine. Nibble on an assortment of appetizers, or go for broke with entrees such as charred rare tuna in a tomato-wasabi vinaigrette — all served family-style.

✗ Campo de Fiori. 205 S. Mill St.; (970) 920-7717 $$$
Innovative Tuscan and Venetian cuisine in a tiny, buzzing room. Outdoor seating in the summer relieves the crowding.

✗ Cowboys Restaurant & Bar. Next to the Silvertree Hotel in Snowmass Village; (970) 923-5249 $$
Dine on "elegant food of the west," including wild game, seafood, and vegetarian specialties. Dance to live music.

✗ Crystal Palace Theatre Restaurant.
Downtown at 300 E. Hyman Ave.;
(970) 925-1455 $$$
The meal is safe, traditional fare, but the servers are talented performers who present a topical review after serving your coffee.

✗ Explore Bistro. 221 E. Main St.; (970) 925-5338 $$
An Old World bistro featuring gourmet

vegetarian fare all day long, located inside and atop the Explore Bookstore.

✗ **Farfalla Trattoria.** 415 E. Main St.; (970) 925-8222 $–$$
Authentic northern and southern Italian cuisine, includes pasta dishes, gourmet entrees and salads, thin-crusted pizza and calzones from the pizza bar; excellent service with an Italian-European smile.

✗ **Flying Dog Brew Pub.** 424 E. Cooper St. (downstairs); (970) 925-7464 $$–$$$
Aspen's only brew-pub pairs porters, stouts, ambers and seasonal beers made on the premises with everything from spicy achiote chicken wings to Rocky Mountain trout.

✗ **Kenichi.** 533 E. Hopkins Ave.; (970) 920-2212 $$$
Top-notch sushi (fish is flown in daily from around the world) and creative, Japanese dishes with Asian influences make this an Aspen hot-spot. The private Tatami room is great for parties.

✗ **Krabloonik.** 1 mile from Snowmass Village on the Divide Rd.; (970) 923-3953 $$$
Expertly prepared game dishes are the draw at this unique restaurant tucked into an historic log building with big views. Also a working kennel, the restaurant offers dog sled rides through the Snowmass wilderness with lunch during the winter. Open winter and summer.

✗ **La Cocina.** 308 E. Hopkins Ave.; (970) 925-9714 $$
A local favorite. Snag a seat at the bar for margaritas with a side of bean dip and guacamole, or put your name in for a seat inside (or on the patio in summer) and plates of blue corn enchiladas and posole.

✗ **L'Hostaria.** 620 E. Hyman Ave.; (970) 925-9022 $$$
A casual place with simple, traditional Italian dishes and a carpaccio bar serving over 30 specialties. Try the bar menu for a lighter, less expensive meal that's equally delicious.

✗ **Little Ollies.** 308 S. Hunter St.; (970) 544-9888 $–$$
Mandarin, Cantonese, Shanghai, Szechuan Chinese food, serving locals and tourists all year round.

✗ **Piñons.** 105 S. Mill St., 2nd fl.; (970) 920-2021 $$$
A "must-do" for anyone aspiring to see and be seen. Or anyone interested in fine cuisine with Colorado touches such as grilled rack of lamb with roasted ratatouille and pheasant breast with foie gras. Exceptional wine list.

✗ **Renaissance.** 304 E. Hopkins Ave.; (970) 925-2402 $$$
Owner-chef Charles Dale, *Food & Wine Magazine's* Best New Chef in 1995, serves modern French cuisine in an elegant, silk-draped setting. Try the tasting menu. Bistro upstairs serves lighter "global" dishes

✗ **The Restaurant at The Little Nell.** 675 East Durant Ave.; (970) 920-6330 $$$
Understated elegance reigns at this sophisticated restaurant where fine American

Alpine cuisine is served within steps of Aspen mountain. Excellent wine list.

✗ **Syzygy.** 520 E. Hyman Ave.; (970) 925-3700 $$$
Contemporary American cuisine with European and Asian influences, a 400-bottle wine list, and after-hour jazz fit the bill at this long-time Aspen Favorite. Book a table near the glass-enclosed waterfall.

✗ **Takah Sushi.** 420 E. Hyman Ave.; (970) 925-8588 $–$$$
First sushi restaurant in town and still there because the locals love it.

✗ **Ute City Bar & Grill.** In the Ute City Building at Hyman and Galena; (970) 920-4699 $$
Housed in a newly renovated rendition of one of Aspen's most historic buildings, the Ute offers everything from fine dining to a unique bar menu.

✗ **Wienerstube.** 633 E. Hyman Ave.; (970) 925-3357 $–$$$
Old World European decor, charm, and food have made this Austrian restaurant a favorite with locals and visitors. Open for breakfast and lunch.

✗ **Woody Creek Tavern.** About three miles before the Snowmass Ski Area off Highway 82 in the Woody Creek Trailer Park; (970) 923-4585 $
Hunter S. Thompson's well-known hangout is the closest thing Aspen has to a neighborhood tavern. This rustic eatery specializes in limousin burgers, thick steaks, and great Mexican dishes.

BASALT
(ROCKY MOUNTAINS)

✗ **Bistro Basalt.** 202 Midland Ave.; (970) 927-2682 $$
A 100-year old red brick building is home to contemporary cuisine with a French flair. Tops for gourmet pizzas and wines by the glass at the granite bar.

✗ **Cafe Bernard.** 200 Midland Ave.; (970) 927-4292 $–$$
A family-owned neighborhood spot "where cowboys eat croissants." Gourmet breakfasts, lunche,s and dinners are presented at eight tables in the tiny, pink-walled space.

✗ **The Rainbow Grill.** 181 Basalt Center Circle; (970) 927-8507 $$
Smack on the banks of the Frying Pan River, this casual eatery serves up hearty, home-style cooking and baked goods, plus 125 different flavors of bottled beer at the sprawling "bear bar."

BOULDER
(FRONT RANGE)

☷ **The Alps Boulder Inn.** 38619 Boulder Canyon Dr.; (303) 444-5445 $$
This restored log cabin tucked into Boulder Canyon served as a stagecoach stop in the 1800s. The innkeepers have preserved the original entryway but have turned the rest of the building into one of the loveliest and coziest bed-and-breakfasts in Boulder.

☷ **Boulder Mountain Lodge.** 91 Four Mile Canyon Dr.; (303) 444-0882 $$
Offers some kitchens and efficiency units; located in Four Mile Canyon.

⌸ Briar Rose Bed and Breakfast. 2151 Arapahoe Ave.; (303) 442-3007 $$-$$$
A quaint, antique-filled inn surrounded by flower gardens. Breakfast consists of homemade breads, croissants, fresh fruit, and granola.

⌸ Goldminer Bed and Breakfast. 601 Klondike Ave. in Eldora; (303) 258-0226/ (800) 422-4629 $-$$
Occupying one of the few original buildings in the old mining town of Eldora, west of Boulder; offers solitude, plenty of outdoor activities, and comfortable rooms.

HOTEL BOULDERADO

⌸ Hotel Boulderado. Near the Mall at 2115 13th St.; (303) 442-4344 $$-$$$
Cherrywood trimmings, stained glass, and other Victorian touches make this 1908 veteran a favorite. The ghost on the fifth floor is pretty harmless, as ghosts of murdered guests go.

⌸ Super 8 Motel. 970 28th St.; (303) 443-7800 $-$$

Standard motel conveniently located opposite the Colorado University campus.

✕ Attusso's of Brooklyn. 1739 Pearl St.; (303) 442-2262 $$
Stop in for a taste of "New York Italian" cuisine, much of which is from recipes passed down through the Impostato family for generations.

✕ Boulder Harvest Restaurant & Bakery. 1738 Pearl St.; (303) 449-6223 $
Specializing in natural, healthy meals and baked goodies that taste sinful.

✕ Daily Bread 1738 Pearl St.; (303) 444-6549 $
Whoever said you can't live by bread alone never made it to this popular local bakery for crusty, hearth-baked breads such as sundried tomato fougasse. Coffee bar and sandwiches, too.

✕ Dandelion. 1011 Walnut St.; (303) 443-6700 $$
Noted chef Kevin Taylor combines international flavors and ingredients in the dishes he serves at this contemporary restaurant with views of the Flatirons.

✕ Dot's Diner. 799 Pearl St.; (303) 449-1323 $
Breakfast and lunch fans groove on the authentic red-eye gravy and grits at this friendly diner located just off the mall.

✕ 15°. 1965 15th St.; (303) 442-4222 $$
From grilled New Zealand venison to halibut with roasted eggplant and garlic puree, 15 Degrees doesn't fail to please. Part of the

new style of Boulder eateries, with an inviting bar and live jazz piano.

✕ **Flagstaff House.** West on Baseline up Flagstaff Mountain, 1138 Flagstaff Rd.; (303) 442-4640 $$$
Perched above the city, the attractive candlelit dining room offers lovely views of Boulder and an eclectic, New American menu. Award-winning wine cellar.

✕ **Full Moon Grill.** 2525 Arapahoe Ave. (in the Village Shopping Center); (303) 938-8800 $$
Northern Italian dishes are prepared with a light touch. The decor follows through. Nice by-the-glass wine list.

✕ **Oasis Brewery.** 11th and Canyon; (303) 449-0363 $–$$
Boulder's largest brewpub bar, featuring five flavors of house-brewed beer on tap. Catch a game on TV, or stop in for Sunday brunch.

✕ **Pasta Jays.** 1701 Pearl St.; (303) 444-5800 $
Piled-high plates of pasta and a variety of pizzas are served up by a friendly staff at this sidewalk café on the Mall.

✕ **Rio Grande.** 1101 Walnut St.; (303) 444-3690 $$
The hot spot for contemporary Mexican food and deadly margaritas (diners are limited to three per evening).

✕ **Siamese Plate.** 1575 Folsom St.; (303) 447-9718 $–$$$
Thai specialities, vegetarian delights, and

sushi, all rolled up in one spot.

✕ **Sink.** 1165 13th St.; (303) 444-7465 $–$$
A legendary CU watering hole that has wetted the whistles and withstood generations of undergrads. Features a full bar, live music, pizza and burgers, and munchies.

✕ **Trio's** 1155 Canyon Blvd; (303) 442-8400 $$
Soothing decor and white linen-topped tables create the perfect setting for contemporary cuisine inspired by the seasons. Over 175 different wines. Lunch, dinner, Sunday brunch.

✕ **Zolo Grill.** 2525 Arapahoe (in the Village Shopping Center); (303) 449-0444 $$
Don't let the location fool you. Once you're inside this Southwestern-style bar and grill, you're in for a treat. We dare you to try the rattlesnake, bean and wild rice cakes. Tamer tastes, too.

BRECKENRIDGE
(ROCKY MOUNTAINS)

⌂ **Beaver Run Resort.** 620 Village Rd.; (970) 453-6000 summer: $$; winter: $$–$$$$
A sprawling complex featuring a variety of hotel rooms and condos that let you ski in and ski out onto Peak 9. Also offers a restaurant, bar, deli, and has conference facilities.

⌂ **Evans House.** 102 S. French St.; (970) 453-5509 $$

A historic operation in the heart of Breckenridge's historic district.

🛏 **Fireside Inn.** In town at 114 N. French St.; (970) 453-6456
summer: $–$$; winter: $–$$$
An original Victorian that has been expanded to offer a bed-and-breakfast experience ranging from full-blown elegant to basic dorm style.

🛏 **The Village at Breckenridge.**
605 S. Park Rd.; (970) 453-2000
summer: $$–$$$; winter: $$$$
A sprawling modern operation that provides a choice of hotel rooms and three types of condos. Located at the base of Peak 9.

🛏 **River Mountain Lodge.** 100 S. Park St.; (970) 453-4711 $–$$$
Condo-style accommodations with a kitchen in each unit and a common sauna and whirlpool for tired skiers.

✕ **Blue River Bistro.** 304 S. Main St.; (970) 453-6974 $$
Locals and visitors alike pack in for steaming plates of pasta (tortellini, ravioli, linguini, fettuccine), plus chicken, veal and casserole specialties. Great bar in the back.

✕ **Breckenridge Brew Pub.**
600 S. Main St.; (970) 453-1550 $
A variety of freshly brewed beers and a wonderful root beer. The lunch menu offers tasty burgers, sandwiches, vegetarian burritos, soups, and salads. Nightly specials include elk medallions and meatloaf.

✕ **Cafe Alpine.** 106 E. Adams Ave.; (970) 453-8218 $$$
Continental cuisine served up in a historic 1885 home. Full menu, or sample "little meals" at the tapas bar.

✕ **The Dredge Boathouse & Restaurant**
180 W. Jefferson Ave.; (970) 453-4877
$–$$
A replica of the gold dredge of yesteryear, this is one ton of floating restaurant and bar in the middle of the Blue River.

✕ **Hearthstone.** 130 South Ridge; (970) 453-1148 $$$
Step back in time at this Victorian-style restaurant set in a 100-year old Victorian home. Regional specialties include rack of elk and Rocky Mountain trout.

✕ **Horseshoe II Restaurant.** 115 S. Main St.; (970) 453-7463 $–$$
Upscale American food for breakfast, lunch, and dinner served in a restored nineteenth-century barroom.

✕ **St. Bernard Inn.** 103 S. Main St.; (970) 453-2572 $$
Home of the Julius Caesar Lounge, this cozy spot features Northern Italian dishes and homemade pasta, bread, and desserts.

✕ **Top of the World.** 112 Overlook Dr. in the Lodge at Breckenridge; (970) 453-9300 $$
Exceptional views compete for attention with gourmet dishes such as oven-roasted venison and Pacific swordfish filet.

CARBONDALE
(ROCKY MOUNTAINS)

✗ **Jose Penas.** In the Sopris Village Shopping Center; (970) 963-5866 $
Inspired by the coastal restaurants of Mexico, this colorful spot is highly regarded for its delicious (and spicy) seafood dishes, including fresh oysters. Traditional Mexican fare, too.

✗ **Sezen Restaurant.** In the Sopris Shopping Center; (970) 963-2385 $–$$
15 different sushi rolls and authentic Asian cuisine rule at this busy Japanese hot spot.

✗ **Village Smithy.** 26 S. Third St.; (970) 963-9990 $
The local favorite for fast, filling breakfast and lunch, served in a comfortably remodeled old home with patio seating in the summer.

COLORADO SPRINGS
(FRONT RANGE)

🗊 **The Antlers Doubletree Inn.** The corner of Pikes Peak and Cascade Blvds.; (719) 473-5600 $$–$$$
A classy, refined, full-service hostelry in the heart of town at the Palmer Center.

🗊 **Broadmoor Hotel.** Southwest of town at 1 Lake Ave.; (719) 634-7711; (800) 634-7711 summer: $$$$; winter: $$$
Opened in 1918, the Broadmoor is a mega-resort complex catering to every visitor's whim, from golf to swimming to ice skating.

🗊 **El Colorado Lodge.** 23 Manitou Ave., Manitou Springs; (719) 685-5485 $
Southwestern-style cabins include kitchenettes, fireplaces, and beamed ceilings. Cabins vary in size and can accommodate from two to six guests.

🗊 **Gray's Avenue Hotel.** 711 Manitou Ave., Manitou Springs; (719) 685-1277 $
One of the original hotels in Manitou Springs, this Victorian-style B&B is clean and comfortable and has great views.

🗊 **Hearthstone Inn.** 506 N. Cascade Ave.; (719) 473-4413/ (800) 521-1885 $$
Two Victorian houses comprise this charming bed-and-breakfast, listed on the National Register of Historic Places. The guest rooms are decorated with furnishings from the 1880s and old photographs. Gourmet breakfast included.

🗊 **Town-n-Country Cottages.** 123 Crystal Park Rd., Manitou Springs; (719) 685-5427 $$
Large rooms nicely designed to accommodate families. Close to Garden of the Gods.

BROADMOOR HOTEL

✕ **Broadmoor Hotel.** Southwest of town off Interstate 25 to Highway 122, 1 Lake Ave.; (719) 634-7711/ (800) 634-7711 $–$$$

The eight restaurants at the Broadmoor provide a day-long choice of settings and food ranging from an English pub to elegant gourmet dining (ties and dresses, please) to international cuisine.

✕ **County Line Restaurant.** 3350 N. Chestnut Ave.; (719) 578-1940 $$

Barbecue is the big draw but the steaks and seafood are equally delicious.

✕ **Edelweiss Restaurant.** 34 E. Ramona Ave.; (719) 633-2220 $$

As the name implies, Old World German and continental fare, in an authentic Bavarian-style setting.

✕ **Giuseppe's Old Depot.** Downtown at 10 S. Sierra Madre; (719) 635-3111 $–$$

Housed in a renovated train station, Giuseppe's pleases train fans and Italian-food fanatics with its fascinating photos of vintage trains and variety of pasta dishes and stone-baked pizzas. Steaks and prime rib are also on the menu.

✕ **Judge Baldwin's Brewing Company.** Antlers Hotel, Pikes Peak and Cascade; (719) 473-5600 $

Freshly brewed beer and a selection of soups, sandwiches, and salads for lunch and dinner.

✕ **The Mason Jar.** 2925 W. Colorado Ave.; (719) 632-4820 $

Home-style cooking, family atmosphere, and famous chicken-fried steak.

✕ **Phantom Canyon Brewing Co.** 2 E. Pikes Peak Ave. at Cascade Blvd.; (719) 635-2800 $$

Micro-brews and English food (fish & chips, shepherd's pie) doled out in a restored turn-of-the-century building with a great view.

COPPER MOUNTAIN
(ROCKY MOUNTAINS)

🛏 **Copper Mountain Resort.** I-70 exit 195; (970) 968-2882 $$$

Large, modern resort complex with all the amenities, right at the base of the slopes.

COPPER MOUNTAIN RESORT

CORTEZ
(SAN JUAN MOUNTAINS)

✕ **Francisca's.** 125 E. Main St.; (970) 565-4093 $–$$

Traditional Mexican food, family atmosphere, and sopaipillas to die for.

✗ **Homesteaders Restaurant.** 45 E. Main St.; (970) 565-6253 **$**
Casual, traditional American family fare served in a dining room that looks suspiciously barn-like.

CRAIG
(WESTERN SLOPE)

✗ **The Galaxy.** 524 Yampa Ave.; (970) 824-8164 **$**
Watch cowboys wield chopsticks on great Chinese lunches and dinners.

✗ **Signal Hill.** 2705 W. Victory Way; (970) 824-6682 **$$–$$$**
A family, restaurant featuring steaks and prime rib served in a rustic old ranch house.

CRESTED BUTTE
(SAN JUAN MOUNTAINS)

▦ **Claim Jumper.** 704 Whiterock; (970) 349-6471 **$$**
Brass beds and other nineteenth-century touches make this bed-and-gourmet-breakfast a blast from the past, while the hot tub and sauna let visitors pamper themselves and rest up for future ski runs.

▦ **Crested Butte Marriott Resort Hotel.** 500 Gothic Rd.; (970) 349-4000 **$$$$**
Every guest room in this enormous hotel includes a private balcony, wet bar, and Jacuzzi bath. The resort also offers an indoor swimming pool, two outdoor hot tubs, ski shop, and ice-skating rink on the premises.

▦ **Nordic Inn.** At the base of Mt. Crested Butte; (970) 349-5542 summer: **$**; winter: **$$$**
Cuddle up by the fireplace in the lobby for aprés-ski relaxing in this comfortable, modern inn.

✗ **Donita's Cantina.** At the corner of 4th and Elk; (970) 349-6674 **$$**
The scene is in the lively bar for chili con queso and perfect margaritas. Move into the dining room for traditional Mexican faves.

✗ **Gourmet Noodle.** 411 S. 3rd St.; (970) 349-7401 **$$**
Homemade pasta and Italian cuisine in a stylish old home. Closed in the off season.

✗ **Idlespurl/Crested Butte Brewery & Pub.** 226 Elk Ave.; (970) 349-5026 **$$**
There's chicken, ribs, and Mexican food to wash down the latest micro-brew.

✗ **The Slogar.** Second and Whiterock; (970) 349-5765 **$$**
"Miner's saloon design" is the setting for family-style dinners of skillet-fried chicken with all the fixings.

CRESTED BUTTE MARRIOTT RESORT

✕ **Soupçon.** 127A Elk Ave.; (970) 349-5448 $$$

Chef-owner Mac Bailey's innovative French cuisine is served in style in a charming —and tiny—log cabin. Very romantic.

✕ **Timberline.** 21 Elk Ave.; (970) 349-9831 $$$

This historic clapboard house at the end of the street is known for skillfully prepared and artfully presented New American Cuisine.

✕ **Wooden Nickel.** 222 Elk Ave.; (970) 349-6350 $–$$

Enjoy beers, burgers, prime rib, and shrimp around the big fireplace.

C R I P P L E   C R E E K
(R O C K Y   M O U N T A I N S)

⌾ **Imperial Casino Hotel.** 123 N. 3rd St.; (719) 689-2922 $

Golden charms remain via an outstanding collection of antiques that let you glimpse at the past while enjoying present-day services.

D E N V E R
(F R O N T   R A N G E)

⌾ **Brown Palace.** Near downtown at 321 17th St.; (303) 297-3111 $$$$

A triangular gem that hasn't lost its elegance since opening in 1892. Rooms ring a central atrium, and the shining brass and polished surroundings remind guests of golden and silver days. There are over 200 guest rooms at this grand old hotel (refurbished in 1995) and four restaurants including the well regarded, Palace Arms (see following page).

⌾ **Holiday Chalet.** 1820 E. Colfax Ave.; (303) 321-9975 $

Stained glass, chandeliers, and a general sense of coming to stay at your refined aunt's house make this one of the city's best bed-and-breakfast deals. Rooms are decorated with French and English antiques.

⌾ **Loews Giorgio Hotel.** 4150 E. Mississippi Ave.; (800) 345-9172 $$$$

Ultra-modern and dark on the outside, northern Italian on the inside (don't ask me), this is a complete upscale operation. Rooms are spacious and elegant.

BROWN PALACE

⌾ **Queen Anne Inn.** 2147 Tremont Pl.; (303) 296-6666 $$–$$$

This three-story home built in 1879 has ten

rooms with various decors. Downtown location; afternoon tea and wine.

QUEEN ANNE INN

☎ **Victoria Oaks.** 1575 Race St.; (303) 355-1818 **$$**
This Victorian-style residence offers nine rooms, some with shared baths. Free breakfast, as well as afternoon tea.

✕**Aubergine Cafe.** 225 E. 7th Ave.; (303) 832-4778 **$$**
This intimate (15 tables) restaurant is the kind of place you'll come back to again and again for Provencal/Mediterranean dishes such as crispy fried artichokes with aioli and mussel stew.

✕ **Barolo Grill** 3030 E. 6th Ave.; (303) 393-1040 **$$$**
A warm, attractive trattoria in the style of Northern Italy. Many dishes, such as duckling in Barolo sauce, are prepared with a touch of wine. A 500-bottle list.

✕ **Breckenridge Brewery.** 2220 Blake St.; (303) 297-3644 **$**
Freshly brewed beer, barbeque and classic pub fare, within walking distance of Coors Field.

✕ **Buckhorn Exchange.** 1000 Osage St.; (303) 534-9505 **$$–$$$**
Specializes in wild game and exotic meat dishes—elk, deer, pheasant, alligator, and more.

✕ **Champion Brewing Company.** 1442 Larimer Square; (303) 534-5444**$**
A micro-brewery that also offers an innovative menu featuring grilled specialties and regional treats.

✕ **Cliff Young's.** 700 E. 17th Ave.; (303) 831-8900 **$$$**
Five-star, gourmet dining in an elegant setting. Extensive wine cellar. Music nightly.

✕ **The Denver Chop House & Brewery.** 1735 19th St.; (303) 296-0800 **$$**
Fresh beer (you can check out the brewery in the back) and all-American dishes go a long way in this stylish LoDo hot spot.

✕ **El Chapultepec.** 1962 Market St.; (303) 295-9126 **$$**
A downtown mainstay, thanks to hot Mexican food and cool jazz every night.

✕ **Healthy Habits.** 865 S. Colorado Blvd.; (303) 733-2105 **$**
As the name implies, healthy food you can proudly offer to your vegetarian friends along with healthy food for meat eaters. Served buffet style.

✗ **Joe's Buffet.** 753 Santa Fe Dr.;
(303) 571-5637 **$**
Say "Buff-it" or you'll be tossed out immediately. Undecorated authentic Mexican food.

✗ **Little Ollies.** 303 3rd & Josephine,
Cherry Creek area; (303) 316-8888
$–$$
Asian cuisine: Mandarin, Cantonese, Shanghai, Szechuan Chinese food, Thai & Vietnamese.

✗ **Little Russian Café.** 1424-H Larimer
St.; (303) 595-8600 **$$**
Old-world flair and Russian fare such as beef stroganoff and stuffed cabbage.

✗ **The Market.** 1445 Larimer St.;
(303) 534-5140 **$**
A mix between a European-style coffee house and old general store, featuring flavored coffees, homemade pastries, sandwiches, and hot meals seved all day long, patio dining, and a store section where you can buy goodies in bulk.

✗ **McCormick's Fish House & Bar.** 1659
Wazee; (303) 825-1107 **$$$**
This classic establishment pays homage to seafood, with over 30 fresh items and a menu that changes daily.

✗ **Mel's Bar & Grill.** 235 Filmore St.;
(303) 333-3979 **$$$**
Don't let the casual name fool you, this is one of the Colorado's best restaurants, serving inspired modern American cuisine in a delightful setting.

✗ **Morton's of Chicago.** Across from the
train station, 1710 Wynkoop;
(303) 825-3353 **$$$**
Steaks, steaks, and more steaks is what this chain has staked its reputation on, and it's worked for years. The best in town, say many.

✗ **My Brother's Bar.** 2376 15th St.;
(303) 455-9991 **$**
Burgers, Beethoven, and great lunches attract everyone from construction workers to bank presidents to this comfortable joint.

✗ **Palace Arms Restaurant.** 321 17th St.;
(303) 297-3111 **$$$**
In the historic Brown Palace Hotel, this richly decorated restaurant offers a deluxe dining experience. Coat and tie required.

✗ **Reese Coffee Shop.** 1435 Curtis St.;
(303) 534-4304 **$**
Breakfast, 24 hours a day, with lunch and dinner squeezed in, too.

✗ **Tante Louise Restaurant.** 4900
E. Colfax; (303) 355-4488 **$$$**
Mon.-Sat. dinners featuring contemporary American cuisine with innovative light sauces in restored turn-of-the-century bungalows.

✗ **Rock Bottom Brewery.** 1001 16th St.;
(303) 534-7616 **$–$$**
Outdoor cafe, walking distance from the Denver Performing Arts Complex. Great microbrews.

✕ **Tommy Tsunami's Pacific Diner.** 1432 Market St.; (303) 534-5050 $–$$$
Sushi bar where you can order a huge "boat of sushi", specializing in Pacific-Rim cuisine, award-winning interior; separate party rooms with shoji screens and tatami mats, around the corner from Larimer Square.

✕ **Wazee Supper Club.** 1600 15th St.; (303) 623-9518 $$
The best pizza downtown, served in a casual, fun-filled barroom atmosphere.

✕ **Wynkoop Brewing Company.** 1634 18th St.; (303) 297-2700 $$
A classic brew pub serving lunch, dinner, and Sunday buffet along with its variety of newly brewed brews. On the bottom of the three-story fun house is the **Comedy Sports**, featuring all manner of live performances. The top story is home to **Wynkoop Billiards**, offering over 20 tables and a deli.

DURANGO
(SAN JUAN MOUNTAINS)

🛏 **Country Sunshine Bed & Breakfast.** Thirteen miles north of Durango, 35130 Hwy. 550 N.; (970) 247-2853 $$
Intimate, friendly accommodations in a country setting.

🛏 **General Palmer Hotel.** 567 Main Ave.; (970) 247-4747 $$$
Charmingly restored Victorian hotel next door to the Durango & Silverton Narrrow Gauge Depot.

🛏 **Jarvis Suite Hotel.** In town at 125 W. 10th St.; (800) 824-1024, or (970) 259-6190 $$–$$$
A unique idea: converting a nineteenth-century theater into a set of suites and rooms complete with kitchens and baths and all sorts of combo rates that include either train tickets or lift tickets.

🛏 **Rochester Hotel.** 721 E. 2nd Ave.; (970) 385-1920 $$$
Built in 1892, this cowboy lover's getaway is devoted to Hollywood Westerns. Request the Butch Cassidy room.

STRATER HOTEL

🛏 **Strater Hotel.** 699 Main Ave.; (800) 247-4431 $$–$$$
A mixture of history and Victorian charm. Will Rogers, John F. Kennedy, and western writer Louis L'Amour have all tasted the Strater's charms. Honky-tonk piano pounds from the Diamond Belle Saloon and boos and hisses accompany the summertime melodramas in the Diamond Circle Theatre.

✗ **Bar D Chuckwagon Suppers.** 8080 County Road 250; (970) 247-5753 $$ Old West dinners served as if you were a wrangler on the range, includes Western entertainment. Reservations required.

✗ **Carver's Bakery & Brew Pub.** 1022 Main Ave.; (970) 259-2545 $ A locals' favorite. Don't miss the chicken stew served in a fresh-baked bread bowl—with a pint of ale from the on-site brewery.

✗ **Durango Diner.** 957 Main Ave.; (970) 247-9889 $ Basic breakfast, lunch, and locals chewing the fat and chowing down. Gotta love it.

✗ **Edgewater Grill.** 501 Camino del Rio; (970) 259-6580 $–$$ In the Doubletree Inn, on the banks of the Animas River, offering simple breakfast and lunch fare on the patio, more elaborate dinners and a Sunday brunch.

✗ **Gazpacho.** 431 E. Second Ave.; (970) 259-9494 $ A lively crowd gathers here for traditional New Mexican cooking (heavy on the green chiles), sensational sopaipillas, and great margaritas.

✗ **Griego's.** 2603 N. Main Ave.; (970) 259-3558 $ Get ready for this: a drive-in Mexican restaurant in an old A&W with good food and sweat-producing green chile.

✗ **Henry's at the Strater Hotel.** 699 Main St.; (970) 247-4431 $–$$ Breakfast, lunch, and dinner are served in this historic hotel dining room. Henry's also hosts an elegant Sunday brunch and a summertime all-you-can-eat prime rib buffet.

✗ **Mr. Rosewater's Delicatessen.** 552 Main St.; (970) 247-8788 $ Healthy deli fare and quick carry out.

✗ **Steamworks Brewing Co.** 801 E. Second Ave.; (970) 259-9200 $-$$ Southwestern cuisine and homemade pizza with plenty of beer to wash it down. The brewing operation is visible in the large, warehouse-type building with hip industrial decor.

EL JEBEL
(ROCKY MOUNTAINS)

✗ **Blue Creek Grill.** 68 El Jebel Rd; (970) 963-3946 $$ Pull open the door by the over-sized fork handle and enter a world of home-style cooking that runs the gamut from duck and sausage gumbo to cornmeal-crusted trout.

✗ **Breakfast In America.** 19125 Hwy. 82 (970) 963-2739 $ Breakfast served 'til mid-afternoon. Grab a stool at the u-shaped counter and watch the show while you wait for your biscuits 'n gravy or huevos rancheros. Starbucks coffee, too.

EMPIRE
(FRONT RANGE)

Mad Creek B&B. 167 Park Ave., off Hwy. 40, two miles from I-70 exit 232 to Winter Park; (303) 569-2003 $
This small Victorian inn is a perfect place to escape to. In addition to comfortable rooms and great meals, mountain bikes or cross-country skis are part of the deal.

ESTES PARK
(ROCKY MOUNTAINS)

Aspen Lodge. Eight miles south of Estes Park, at 6120 on Hwy. 7; (970) 586-8133 $$$
A real "family resort" that offers several family reunion packages.

Romantic Riversong Bed and Breakfast. Box 1910; (970) 586-4666 $$–$$$
This elegant and romantic inn is furnished with antiques; bedrooms have fireplaces, and even sunken bathtubs in some cases.

STANLEY HOTEL

Stanley Hotel. 333 Wonderview Ave.; (970) 586-3371 $$
Located on a hill above town, this charming hotel was built by F. O. Stanley, co-inventor of the Stanley Steamer, and opened in 1909. The sprawling, sparkling white, and renovated Stanley of today hosts a summer theater program and other musical events to go with the scenery.

Telemark Resort. Hwy. 36; (970) 586-4343 $–$$
Seventeen rustic cabins with screened-in porches and fireplaces, located just west of the Estes Park and bordering the Big Thompson River.

Whispering Pines Cottages. 2646 Big Thompson; (970) 586-5258 $–$$
Fifteen cottages located among the pines along the Big Thompson River. You might even hook a trout from your patio.

FORT COLLINS
(EASTERN PLAINS)

Edwards House Bed & Breakfast. 402 W. Mountain Ave.; (970) 493-9191 $
A fashionable turn-of-the-century structure with a neo-classical twist.

CooperSmith's Pub & Brewing. 5 Old Town; (970) 498-0483 $
One of the Colorado's original brew pubs. The fare is excellent—they even put their brews in some of the dinner entrees. Blackboard specialties change daily. Try the homemade root beer, ginger ale, or cream soda.

Lone Star Steakhouse & Saloon. 100 W. Troutman Pkwy.; (970) 225-6284 $$

Mesquite grilled delights and atmosphere remind you of a Texas roadhouse.

✗ **Nico's Catacombs.** 115 S. College Ave.; (970) 482-6426 **$$$**
Upscale American and Continental dinners and an extensive wine cellar in a refined, softly lit setting.

✗ **Silver Grill Café.** 218 Walnut St.; (970) 484-4656 **$**
Locals' hangout for breakfast and lunch. Are the cinnamon rolls good? Well, they crank out 8,000 a month and have a cinnamon roll award on the wall.

FRISCO
(FRONT RANGE)

✗ **Butterhorn Bakery & Deli.** 408 Main St.; (970) 668-3997 **$**
An airy enclave featuring gourmet coffee and organic baked goods for breakfast and lunch.

✗ **Claimjumper Restaurant.** Frisco Plaza Center; (970) 668-3617 **$$**
Casual Amerian fare. Hickory smoked dinners are the house specialties.

✗ **El Rio.** 450 W. Main St.; (970) 668-5043 **$–$$**
Solid Mexican food in a festive setting on the river's edge.

✗ **Golden Annie's.** 603 Main St.; (970) 668-0345 **$–$$**
Fine fajitas, barbecue ribs, and fresh seafood make this the spot for aprés-ski dinner in the winter or patio lunches aprés boating on Dillon Reservoir in the summer.

✗ **Moose Jaw.** 208 Main St.; (970) 668-3931 **$**
The local hangout for playing pool, chowing down on giant hamburgers and fries, along with the usual assortment of saloon eats.

GEORGETOWN
(FRONT RANGE)

⌂ **Hardy House.** 605 Brownell St.; (800) 490-4802 **$–$$**
A Victorian bed-and-breakfast complete with a parlor and wood-burning stove and comfortable antique furnishings. Full, candle-lit breakfasts served are just one of the charming details.

HARDY HOUSE

✗ **The Red Ram Bar and Restaurant.** 606 6th St.; (303) 569-2300 **$–$$**
The Red Ram is a cozy establishment that hasn't been restored to the point of losing its Victorian character, serving burgers, fajitas, ribs.

GLENWOOD SPRINGS
(ROCKY MOUNTAINS)

☲ **Hotel Colorado.** 526 Pine St.; (970) 945-6511 **$$**

Opened in 1893 just across the street from the famous hot springs pool and fashioned after a Medici palace, this recently renovated hotel has hosted presidents, gangsters, and socialites who've come to "take the waters."

HOTEL COLORADO

☲ **Hot Springs Lodge.** 415 E. 6th St.; (970) 945-7428 **$$**

Next to the Hotel Colorado, this modern lodge has tapped into the nearby hot springs to become one of the world's largest geothermally heated buildings.

HOT SPRINGS LODGE

☲ **Riverside Cottages.** On Old Hwy. 82 south of Glenwood Springs; (970) 945-5509 **$$–$$$**

Against the banks of the Roaring Fork River, just two miles from the hot springs. These kitchen-equipped cottages are several shapes and sizes and are sprinkled over four acres of well-kept grounds.

✕ **Bayou.** 52103 US 6 in West Glenwood; (970) 945-1047 **$$**

Funhouse Cajun dinners (motto: Food So Good You'll Slap Yo Mamma); ask for "The Abuse Room" in winter, the patio in summer.

✕ **Daily Bread Bakery/Café.** Downtown at 729 Grand Ave.; (970) 945-6253 **$**

Offering breakfast/lunch and all-natural homemade baked goods made fresh daily.

✕ **Florindo's Fine Italian Cuisine.** 721 Grand Ave.; (970) 945-1245 **$–$$**

Real Italian food prepared by real Italian owners who really came out West from New York. Everything, from the pasta to the veal, is saucy and scrumptious. Dinners nightly and lunch during the week.

✕ **Restaurant Sopris.** About seven miles south of Glenwood on Hwy. 82; (970) 945-7771 **$$–$$$**

Consistently good continental cuisine —veal, seafood, and wienerschnitzel—in a spacious, gracious dining room.

GRAND JUNCTION
(WESTERN SLOPE)

☲ **The Orchard House.** About 20 minutes from Grand Junction on the mesa four

miles south of Palisade at 3573½ East Rd.; (970) 464-0529 $
Hit at harvest time and you can pick fruit from the orchard alongside this pleasant bed-and-breakfast.

✕ **Enstrom Candies.** 200 S. 7th St.; (970) 242-1655.
A local operation famous for its Almond Toffees, which are sold everywhere in town.

✕ **Far East.** 1530 North Ave.; (970) 242-8131 $–$$
Authentic Cantonese, Szechuan, and Mandarin dishes for lunch and dinner served in a palatial setting.

✕ **G. B. Gladstones.** Between town and the airport, corner of 12th St. and Patterson Dr.; (970) 241-6000 $–$$
Good American lunch and dinner in a lively, fern-filled dining room.

✕ **Good Pastures.** 753 Horizon Ct.; (970) 243-3058 $–$$
Healthy food that tastes good for breakfast, lunch, or dinner. By the airport.

✕ **W. W. Peppers.** 753 Horizon Ct.; (970) 245-9251 $$
Distinctive Southwestern cuisine.

G R A N D   L A K E
(R O C K Y   M O U N T A I N S)

🛏 **Grand Lake Lodge.** 15500 US Hwy. 34; (970) 627-3967 in summer
(303) 759-5848 in winter (closed) $
Built in 1925 of lodgepole pine, this lodge boasts terrific views of Grand and Shadow

Mountain lakes. There are also 66 cabins, a swimming pool, and a restaurant. Open summers only.

GRAND LAKE LODGE

🛏 **Lemmon Lodge.** Box 514; (970) 627-3314 in summer; (970) 725-3511 in winter $$–$$$
The five-bedroom lodge and 19 cabins (each sleeps four to ten) are situated on secluded banks of the lake itself. The lodge features a sandy beach, as well as a private dock for guests who bring their boats. Open summers only.

🛏 **Shadowcliff Lodge.** PO Box 658; (970) 627-9220 $
This quiet retreat has spectacular views, and each bedroom in the 12- and seven-room lodges offers one double bed and two bunk beds, although baths are shared. Perfect for large groups. Open summers only.

G U N N I S O N
(S A N   J U A N   M O U N T A I N S)

🛏 **Mary Lawrence Inn.** 601 N. Taylor St.; (970) 641-3343 $$
A two-story Victorian home stylishly converted into a comfortable B&B.

✗ **Cattleman Inn.** 301 W. Tomichi Ave.; (970) 641-1061 $–$$
The two restaurants in the inn serve breakfast, lunch, and dinner. Steaks and prime rib are the big draws but the menu also includes seafood, burritos, soup, and a salad bar.

✗ **Mario's Pizza.** 213 W. Tomichi Ave.; (970) 641-1374 $–$$
The pizzas here have kept generations of college students alive.

IDAHO SPRINGS
(FRONT RANGE)

☷ **Indian Springs Resort.** 302 Soda Creek Rd.; (303) 989-6666 $
South of town, this nineteenth-century resort is still thriving and offers a mineral pool, vapor tunnel, and solitude to bask in.

✗ **Beau Jo's.** 1517 Miner St.; (303) 573-6924 $–$$
Could just be the best pizza joint in the state, featuring five types of crusts and countless toppings. You can order one-, two-, and five-pound pizzas.

✗ **Buffalo Bar & Restaurant.** 1617 Miner St; (303) 567-2729 $
Heaping bowls of chili, buffalo burgers, and homemade potato chips are worth a stop, especially if you eat them at the hulking old bar.

KEYSTONE
(ROCKY MOUNTAINS)

☷ **Keystone Lodge.** (970) 468-2316 $$$$
Right at the base of the Keystone ski area, this luxurious resort affords mountain views from every guest room. Heated indoor–outdoor pool, sauna, whirlpool.

✗ **Alpenglow Stube.** Atop North Peak; (800) 354-4FUN $$$
North America's highest gourmet restaurant. Hop the Keystone gondola (and then another) for fine Bavarian-style cuisine in an elegant mountain setting.

ALPENGLOW STUBE

✗ **Keystone Ranch** Keystone Resort; (800) 354-4FUN $$$
Indulge in six-course gourmet dinners in this elegant mountain restaurant. Save room for the sumptuous soufflés, served by the fire in the living room.

✗ **Ski Tip Lodge** Keystone Resort; (800) 354-4FUN $$
Formerly an 1880s stagecoach stop, this lovely, rustic inn serves top-notch breakfasts and dinners.

LAKE CITY
(SAN JUAN MOUNTAINS)

✗ **Lake City Café & Bar.** At the corner of 3rd and Gunnison, just off town square; (970) 944-2733 $–$$

They like to joke about serving their fellow man, but offer the basics like fast breakfasts, burgers, pizza, and steaks.

LEADVILLE
(ROCKY MOUNTAINS)

🏨 **Delaware Hotel.** 700 Harrison Ave.; (719) 486-1418/(800) 748-2004 $–$$
A recently restored, 100-year-old building with unique Queen Anne masonry and French mansard design. Breakfast included.

DELAWARE HOTEL

✕ **The Grill.** 715 Elm St; (719) 486-9930 $
The favorites at this friendly Mexican restaurant include homemade tortillas, stuffed sopaipillas, and chicken and beef flautas.

LOUISVILLE
(FRONT RANGE)

✕ People come from Denver, Boulder, and Rome to eat the homemade Italian food at the two following restaurants:

The Blue Parrot Café. 640 Main St.; (303) 666-0677 $$

Colacci's. 816 Main St.; (303) 673-9400 $$

MANITOU SPRINGS
(FRONT RANGE)

✕ **Stagecoach Steak & Ale House.** 702 Manitou Ave.; (719) 685-9400 $$
Great steak and seafood in a rustic setting. Dine by the banks of Fountain Creek.

MEEKER
(WESTERN SLOPE)

🏨 **Meeker Hotel.** 560 Main St.; (970) 878-5255 $
The lobby displays the bounty of surrounding forests via the herd of heads mounted on the walls. Big-game animal heads, of course. You can stay in regular rooms, the suite Teddy Roosevelt occupied, or dorm-style rooms.

MEEKER HOTEL

✕ **Sleepy Cat Guest Ranch.** Open daily in summer, weekends in winter. (970) 878-4413 $$
Just 18 miles east of town, and worth the drive. A bar full of real cowboys, tables in cozy little rooms, lots of hunting trophies, and good beef, pork, and lamb.

MONTROSE
(WESTERN SLOPE)

✕ **Glen Eyrie.** 2351 S. Townsend Ave.;
(970) 249-9263 $$

Housed in a colonial farmhouse, this enchanting restaurant offers garden tables in the warmer seasons and tables by the fireplace year-round. Classic continental/ American cuisine and a delightful Sunday brunch.

NEDERLAND
(FRONT RANGE)

✕ **Pioneer Inn.** First St. (you can't miss it);
(303) 258-7733 $–$$

A mingling of old hippies, cowboys, and yuppies enjoying standard American fare for lunch and dinner in a rustic setting.

OURAY
(FRONT RANGE)

⌂ **Box Canyon Lodge and Hot Springs.**
45 3rd Ave.; (970) 325-4981 $

Soak in a hot tub filled with natural hot springs water while enjoying the view of Box Canyon.

⌂ **The St. Elmo Hotel.** 426 Main St.;
(970) 325-4951 summer: $$; winter: $

"Aunt" Kitty Heit built the St. Elmo in 1898 and rarely turned away a hungry miner from her adjoining restaurant, the Bon Ton. The St. Elmo was once bet and lost in a poker game; today it's a charming bed-and-breakfast, complete with a good-natured ghost who seems content to rattle dishes.

⌂ **Wiesbaden Hot Springs Spa and Lodgings.** At the corner of 6th and 5th;
(970) 325-4347 summer: $$$; winter: $$

Combine a vapor cave, hot springs pool, and massage with comfortable rooms and you have a great stress-reduction package.

✕ **Bon Ton Restaurant.** 426 Main St.;
(970) 325-4951 $$

Located in the historic St. Elmo Hotel, this historic restaurant serves northern Italian food in a colorful Victorian atmosphere.

✕ **The Outlaw.** 610 Main St.;
(970) 325-4366 $$

Steak and seafood are the order of the day, with an outdoor barbecue and lunch available in the summer. The Duke (John Wayne) left his hat here during the filming of *True Grit* so now everyone does.

✕ **Silver Nugget Café.** 746 Main St.;
(970) 325-4100 $

Belly up to the counter at this all-American café where unpretentious food, coffee, and conversation replace "atmosphere."

PUEBLO
(FRONT RANGE)

⌂ **Abriendo Inn.** 300 W. Abriendo Ave.;
(719) 544-2703 $$

Built by brewing magnate Martin Walter, this 1906 mansion is decorated with period antiques including four-poster beds and oak-wainscoted trimmings.

ABRIENDO INN

✕ **Gaetano's Restaurant.** 910 Hwy. 50 West; (719) 546-0949 $$
Italian food in a classy setting.

✕ **Gus' Restaurant.** 1201 Elm St.; (719) 542-0756 $
All-day Dutch lunch: they spread out the goodies, you grab as much as you can, including huge schooners of beer.

✕ **Ianne's Pizzeria.** 515 W. Northern Ave.; (719) 542-5942 $–$$
The "grinder" sandwich with hot peppers is a legend.

✕ **Nacho's.** 409 N. Santa Fe Dr.; (719) 544-0733 $
Authentic Mexican food. Mariachi bands on the weekends.

✕ **The Renaissance.** 217 E. Routt Ave.; (719) 543-6367 $$–$$$
This restored old church is now home to a classy restaurant offering an array of five-course American meals.

REDSTONE/MARBLE
(ROCKY MOUNTAINS)

⌂ **Redstone Castle.** Located one mile south of Redstone. 58 Redstone Blvd.; (970) 963-3463 $$–$$$
This huge, 42-room, lavishly appointed and decorated Victorian mansion (once the home of industrialist John Osgood) is now a bed-and-breakfast and available for special events.

REDSTONE CASTLE

⌂ **Redstone Inn.** 82 Redstone Blvd.; (970) 963-2526 $–$$
Built by industrialist John Osgood in the early 1900s as a dorm and recreation center for his coal miners, the inn is now a comfortably restored retreat and spa that can't be missed, thanks to its imposing clock tower.

✕ **Redstone Inn.** 82 Redstone Blvd.; (970) 963-2526 $–$$
Sunday buffet is the summer treat in this historic Tudor-style inn. The inn's Grille and Redstone Room are open all year.

SALIDA
(ROCKY MOUNTAINS)

✗ **Il Vicino Restaurant & Brewery.** 136 E. 2nd St.; (719) 539-5219 $-$$
Featuring homemade, wood-oven-baked pizza and fresh-brewed microbrews.

SAN LUIS
(SOUTHERN)

☷ **El Convento Bed and Breakfast.** 512 Church Place; (719) 672-4223 $
This adobe structure in the middle of town across from the Catholic church was first a school, then a convent, before its current incarnation as a bed-and-breakfast. Local artists work and sell their art here in the downstairs space.

SILVERTHORNE
(ROCKY MOUNTAINS)

✗ **Arapahoe Cafe & Pub.** 626 Lake Dillon Dr.; 970-468-0873 $$
Wrap your mouth around a "guacabaca-chezzaburgah" (if you can!).

✗ **The Historic Mint.** 347 Blue River Parkway; (970) 468-5247 $$
Pick your own prime cut of beef, chicken, or seafood, and cook it yourself at a "lava rock" table.

✗ **Sunshine Cafe.** Summit Place Shopping Center (right beside the Silverthorne exit off I-70); (970) 468-6663 $
Great bakery and a variety of healthy yet tasty food for breakfast, lunch, and dinner. Mom would be jealous of their homemade cookies.

SILVERTON
(SAN JUAN MOUNTAINS)

☷ **The Grand Imperial Hotel.** (970) 387-5527 $-$$
The vintage 1880s' cherry-wood back-bar made in London and shipped around Cape Horn is one of the hotel's many elegant Victorian touches. Built in 1882, the three-story hotel impressed Diamond Jim Brady and Lillian Russell and still shines today. It's the biggest building in town; you can't miss it.

✗ **French Bakery Restaurant.** 1250 Greene St.; (970) 387-5423 $
The name says it all: a great bakery and eating establishment on the ground floor of the Teller House Hotel.

STEAMBOAT SPRINGS
(ROCKY MOUNTAINS)

☷ **Harbor Hotel.** 703 Lincoln Ave.; (800) 334-1012 in Colorado; (800) 543-8888 nationwide; (970) 879-1522 from any bar in Steamboat. summer: $-$$; winter: $$-$$$$
Antiques and a 50-year history add character to the Harbor amid the sea of new condos. Characters as diverse as Jack Dempsey and Shirley Temple have liked the place, which has been remodeled, so it's probably got something for everyone.

☷ **Inn at Steamboat Bed & Breakfast.** 3070 Columbine Dr.; (970) 879-2600 $$$
Great views and personalized service at this spacious ranch-style bed-and-breakfast.

Stone fireplace. Private ski shuttle to the mountain, offers ski-tuning services. Quaint dining room. Etched pine decor.

☨ **Ptarmigan Inn.** 2304 Apres Ski Way; (970) 879-1730 $$$
Comfortable, tasteful rooms at the base of the ski hill and next to the Silver Bullet Gondola.

☨ **Rabbit Ears Motel.** 201 Lincoln Ave.; (970) 879-1150 $$
Nice rooms with a view of the Yampaha River, located next to the municipal hot springs pool.

☨ **Scandinavian Lodge.** 2883 Burgess Creek Rd.; (970) 879-0517 summer: $; winter: $–$$$
This newly renovated lodge offers suites and regular rooms. You don't have to ski in, but you can.

✗ **Antares.** 57½ 8th St.; (970) 879-9939 $$
Housed in a historic 1903 building rumored to have its own ghost, with an eclectic menu showing international influences. Check the blackboard for specials.

✗ **The Chart House.** 2165 Pine Grove Rd.; (970) 879-6976 $$$
The Chart House chain has built an enviable reputation for fine steaks, prime rib, and seafood.

✗ **La Montana.** 2500 Village Dr.; (970) 879-5800 $$$
Tex-Mex and Southwestern cuisine. Everything is made from scratch, including the tortillas.

✗ **La Pogée.** 911 Lincoln Ave.; (970) 879-1919 $$–$$$
Contemporary and classic French cuisine with a wide choice of wine in cowboy country and a more eclectic menu in the adjoining Harwig's Bar and Grill.

✗ **Mattie Silk's.** On Mt. Werner at Ski Time Square, 1890 Mt. Werner Rd.; (970) 879-2441 $$
The candlelit dining room serves veal, seafood, lamb, and steaks with 50 imported beers in a building named after an infamous lady of the evening.

✗ **The Shack Café.** 740 Lincoln Ave.; (970) 879-9975 $
Quick and tasty breakfast and lunch.

✗ **Steamboat Smokehouse.** 912 Lincoln Ave.; (970) 879-RIBS $
Hickory-smoked brisket, pulled pork, ribs, jalapeno sausage, mashed potatoes, "road kill" specials. Need we say more?

T E L L U R I D E
(SAN JUAN MOUNTAINS)

☨ **Bear Creek Bed & Breakfast.** 221 E. Colorado Ave.; (970) 728-6681 $$–$$$
Sun yourself on the rooftop sundeck and get a stunning view, too.

☨ **Ice House.** 310 S. 1st St.; (970) 728-6300 summer: $$–$$$$; winter: $$$$
A modern luxury hotel near downtown with all the amenities a skier or festival-goer could want.

☎ **Johnston Inn.** 403 W. Colorado Ave.; (970) 728-3316 $$
An intimate Victorian-style bed and breakfast with modern amenities. Eight guest rooms.

NEW SHERIDAN HOTEL

☎ **New Sheridan Hotel.** Downtown at 231 W. Colorado St.; (970) 728-4351 $$–$$$$
Opened in 1895, the Sheridan soon vied with the best of the nineteenth century's hotels. William Jennings Bryan repeated his impassioned "Cross of Gold" speech at the hotel to a rapt audience in 1903.

☎ **Peaks at Telluride.** 136 Country Club Dr.; (970) 728-6800 $$$$
The ultimate ski resort hotel. The decor is stylishly southwestern—stonework, soothing colors, overstuffed sofas, kilim pillows. Most guest rooms have private terraces and stunning views of the San Juans.

☎ **Pennington's Mountain Village Inn.** 100 Pennington Ct.; (970) 728-5337 $$$$

A small and elegant bed-and-breakfast decorated in French country-style.

☎ **San Sophia.** 330 W. Pacific Ave. (970) 728-3001 or (800) 537-4781 summer: $$$; winter: $$$–$$$$
This modern, lavish, and spacious bed-and-breakfast offers a range of room sizes and styles. Classy and comfortable.

☎ **Victorian Inn.** 401 W. Pacific Ave.; (970) 728-6601 summer: $; winter: $$
Located in the center of town, this "new" Victorian built in 1976 has a sauna and hot tub. Continental breakfast included.

✕ **Campagna.** 435 W. Pacific Ave.; (970) 728-6190 $$$
Tuscan dishes served in a Victorian setting. Fine food enhanced by an fine wine list.

✕ **The Cosmopolitan.** In the Hotel Columbia at foot of the gondola; (970) 728-1292 $$$
Chef Chad Scothorn works his magic in the exhibition-style kitchen of this neo-Victorian establishment, turning out dishes like pepper-encrusted tuna with lobster mashed potatoes.

PEAKS AT TELLURIDE

✕ **Floradora.** 103 W. Colorado Ave.;
   (970) 728-3888 $–$$

Quick lunches and a full dinner menu offering standard American fare. The hand-squashed burgers and steaks are a hallmark.

✕ **La Marmotte.** 150 W. San Juan St.
   (970) 728-6232 $$–$$$

Fine French country cuisine. Dinner only.

✕ **Legends**. At The Peaks Resort & Spa in
   Telluride Mountain Village;
   (970) 728-2512 $$–$$$

A spacious, comfortable restaurant with views of the ski slopes. Ample breakfast and lunch buffets. Elegant dining at night. Performance Spa Cuisine is so good, you won't know it's low-fat.

✕ **Powderhouse.** 226 W. Colorado Ave.;
   (970) 728-3622 $–$$

A wide range of dinner entrees from wild game to pasta to seafood to steak in an upscale setting.

V A I L / B E A V E R   C R E E K
(R O C K Y   M O U N T A I N S)

☗ **Holiday Inn Chateau Vail.** 13 Vail Rd.;
   (970) 476-5631/ (800) 451-9840 $$$

Enjoy a quaint Bavarian motif set off with antiques.

☗ **Hyatt Regency Beaver Creek.** 136 E.
   Thomas Place; (970) 949-1234/ (800)
   233-1234 winter: $$$$; summer: $$$

A blend of Alpine and Rocky Mountain architecture, this lovely hotel is rustic and elegant (e.g. the lobby's stunning chandelier of antlers from found, not hunted elk). Ski-in,

ski-out convenience at the base of the Beaver Creek ski area.

HYATT REGENCY BEAVER CREEK

☗ **Lodge at Vail.** 174 E. Gore Crk. Dr.;
   (970) 476-5011 summer: $$$; winter:
   $$$$

The exterior retains the distinctive European chalet design that was part of the resort's original allure, while inside is a full-service hostelry.

☗ **Park Plaza.** 46 Avondale Ln.;
   (970) 845-7700 $$$$

Intimate and luxurious.

☗ **Roost Lodge.** 1783 N. Frontage Rd.;
   (970) 476-5451 summer: $; winter: $$

A bit farther out from the middle of town, this is a favorite with families.

☗ **Sitzmark Lodge.** 183 Gore Creek Dr.;
   (970) 476-5001 $$

Just a block's walk from the lifts in the center of Vail.

☗ **St. James Place.** 210 Offerson Rd.;
   (970) 845-9300 $$$$

Two and three bedroom suites less than a block from the slopes in Beaver Creek.

☎ **Vail Athletic Club.** 352 E. Meadow Dr.; (970) 476-0700/ (800) 822-4754 $$$$
If you want to work out after skiing and then collapse in a comfortable room, this is the place for you.

✗ **Beano's Cabin.** Foot of Larkspur Lift, Beaver Creek Mountain; (970) 949-9090 $$$
Ride a snowcat-pulled sleigh in winter, or travel by horseback in summer, to this contemporary version of a homesteader's cabin for upscale cuisine from wood-burning ovens, grills, and rotisseries. Reservations are a must.

✗ **Campo di Fiori.** 100 E. Meadow Drive; (970) 476-8994 $$$
A sister restaurant to the original in Aspen, serving innovative Tuscan and Venetian cuisine. Marvelous murals on walls, floor, and ceiling.

✗ **Cucina Rustica.** 174 E. Gore Creek Dr.; (970) 476-5011 $$$
The stunning dining room in The Lodge at Vail, reminiscent of an Italian marketplace, serves superb buffet breakfasts and lunches. Dinner winter only.

✗ **Gashouse.** 34185 Hwy. 6 (in the heart of Edwards, 13 miles from Vail and four miles from Beaver Creek); (970) 926-3613 $–$$
This homey establishment in an old gas station is where the locals go to escape the glitz of Vail and Beaver Creek. Great lunch burgers and dinners of baby-back ribs, steak, seafood, and quail.

✗ **Gasthof Gramshammer.** 231 E. Gore Creek Dr., Vail; (970) 476-4671 $$–$$$
Continental cuisine in one dining room and wild game in another make the Gasthof stand out.

✗ **Grouse Mountain Grill** In the Pines Lodge, 141 Scott Hill Rd., Beaver Creek; (970) 949-0600 $$$
The progressive American fare and impressive wine list are topped only by the lovely views of Beaver Creek ski area. Reservations required.

✗ **Hubcap Brewery & Kitchen.** Crossroad Shopping Center; (970) 476-5757 $
Great lunches and fresh micro-brews. Homemade beer bread accompanies dinner entrees. Don't miss the jalapeno "poppers" and Extra Special Bitter.

✗ **The Left Bank.** In the Sitzmark Lodge, 183 Gore Creek Dr.; (970) 476-3696 $$–$$$
Fine French cuisine and an award-winning wine list.

✗ **Mirabelle's.** 55 Village Rd., Beaver Creek; (970) 949-7728 $$$
Some of the best French food in the region, if not the state, resides in this rambling farmhouse. Closed in the spring.

✗ **SaddleRidge.** 44 Meadow Lane, Beaver Creek; (970) 845-5450 $$$
Contemporary cuisine is served in one of the most impressive dining rooms in the area, with museum quality western artifacts and mountain views.

✕ **Sweet Basil.** 193 E. Gore Creek Dr.,
  Vail; (970) 476-0125 $$–$$$
Noted for homemade desserts and an eclectic dinner menu featuring creative American cuisine. Beautiful decor with views.

✕ **The Tyrolean Inn Restaurant.** 400 E.
  Meadow Dr.; (970) 476-2204 $$$
Continental and New American cuisine and wild game dishes in an alpine setting. Summer dining on the patio.

✕ **Zino Ristorante.** At River Walk, 27
  Main St., Edwards (on CO 6, 13 miles from Vail; 4 miles from Beaver Creek); (970) 926-0444 $$
A booming, bi-level eatery serving casual Italian food. Check out the action at the Z Bar.

W I N T E R   P A R K
(R O C K Y   M O U N T A I N S)

⛆ **Iron Horse Resort Retreat.** 257 Winter
  Park Dr.; (970) 726-8851 summer: $$$; winter: $$$$
Gym, full hotel trappings, and Winter Park's only ski-in/ski-out hotel located at the base of the Mary Jane and Winter Park hills.

⛆ **YMCA Snow Mountain Ranch.**
  20 miles north of Winter Park Ski Area, 1101 County Rd. 53 in Granby; (970) 887-2152 $$–$$$
A year-round resort where you can choose between a simple dorm room or a deluxe cabin and partake in everything from swimming to cross-country skiing.

✕ **Crooked Creek Saloon.** 401 Zerex Ave.,
  Fraser; (970) 726-9250 $–$$
American breakfasts, lunches, dinners, and drinks by the Fraser River. The breakfast burritos and frittatas are especially popular.

✕ **Gasthaus Eichler.** 78786 Hwy. 40;
  (970) 726-4244 $$
Authentic German decor and cuisine, including schnitzel, sauerbraten, goulash. Wide German beer selection (some on tap).

✕ **The Last Waltz Kings.** Crossing Shopping Center on Hwy 40; (970) 726-4877 $
Say olé to a crabmeat enchilada or black bean tostada at this long-time locals' favorite with early American decor.

■ GUEST RANCHES

> *Prices per week, one person, three meals per day:*
> $ = up to $500; $$ = $500 to $750; $$$ = over $750

ASPEN

T-Lazy 7 Guest Ranch. 3129 Maroon Creek Rd., Aspen 81611; (970) 925-7254 $$-$$$
No glitz, no glamor, just neat cabins along Maroon Creek, snowmobile and horse trips, and solitude on the edge of the Maroon Bells/Snowmass Wilderness. Closed October through November, April through May.

CORTEZ

Lake Mancos Ranch. 42688 County Rd. N., Mancos 81328; (970) 533-7900; (800) 325-9462 $$$
Strategically located between Cortez and Durango offering a full slate of outdoor activities, including horseback riding. Open June through October.

CREEDE

Wason Ranch. Write: Box 220 Creede, 81130; (719) 658-2413 $-$$$$
Settled along the banks of the Rio Grande River, offering a variety of cabins and great fishing, and cross-country skiing, just two miles from Creede. Open year round.

CRESTED BUTTE

Harmel's Ranch Resort. Write: Box 944, Gunnison 81230; (970) 641-1740 or (800) 235-3402 $$-$$$$
Between Gunnison and Crested Butte on the Taylor River, offering raft trips, fishing, horses, and cabins and rooms on American (includes 3 meals per day) or European plan (meals not included). Open May through November.

DURANGO

Colorado Trails Ranch. 12161 County Rd. 240, Durango 81301; (800) 323-3833 $$$
All the summer fun you could want, from archery to trout fishing. Also offers special children's programs. Open June through September.

ESTES PARK

Wind River Ranch. Box 3410, Estes Park 80517; (970) 586-4212 $$$
Next to Rocky Mountain National Park, this Christian family guest ranch has log cabins anddiversions which include horseback riding, fishing, hiking, and cookouts. Great food, and entertainment. Open June through September.

FORT COLLINS

Sylvan Dale Guest Ranch. 2939 N. County Rd. 31D, Loveland 80538; (970) 667-3915 $$

Gives the feel of a working ranch with its cattle and quarter horses grazing along the Big Thompson River, which you can ride along or fish in. All the basics in a great setting. Open year round.

GRANBY
C Lazy U Ranch. Box 379, Granby 80446; (970) 887-3344 $$$$
Offers everything from live entertainment to a guest "Showdeo." Wranglers take guests on trail rides. Excellent fishing and rafting, and first-rate accommodations and food. Open winter and summer only.

MEEKER
Sleepy Cat Guest Ranch. 16064 County Rd. 8, Meeker 81641; (970) 878-4413 $
Just 16 miles east of Meeker, Sleepy Cat offers unstructured relaxation and great hunting, fishing, and cross-country skiing or snowmobiling. The restaurant is excellent. Open year round.

RIFLE
Coulter Lake Guest Ranch. Box 906, Rifle 81650; (970) 625-1473 $
About 21 miles northeast of Rifle, this ranch is set in the woods and offers fishing, snowmobiling, guided big-game hunts. Open all year except November.

STEAMBOAT SPRINGS
Focus Ranch. Write: Focus Ranch, Slater 81653; (970) 583-2410 $$$
"So you wanna be a cowboy, huh?" Here's the place. Experienced riders help move cows through the national forest on this working ranch near the Colorado/Wyoming border and milk cows and chickens provide part of the grub. Fishing, hunting, and regular horseback trips also available.

TELLURIDE
Skyline Guest Ranch. 7214 Hwy. 145, Telluride 81435; (970) 728-3757 $$
Skyline lets you enjoy the spectacular San Juan Mountains by jeep, horse, mountain bike, or foot. Exceptional cross-country skiing and classic country lodging. Open year round except April, May, and November.

VAIL/BEAVER CREEK
Sweetwater Lake Resort. 3406 Sweetwater Road, Gypsum 81637; (970) 524-7344 $$
Remote lake and stream fishing, trail rides and hikes combined with modern amenities like a hot tub and heated pool. Family-style meals in historic lodge. Open all year except April.

WESTCLIFFE
The Pines Ranch. Box 311 Westcliffe 81252; (719) 783-9261 or (800) 446-9462 $$
This guest ranch has the Sangre de Cristo mountains for a backyard and offers modern cabins, fishing, trail rides, pack trips, and family style meals. Open May through mid-October.

■ FESTIVALS AND EVENTS

JANUARY

Aspen: Aspen/Snowmass Winterskol
Five-day extravaganza of fireworks, parades, all manner of ski races, and an impressive torchlight descent down Aspen Mountain. (970) 925-1940

Breckenridge: Ullrfest and World Cup
Freestyle honor Ullr, the Norse god of snow, with a parade, fireworks, and the best pro freestyle skiers in the nation. (970) 453-6018

Denver: National Western Stock Show
Largest stock show in the U.S., 23 days of rodeos, and a month's worth of all the cowtown ambiance you can handle. (303) 295-1660

Meeker: Two types of snow travel are highlighted: the **Meeker Massacre Sled Dog Race** and the **White River Rendezvous Devil's Hole Hill Climb** for snowmobiles. (970) 878-5510

FEBRUARY

Breckenridge: Fat Tuesday
Mardi Gras comes to the mountains. (970) 453-5521

Delta: North Fork Snowmobile Races and Snowdeo
Snowmobiling fun. (970) 874-8621

Denver: Grand Ball
Traditional gala begins the opera season. (303) 778-1500/(303) 98-MUSIC

Steamboat Springs: Winter Carnival
The oldest winter carnival west of the Mississippi. Features a band on skis, ski jumping, ski jouring (skiers being pulled by horses), and more. (970) 879-0882.

Walsenburg: Ground Hog Brunch
The Walsenburg golf course lets you munch while watching for a certain furry shadow. (719) 738-1065

MARCH

Craig: Greek Festival
This northeastern Colorado town dines on souvlaki, dolmathes, and baklava before dancing Greek folk dances. (970) 824-5689

Denver: Colorado Ballet
Runs for one month at the Denver Performing Arts Complex. (303) 986-8742

Denver: St. Patrick's Day Parade
Allegedly the second longest parade in the nation, due in part to the 5,000 horses.

Monte Vista: Monte Vista Crane Festival
The town welcomes whooping and sandhill cranes returning to the valley for spring. Guided wildlife tours and lectures are featured. (719) 852-3552

San Luis: Stations of the Cross
A Good Friday observance of the traditional Stations of the Cross, which are represented by sculptures along a trail outside of town. (719) 672-3685

Springfield: Spring Equinox Festival

During spring and autumn equinox, the sun turns Crack Cave into Colorado's version of Stonehenge and shines into the cave to reveal the ancient Ogam calendar and writings linked to Celtic roots in fourth-century Eire. (719) 523-4061

Vail/Beaver Creek: American Ski Classic

Hosted by former President Gerald Ford, highlights the Legends of Skiing Competition, honoring past national and world champs. (970) 949-1999

A P R I L

Copper Mountain: The Hot Shot Eenie Weenie Bikini Ski Contest

Both men and women strip down to the least amount of clothing weather will allow for one final race down the slopes. (970) 968-2882

Colorado Springs: Easter Sunrise Service.

Held at the Garden of the Gods.

Georgetown: Poverty Ball

Held after April 15. Attire: old rags. Food: stew and bread. (303) 569-2888

Kit Carson: Mountain Man Rendezvous

Takes you back in time to the days when men matched the mountains by featuring period dress, black powder shooting, and displays of the cooking and crafts of yesteryear. (719) 962-3248

M A Y

Antonito: Cumbres and Toltec Scenic Railroad Season Opening

(719) 376-5483

Boulder: Bolder Boulder 10-K

One of the nation's premier 10-km road races. (303) 444-7223

Boulder: Kinetic Conveyance Sculpture Race

Features the weirdest human-powered vehicles ever to traverse land and water. (303) 444-5600

Cuchara: Cuchara Valley Cowboy Arts

Celebration all things cowboy, from the rustic to the artistic. (719) 742-3676

Denver: Cinco de Mayo.

Civic Center Park converted into a Mexican fiesta replete with food, dance, and costume. (303) 534-8342

Durango: Annual Iron Horse Bicycle Classic

Over 2,000 mountain bikers and road racers compete for three days of pedaling. (970) 259-4621

Fort Garland: Rendezvous of Cultures

Reunites the Hispanic, Indian, and Anglo influences in the San Luis Valley. (719) 379-3461

Ignacio: Annual Bear Dance

A three-day spring celebration marked by traditional Ute dancing, costumes, singing, and ceremonies. (970) 563-0100

Telluride: Telluride Mountain Film Festival

Features outdoor, adventure, and mountain films. (970) 728-4123

J U N E

Aspen: Music Festival and School
Running nine weeks, with performances of everything from opera to jazz to symphonies in the Wheeler Opera House and the Music Tent. (970) 925-9042

Central City: Lou Bunch Day
In honor of the town's last madam. Festivities include bed races and a formal costume ball. (303) 582-5077

Cortez: Arts and Crafts Fiesta
Native American and other artists from throughout the Southwest display and sell their wares. (970) 565-3414

Cripple Creek: Donkey Derby Days.
Donkey races for all ages (donkeys and humans, we assume), greased-pig chase.

Denver: Capitol Hill People's Fair
Over 500 arts and crafts booths and entertainment on three stages. Held at Civic Center Park. (303) 830-1651

Glenwood Springs: Strawberry Days
The state's oldest civic celebration and offers arts and crafts booths, entertainment, a parade, and free strawberries and ice cream. (970) 945-6589

Idaho Springs: Gold Rush Days
Watch mucking and drilling contests and try your hand at panning gold. (303) 567-4382

Julesburg: Pony Express Re-Ride
Aerobic pony express riders change horses in a heartbeat, hold on to the mail pouch, and keep on going without missing a step. (970) 474-3504

Larkspur: Renaissance Festival
Revival of the sixteenth century, complete with jousting, every weekend through July. (303) 688-6010

Salida: FibArk Boat Races
The longest and oldest downriver kayak race in America, with raft races and other entertainment tossed in. (719) 539-2068

Telluride: Bluegrass Festival
A weekend of fiddling, fun, and fandangos. (800) 624-2422

Trinidad: Santa Fe Trail Festival
Two-day celebration of history and art. (719) 846-9285

J U L Y

Aspen: Dance Aspen's Summer Festival
A six-week run of performances by nationally-known dance companies, ranging from ballet to modern to avant-garde. (970) 925-8400.

Boulder: Colorado Shakespeare Festival
One of the nation's top three Bard bashes. Performed under the stars. Dance and music festivals also fill the month. (303) 492-0554

Breckenridge: Bach, Beethoven, and Breckenridge
Classical concerts and workshops run from July to August. (970) 453-2120

Carbondale: Carbondale Mountain Fair
Food, entertainment, and a juried selection of fine professional art and handmade crafts. (970) 963-1890

Central City: Opera Festival
Held in the restored opera house, performances run through August. Classic opera performed in English. (303) 582-5077

Florissant: 1880s Picnic on the Hornbeck Homestead
Held at the Florissant Fossil Beds National Monument. (719) 748-3253

Greeley: Denver Broncos Training Camp
It's more fun to watch the fanatics, er, fans, who flock to watch their heroes prepare for the upcoming season. (970) 351-2007

Greeley: Independence Stampede
The largest Fourth of July rodeo, preceded by a week's worth of barbecues, and parades. (970) 356-2855

La Junta: Bent's Old Fort Fourth of July
Relive the excitement of the fur-trapping era in an authentically restored fort. (719) 384-2596

Lake City: Alfred Packer Trial
Watch the trial of the famed Colorado cannibal as presented by the Western State College Drama Department. Runs through August. (970) 944-2527

Las Animas: Silly Homemade River Raft Race
Crowds of whimsically decorated handmade rafts float along the Arkansas River. Month varies year to year; call ahead. (719) 456-0453

Manitou Springs: Pikes Peak Auto Hill Climb
Over 60 professional race car drivers twist up the 12 miles of gravel to the top of Pikes Peak in this Race to the Clouds. (719) 685-4400

Steamboat Springs: Rodeo
Cowboys and broncos tango every Friday and Saturday night for a thirteen-week run. (970) 879-0880

Vail Valley: Bravo Colorado Music Festival
Chamber, orchestral, and jazz music in various locations throughhout Vail and Beaver Creek. (970) 827-5700

Winter Park: Jazz Festival
Headline jazz artists play outdoors. Food and crafts booths. (800) 903-7275

AUGUST

Castle Rock: International Golf Tournament
Castle Pines Golf Club hosts the PGA's only Colorado stop. (303) 688-4597

Central City: Jazz Festival

Performances by the best jazz jammers from the U.S. and Europe. (303) 582-5077

Cortez: Notah Dineh trading Post Indian Dance and Sing

Traditional Navajo dress, dance, and song. (970) 565-3414

Grand Junction: Palisade Peach Festival

Celebration of the the area's celebrated peaches. (970) 242-3214

Leadville: Boom Days

Celebrates the silver boom with a drilling contest and 22-mile pack burro race over a 13,000-foot mountain. (719) 486-3900

Leadville: Leadville Trail 100

People actually run or bike 100 miles at 10,000 feet above sea level. Spectators free, runners insane. (719) 486-3900

Montrose: Annual Black Canyon Horse and Mule Race Meet

Yes, mules can run, proving burros aren't the only four-legged Colorado athletes. Some years the race is held in July. (970) 249-5000

Pueblo: Colorado State Fair

About two weeks of agricultural ecstasy where everything from strawberry preserves to peaches vie for blue ribbons. Parades, professional rodeo, big-name country-western artists, and nights of carnival lights make this the fairest fair in this fair state. (719) 542-1704

SEPTEMBER

Aspen: Ruggerfest

International rugby teams hit town and each other in this three day bash. (970) 920-1042

Beecher's Island: Beecher's Island Reunion

A remembrance of the Battle of Beecher's Island, one of the last between whites and Native Americans. Attractions include a black powder shoot, crafts, and games. (970) 332-5063

Denver: Festival of Mountain and Plain

Every Labor Day weekend this Taste of Colorado is a great excuse to gorge yourself on every type of food imaginable. (303) 892-7004

Estes Park: Annual Scottish-Irish Highland Festival

Celebration of Scottish and Irish heritage including authentic Celtic music and athletic competitions, kilts. (970) 586-4431

Ignacio: Southern Ute Tribal Fair

Traditional games, exhibits, and ceremonies. (970) 563-0100

Grand Junction: Renaissance Fair

Period costumes, artists, food and entertainment. (970) 242-3214

La Junta: Early Settlers' Day

One of the most popular events in southeast Colorado. Over 140 arts and crafts booths, beer garden, fiddling contests, barbecue. (719) 384-7411

Leadville: St. Patrick's Day Practice Parade
Great excuse for green beer.

Loveland: Stone Age Fair
Displays of ancient Indian artifacts and art. Archaeologists on hand to explain what they mean. (970) 667-6311

Meeker: Sheep Dog Championship Trials
The world's best sheep dogs and handlers attempt to corral ornery Colorado sheep. (970) 878-5510

Steamboat Springs: Steamboat Mountain Road Race and Vintage Auto Race and Concours d'Elegance
Vintage motorcycles and autos challenge a two-mile course and restored exotic sports cars are displayed. (970) 879-0882

Telluride: Film Festival
Premieres and oldies (fee) and the Telluride Hang Gliding Festival (free). Labor Day weekend. (603) 643-1255

Yuma: Ole Threshers Day
Demonstrations of old wheat threshers, corn huskers, and other farm equipment and activities trace the history of farming. (970) 848-2704

O C T O B E R
Durango: Western Arts, Film, and Poetry Gathering
Lectures and demonstrations of cowboy skills, and readings from contemporary cowboy poets. (970) 247-0312

Fort Morgan: Western Barbecue Cookoff
The best barbecue cooks in the area gather to get sauced, barbecue style. (970) 867-6702

D E C E M B E R
La Junta: Bent's Old Fort Christmas 1846
A frontier Christmas celebration. (719) 384-2596

Burlington: Carousel and Old Town Christmas
Burlington Carousel, a national landmark, is the center of the celebration. Features costumed Victorian carolers, and treats. (719) 346-8070

Denver: Parade of Lights
Brightly lit floats and bands converge on the downtown Civic Center, and the Denver City and County Building is set aglow with colored light in every nook and cupola. (303) 534-6161

Pueblo: Posada.
A processional with a living nativity scene and music and song. (719) 542-1704

San Luis: Fiesta de Nuestra Senora de Guadalupe.
Music and prayer. (719) 672-3685

San Luis: Las Posadas
A two-week re-enactment of the journey of Mary and Joseph in search of a room for the Christ Child. (719) 672-3685

■ GOLF COURSES

Most Colorado towns and resorts have at least a nine-hole golf course somewhere in proximity. The following, however, are 18-hole layouts offering either good golfing, great views, or both. Most of the resort courses in the middle of the Rockies open in May, with those in the west and south and even Front Range courses offering almost year-round golfing.

ASPEN/SNOWMASS

Aspen Golf Course. Great views and a challenging layout with lots of hidden ditches and lakes. (970) 925-2145

Snowmass Lodge and Club. More expensive and less challenging than the Aspen 18, but the setting is stunning. (970) 923-5600

BRECKENRIDGE

Breckenridge Golf Club. The only publicly owned Jack Nicklaus–designed course in the world. It plays through the natural terrain, even a beaver pond, and has lots of pesky trees. Reservations suggested. (970) 453-9104

BOULDER

Flatirons Golf Course. Not only popular, but scenic and challenging, thanks to lots of lakes and trees. Call for tee times. (303) 442-7851

CASTLE ROCK

Castle Pines Golf Club. Home of the PGA International Golf Tournament, challenges the pros, so you can imagine what it does to the rest of us. (303) 688-6000

COLORADO SPRINGS

Broadmoor Golf Club. One of the most popular courses in the region, and one of the oldest. Challenging course, beautiful setting. (719) 577-5790

Patty Jewett Golf Club. Definitely mature, since it was built in 1898 and was the first golf course west of the Mississippi. Located in the middle of town with a great view of Pikes Peak, it offers 27 holes. (719) 578-6826

COPPER MOUNTAIN

Copper Creek Golf Club. A Perry Dye design, has the highest altitude of any PGA course in the nation and great views of the Tenmile Range. Reservations suggested. (970) 968-2339

CRESTED BUTTE

Skyland Country Club. Tucked into the base of Mt. Crested Butte and surrounded by high-country scenery, which helps keep your mind off the battle its 18-hole layout presents. (970) 349-6131

DENVER

With over 20 public links to choose from, Denver is not lacking for hacking.

Arrowhead Golf Club, with 76 sand traps and six lakes, not to mention scrub oak and the rock formations of Roxborough Park, is a dandy. Designer Robert Trent Jones, Jr. claims this course is among his favorites. Reservations suggested. (303) 973-9614

Meadow Hills Golf Course. Isn't as challenging or expensive, but is still a good play, with plenty of mature trees and geese creating most of the obstacles, (303) 690-2500.

Wellshire Golf Course is full of trees and very long (over 6,500 yards), but at a mile high you can slash away and hope for altitude assistance to improve your score. (303) 757-1352

D U R A N G O
Hillcrest Golf Course. On the Fort Lewis College Mesa, gives you a peek at the La Plata Mountains, and some good mountain golfing. (970) 247-1499

G R A N D   J U N C T I O N
Tiara Rado Golf Course. A young tough near the entrance to the Colorado National Monument, assuring nice views. (970) 245-8085

G R A N D   L A K E
Grand Lake Golf Course. On the western edge of Colorado National Park, has tight fairways and tons of trees, so you have to keep it on the straight and narrow or bring lots of balls. But at an altitude of 8,400 feet, things really fly. (970) 627-8008

P U E B L O
Pueblo West Golf Club. The second highest rated course in the state is a good test of all your golfing skills, cursing included. (719) 547-2280

R I F L E
Rifle Creek Golf Course. Located at the base of Rifle Gap, where artist Cristo hung a short-lived red curtain from rim to rim. The 18-hole layout is short, but steep, and tricky. (970) 625-1093

S T E A M B O A T   S P R I N G S
Steamboat Golf Club. Designed by Robert Trent Jones, Jr., and one of the toughest in the state, regardless of the views of Mt. Werner and the Yampa River Valley. Reservations are suggested. (970) 879-4295

V A I L / B E A V E R   C R E E K
Vail Golf Club. This municipal course is flank to shank with the Gore River and Vail Mountain. Call for tee times, (970) 479-2260.

Beaver Creek Resort Golf Club. Limited public tee times, but it's worth the wait to tackle this rolling, sand-trapped terror at the base of Beaver Creek ski hill. Reservations advised. (970) 949-7123

■ HISTORIC RAILROADS

Narrow-gauge tracks laid precariously along mountainsides, over trestles, or though rolling forests still carry sturdy steam locomotives and their string of passenger cars, reminding visitors what the world was like before the automobile and freeway. Plumes of steam spewing from the smokestack, sparks, and soot spraying the summer air with their unique smell mark the passage of Colorado's most famous, scenic, and delightful historic train rides.

Cumbres & Toltec Scenic Railroad, the longest and highest narrow-gauge line in North America, stretches 64 miles from Antonito, Colorado, to Chama, New Mexico. From Antonito, the train starts a slow chug up the rolling high country, passing through the dramatic Toltec Gorge of the Los Pinos River before cresting out at a heady 10,015 feet atop Cumbres Pass. Then it's all downhill, at a four-percent grade, into Chama. The trip along rivers and over mountains has made many agree that the Cumbres & Toltec was one of the most spectacular feats of mountain railroad building ever undertaken. Located along the isolated Colorado/New Mexico border, the train is off the beaten track, but once you get on its tracks, you can rest assured it's well worth it. Coming from Colorado, you can take US 285 south from Denver through Alamosa to the Antonito station. From Santa Fe, hit 285 north to Espanola, then U.S. 84 to the Chama station. The enclosed coaches feature windows that can be open or closed, weather allowing. A completely open sightseeing coach is available to all, with on-train refreshments. Cars are not heated, so be prepared with your own warmth. The train stops in Osier for lunch, or you can hop off at Osier and head back to where you started. **Season and information:** June to mid-October. *For information: Antonito Depot, Box 668, Antonito, CO 81120, (719) 376-5483, Chama Depot, Box 789, Chama, NM 87520,(505) 756-2151.*

Cripple Creek/Victor Narrow Gauge Railroad takes you on a four-mile round trip through the gold town of Cripple Creek. **Season and information:** Memorial Day until mid-October. *Box 459, Cripple Creek, CO 80813, or call (719) 689-2640.*

Durango & Silverton Narrow Gauge Railroad takes you 45 miles through the heart of southwestern Colorado's stunning San Juan National Forest and past remnants of the state's mining past and living reminders of its mining present. Over $300 million in gold and silver were hauled on the narrow-gauge tracks in mining's heyday, and those days can now be relived in a number of ways on the current train. A choice of authentically restored 1880 passenger cars is available, ranging from the opulent private Cinco Animas car (for charter only) to standard covered coach to an open-air gondola car. Refreshments are served in the Alamosa Parlour Car. Along the way hearing the shriek of the steam whistle, seeing abandoned mine sites, and miles of roadless, virgin forest make for an unforgettable journey. The entire trip from Durango to Silverton takes most of a day, so many opt for staying the night in Silverton, which started as and remains a mining town, and returning to Durango the next day. **Season and information**: May to late October, depending on the length of trip. Reservations are strongly recommended. Call for an order form/brochure and then pick up your tickets in advance, especially if you are planning a fall trip to view the spectacular fall foliage. *For information: 479 Main Ave., Durango, CO 81301, (970) 247-2733 or (888) 872-4607.*

Georgetown Loop Railroad winds its way back to glory days of Colorado's gold boom by taking travelers on an hour-long, steam-powered ride. Starting from Georgetown, the narrow-gauge tracks cross the rebuilt 95-foot high Devil's Gate Bridge (called the Eighth Wonder of the World when it was completed in 1888), then take 14 twisting turns before hitting Silver Plume. A brief rest and you're back aboard for the return trip which closes the loop. The rolling stock, engines, and restored passenger cars (some of which are open to the mountain air, so don't forget a jacket), are immaculate and the crews helpful and enthusiastic. You can board at either Georgetown, an hour's

drive west from Denver on Interstate 70, or Silver Plume, another half hour away on the interstate. **Season and Information:** Trains run every day from late May to early October. *Box 217, Georgetown, CO 80444; (303) 569-2403 from Georgetown/Silver Plume; (303) 670-1686, from Denver.*

Leadville Colorado and Southern Railroad runs from Leadville to the Climax Mine, giving riders a panoramic view of this once booming valley of silver. *Information, 326 E. 7th. St., Leadville, CO 80461, (719) 486-3936.*

Lebanon Mine and Mill Tour lets you delve even deeper into the golden era by taking you inside an old mine and mill, accessible only by train, which you can do as a part of the Georgetown Loop trip or independently. Be sure to bring a jacket (the mine is a constant 44 degrees (7°C) and walking shoes for this hour and a half tour. Reservations are also suggested if you want to combine the tour and train ride. **Schedule and information:** see "Georgetown Loop Railroad," above.

Manitou & Pikes Peak Cog Railway is a modern people-mover that makes a three-hour round trip from Manitou Springs to the top of Pikes Peak. Gaining 8,000 feet in altitude during the nine-mile trip through aspens and pines to timberline, once atop the peak you can see the purple mountains' majesty and amber waves of grain that inspired Katherine Lee Bates to pen "America the Beautiful." **Season and information:** May through October with hourly departures during peak (that's not a pun) seasons. *Contact either Cog Road Depot, 515 Ruxton Ave., Manitou Springs, CO 80829, (719) 685-5401; or Box 1329, Colorado Springs, CO 80901.*

Royal Gorge Scenic Railway snakes along the top of the imposing Royal Gorge, in modern, open-air cars and stops for peeks over the edge that make you want to get back in you seat. **Information:** *Box 1387, Canon City, CO 81212, (719) 275-5485.*

Royal Gorge Aerial Tram and the **Royal Gorge Incline Railway** will give you two views of this monstrous crack in the earth spanned by the world's highest suspension bridge. Up to 35 passengers without a fear of heights can look down 1,200 feet into the bottom of the gorge from the safety of the comfortable tram cars chugging across the top of the gorge. For those who want to take a closer look, the railway, steepest in the world, takes you right to the bottom. **Season and information:** Open year round, depending on weather. *Royal Gorge Bridge Co., Box 594, Canon City, CO 81212, (719) 275-7507.*

The Ski Train is not a narrow-gauge railroad, but it is historic: since 1941 it's been delivering skiers from Denver to the base of the Winter Park slopes. **Season and information:** *Saturdays and Sundays, mid-December through mid-April, Fridays as well, after February 13 $35–$60 round trip. P.O. Box 481234, Denver, CO, 80248; (303) 296-4754.*

The Silverton branch of the Denver & Rio Grande Railroad traverses the High Line around 1885. (Denver Public Library, Western History Department)

■ INFORMATION SOURCES

STATEWIDE INFORMATION

Colorado Ski Country USA is the promotional association for all of the state's ski areas. It produces a slick, 100-page magazine describing every ski area, how to get there, and listings of accommodations and other nearby amenities. Call (303) 837-0793 for more information.

Colorado Travel and Tourism Authority will send you the official state vacation guide. Included in the guide are phone numbers and addresses for everything from government offices to all the state's chambers of commerce and national parks and recreation areas. To order, call (800) 433-2656.

Weather Reports Road Conditions Statewide: (303) 639-1111/(303) 639-1234

OUTDOOR RECREATION ORGANIZATIONS

Colorado Association of Campgrounds, Cabins, and Lodges. Canon City, (719) 275-0506
Colorado Dude/Guest Ranch Association, Tabernash; (970) 724-3653
Colorado Golf Resort Association, Denver; (303) 699-4653
Colorado Outfitters Association, Parker; (303) 841-7760

Colorado Plateau Mountain Bike Trail Association; (970) 243-5602
Colorado Reservation Service, (800) 777-6880
Colorado Snowmobiling Association, Golden (303) 279-8436
Colorado Tennis Association, Denver; (303) 695-4116

HUNTING AND FISHING INFORMATION

The Colorado Devision of Wildlife (DOW) produces a number of comprehensive brochures which outline in detail every aspect of the state's hunting and fishing regulations and rules. The DOW also publishes *Colorado Outdoors,* a bimonthly, full-color magazine "dedicated to the conservation and enjoyment of Colorado outdoors—its animals, fish, soil, forests, prairies, and waters." For a subscription, write to *Colorado Outdoors,* 6060 Broadway, Denver CO 80216, or call (303) 291-74\69 for a subscription or sample copy. If you wish to order publications or to get information on hunting, fishing, or wildlife watching, the following numbers will set you in the right direction. For general information call (303) 297-1192; for recorded information on fishing and hunting call (303) 291-7299, and for information on wildlife watching call (303) 291-7518.

RECOMMENDED READING

■ HISTORY

Borland, Hal. *High, Wide, and Lonesome*. Philadelphia, New York: J. B. Lippincott Company, 1956.

Fay, Abbott. *Ski Tracks in the Rockies: A History of Skiing in Colorado*. Evergreen, CO: Cordillera Press, Inc., 1984.

Fradkin, Philip L. *A River No More: The Colorado River and the West*. Tucson, Arizona: University of Arizona Press, 1984. How the state and its mighty Colorado River have become interwoven into the politics and problems of the West.

Neihardt, John G. *Black Elk Speaks*. New York: William Morrow & Co., 1932.

Parkman, Francis. *The California and Oregon Trail*. New York: Thomas Y. Crowell & Co., 1849.

Ubbelohde, Carl, Maxine Benson, and Duane A. Smith. *A Colorado History*. 6th ed. Boulder: Pruett Publishing Co., 1988.

Vandenbusche, Duane. *A Land Alone, Colorado's Western Slope*. Boulder: Pruett Publishing Co., 1980.

Note: Caroline Bancroft is Colorado's best-known and most prolific citizen historian. She has written dozens of short histories, pamphlets, and profiles on almost every aspect of the state and its many colorful characters. Her efforts afford the visitor a quick, colorful glimpse into the state's past.

■ GUIDEBOOKS

Borneman, Walter R., and Lydon J. Lampert. *Climbing Guide to Colorado's Fourteeners*. Boulder: Pruett Publishing Co., 1989.

Borneman, Walter, R. *Colorado's Other Mountains: A Climbing Guide to Selected Peaks Under 14,000 Feet*. Evergreen, CO: Cordillera Press, Inc., 1984.

Cahill, Rick. *Colorado Hot Springs Guide.* Boulder, Colorado: Pruett Publishing Company, 1986.

Caughey, Bruce, and Dean Winstanley. *The Colorado Guide: Landscapes, Cityscapes, Escapes.* Golden, CO: Fulcrum, Inc., 1991.

Fidler, John, and M. John Fayhee. *Along the Colorado Trail.* Englewood, CO: Westcliffe Publishers, 1992. Over 120 photos accompany text that guides you along the 470 miles of hiking on the Colorado Trail.

Gray, Mary Taylor. *Colorado Wildlife Viewing Guide.* Helena, MT: Falcon Press, Inc., 1992. Photos, maps, and illustrations of the state's wildlife and where to go to see them.

Keilty, Maureen. *Best Hikes with Children in Colorado.* Seattle: The Mountaineers, 1991.

Litz, Brian. *Colorado Hut to Hut: A Guide to Skiing and Biking Colorado's Backcountry.* Englewood, CO: Westcliffe Publishers, 1992. Color photos, topo maps, and advice on hut-hopping Colorado style.

Rye, David. *Colorado's Guide to Fishing.* Denver: Mountain Peaks, Inc., 1991. If there's a fish in water, this book will show you where it is and how to catch it.

Wilson, D. Ray. *Colorado Historical Tour Guide.* Carpentersville, IL: Crossroads Communications, 1990. The state's every visible historical site, plaque, museum, digging, or roadside attraction.

■ FICTION

Abbey, Edward. *The Monkey Wrench Gang.* Philadelphia: J. B. Lippincott Co., 1975. The seminal work on acting out the West's eco-outrage.

Cather, Willa. *Song of the Lark.* Boston and New York: Houghton Mifflin Co., 1932.

Guthrie, A. B., Jr. *The Big Sky.* Forward by Wallace Stegner. Boston: Houghton Mifflin Co., 1952. The best novel written about Mountain Men, their way of life, and the mountains which provided their livelihood.

Michener, James A. *Centennial.* New York: Random House, Inc., 1974. Michener applies his exacting research and storytelling gifts to Colorado's vibrant past.

I N D E X

COMPASS AMERICAN GUIDES

Critics, Booksellers, and Travelers All Agree: You're Lost Without a Compass.

Compass American Guides are compelling, full-color portraits of America for travelers who want to understand the soul of their destinations. In each guide, an accomplished local expert recounts history, culture, and useful information in a text rife with personal anecdotes and interesting details. Splendid four-color images by an area photographer bring the region or city to life.

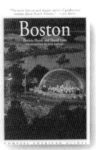

Boston (1st Edition)
1-878-86776-8
$18.95 ($26.50 Can)

"This splendid series provides exactly the sort of historical and cultural detail about North American destinations that curious-minded travelers need."
—*Washington Post*

Minnesota (1st Edition)
-878-86748-2
18.95 ($26.50 Can)

"This is a series that constantly stuns us; our whole past book reviewer experience says no guide with photos this good should have writing this good. But it does."
—*New York Daily News*

"Of the many guidebooks on the market few are as visually stimulating, as thoroughly researched or as lively written as the Compass American Guides series."
—*Chicago Tribune*

Pacific Northwest (1st Edition)
1-878-86785-7
$19.95 ($27.95 Can)

"Good to read ahead of time, then take along so you don't miss anything."
—*San Diego Magazine*

"Compass has developed a series with beautiful color photos and a descriptive text enlivened by literary excerpts from travel writers past and present."
—*Publishers Weekly*

Alaska (1st Edition)
-878-86777-6
18.95 ($26.50 Can)

Compass American Guides are available in general and travel bookstores, or may be ordered directly by calling (800) 733-3000. Compass American Guides are available at special discounts for bulk purchases for sales promotions or premiums. Special editions, including personalized covers and corporate imprints, can be created in large quantities for special needs. For more information, write to Special Marketing, Fodor's Travel Publications, 201 E. 50th St., New York, NY 10022; or call (800) 800-3246.

COMPASS AMERICAN GUIDES

Critics, Booksellers, and Travelers All Agree You're Lost Without a Compass

Arizona (4th Edition)
0-679-03388-2
$18.95 ($26.50 Can)

Chicago (2nd Edition)
1-878-86780-6
$18.95 ($26.50 Can)

Colorado (4th Edition)
0-679-00027-5
$18.95 ($26.50 Can)

Hawaii (3rd Edition)
1-878-86791-1
$18.95 ($26.50 Can)

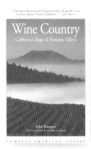

Wine Country (2nd Edition)
0-679-00032-1
$18.95 ($26.50 Can)

Montana (3rd Edition)
1-878-86797-0
$18.95 ($26.50 Can)

Oregon (3rd Edition)
0-679-00033-X
$18.95 ($26.50 Can)

New Orleans (3rd Editi
0-679-03597-4
$18.95 ($26.50 Can)

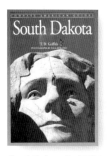

South Dakota (2nd Edition)
1-878-86747-4
$18.95 ($26,50 Can)

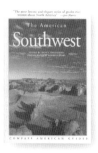

Southwest (2nd Edition)
0-679-00035-6
$18.95 ($26.50 Can)

Texas (2nd Edition)
1-878-86798-9
$18.95 ($26.50 Can)

Utah (4th Edition)
0-679-00030-5
$18.95 ($26.50 Can)

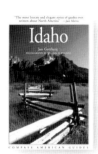

Idaho (1st Edition)
1-878-86778-4
$18.95 ($26.50 Can)

New Mexico (3rd Edition)
0-679-00031-3
$18.95 ($26.50 Can)

Maine (2nd Edition)
1-878-86796-2
$18.95 ($26.50 Can)

Manhattan (2nd Edition)
1-878-86794-6
$18.95 ($26.50 Can)

Las Vegas (5th Edition)
0-679-00015-1
$18.95 ($26.50 Can)

San Francisco (4th Edition)
1-878-86792-X
$18.95 ($26.50 Can)

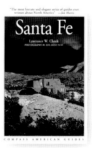

Santa Fe (2nd Edition)
0-679-03389-0
$18.95 ($26.50 Can)

South Carolina (2nd Edition)
0-679-03599-0
$18.95 ($26.50 Can)

Virginia (2nd Edition)
1-878-86795-4
$18.95 ($26.50 Can)

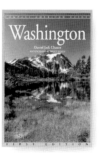

Washington (1st Edition)
1-878-86758-X
$17.95 ($25.00 Can)

Wisconsin (2nd Edition)
1-878-86749-0
$18.95 ($26.50 Can)

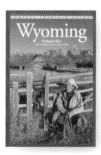

Wyoming (3rd Edition)
0-679-00034-8
$18.95 ($26.50 Can)

■ ABOUT THE AUTHOR

Jon Klusmire was born in Aspen and raised in numerous towns up and down the Roaring Fork and Colorado River valleys. He received a degree in history from Western State College in Gunnison, Colorado, and started his journalism career as a reporter for the *Weekly Newspaper* in Glenwood Springs, later to become its editor. He is currently editor-in-chief of *Trilogy,* a national magazine focusing on the connections between recreation, the environment, and industry and technology. Klusmire is currently a regional correspondent for the *Rocky Mountain News* and *Colorado Business* magazine; he writes a regular column for the *Aspen Times* and has been listed in *Who's Who in the West.* His freelance work has appeared in such publications as the *High Country News,* the *Los Angeles Times,* and the *National Catholic Reporter.*

■ ABOUT THE PHOTOGRAPHER

Paul Chesley has been a freelance photographer with the National Geographic Society since 1975, traveling regularly throughout Europe and Asia. He was recently honored by the inclusion of his work in the Society's first major exhibition, "The Art of Photography at National Geographic: A 100 Year Retrospective" at the Corcoran Gallery of Art in Washington, D.C. Solo exhibitions of his work have appeared in museums in London, Tokyo, and New York; and his photographic essays are regularly featured in such magazines as *LIFE, Fortune, Bunte, Paris Match,* and *Connoisseur.* Over the past six years he has participated in ten *Day in the Life* projects. He currently resides in Aspen.